SEVENOAKS PEOPLE AND FAITH
Two Thousand Years of Religious Belief and Practice

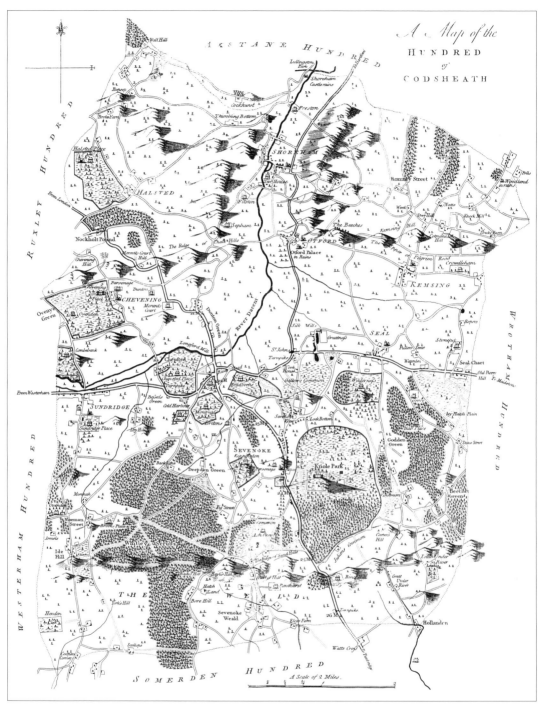

MAP 1 *The Hundred of Codsheath. The area covered by this book approximates to the old hundred, a pre-Conquest division of Kent. The hundred had a military, judicial, and administrative function. In Anglo-Saxon times the meeting place for the men of the hundred was in all probability away from existing settlements and on the wooded chart lands near the present site of Sevenoaks. This map is taken from Edward Hasted,* The History and Topograpical Survey of the County of Kent *(London, 1797).*

SEVENOAKS PEOPLE AND FAITH

Two Thousand Years of Religious Belief and Practice

EDITED BY

DAVID KILLINGRAY

Phillimore

2004

Published by
PHILLIMORE & CO. LTD
Shopwyke Manor Barn, Chichester, West Sussex, England

© Sevenoaks Historical Society, 2004

ISBN 1 86077 297 8

Printed and bound in Great Britain by
BIDDLES LTD.
www.biddles.co.uk

CONTENTS

List of Illustrations

List of Maps

ACKNOWLEDGEMENTS

This book is the work of many minds and hands as is indicated by the names that head the various contributions. I am grateful to all those who have contributed to the book for being so understanding and helpful in the face of my suggestions of amendments to their texts. As editor I have received help from a number of friends who have kindly read and rigorously commented upon sections of the text. My grateful thanks go to Christopher Bell, Professor Sam Berry, Dr John Coffey, Dr Gillian Draper, Professor Paul Fouracre, Margaret Killingray, Revd Angus MacLeay, Dr Mark Smith, Dr Jennifer Ward, and Professor John Wolffe. Further thanks go to my former colleague Dr Jeremy Goring for permission to use a few neatly formulated sentences accompanying a table in his excellent book *Burn Holy Fire. Religion in Lewes since the Reformation* (2003), p.110.

The Sevenoaks Historical Society is most grateful for two generous grants that have made possible the publication of this book: from the Allen Grove Memorial Fund, administered by the Kent Archaeological Society; and an Awards for All grant from the Lottery Grants for Local Groups. The Society is grateful to Rod Shelton and the Otford Heritage Centre for permission to use illustration 11, and to Derek Lucas for illustration 96. Illustrations 24 and 25 come from Margaret Killingray, *I am an Anglican* (Franklin Watts, 1986). Every effort has been made to gain consent for use of copyright material but in some cases it has not been possible to locate the holder, and for this we ask forbearance.

LIST OF SUBSCRIBERS

PAUL & CATHY ALFORD

MR & MRS F AMOTT

LIBBY ANCRUM

MR & MRS D S C ASHENDEN

DIANA ATKINSON

JOHN BAILEY

DR MURRAY BAKER

R & M VAN ZINDEREN BAKKER

G D BALL

DR SARAH BASHALL

PAUL & JANET BATCHELOR

LEONARD BECKETT

ANN & CHRISTOPHER BELL

MR & MRS NIGEL BELLE

PROF & MRS R J BERRY

MR & MRS L P BEST

MR & MRS D BESTWICK

ANTHONY BEWES

ISOBEL BLAND

MAURICE BONNETT

ANDREW & DIANE MCKENZIE BOYLE

NIGEL & NANCY BRANSON

ISOBEL M BROUGHAM

I JOAN E BROWN

MRS M J CARPENTER

MR & MRS J R CHEESEMAN

ANDY & FIONA CLARKE

ROSEMARY CLARY

ALAN & CAROL COLLARD

HELEN & NIGEL COOKE

JOHN W COOMBER

JOHN CORNWELL

HEATHER CORNWELL-KELLY

JAMES COUCHMAN

MARGARET & ALAN COULSON

MR & MRS D G CRACKNELL

JOHN F CRAIG

DAVID & ROSEMARY CRANFIELD

GODFREY CROUGHTON

REV JOHN S CURNOW

DR T DALTON

DAVID DAVIES

PAT DAVIES

MR NOEL F DAWES

FR CHRISTOPHER DAWSON

PHILIP DAY

PETER DEANS

IAN DOBBIE

KATHARINE DRAPER

KATHLEEN DRAPER

PROFESSOR PETER DRAPER

BERYL DUNCAN

PAUL & PAM DUNN

MR & MRS ANDREW DURANT

DAVID JOHN EDMEADS

DONALD ALAN ELEY

HELEN W ELLIS

ELLEN D EXCELL

NEIL & JENNIFER FAIR

ANTHONY FINNEY

MR & MRS D J FOWDREY

K C FOWLER

JEAN FOX

J JILL GARNER

L E & J R GAVIN

JOHN PHILIP GILBODY

MR & MRS K E GRAFTON

DAVID GREENSLADE

MARTIN GREENSLADE

MARK HARDING

SUSAN HARLAND

MR & MRS P HARLOW

MISS V C HARRISON

TREVOR A HARVEY

MR & MRS MICHAEL HARWOOD

M & P HEAPS

BERYL HIGGS

MRS SHIRLEY HILL

M & B HORRIDGE

DR BRIAN J HOUGHTON

JOHN HUMPHREY

REV JAMES B HURLEY

BRIAN & JENNIFER JACKSON

EDWARD JAMES

REVD & MRS D JOHNSON

DR ROGER JOHNSON

ANITA JONES

PAUL & CAROLINE JULIUS

KEMSING HERITAGE CENTRE ASSOCIATION

KEMSING HISTORICAL & ART SOCIETY

UNIVERSITY OF KENT

ERIC KEYS

GEOFFREY KITCHENER

EDWARD LADE

MR & MRS N LIGHTFOOT

JOHN LONDON

D E LOVETT

JOHN LURCOOK

V LUTTON

JEAN MAIR

EVA E MAJOR

IVY MARRIOTT

JILL & BRYAN MARSON-SMITH

LINDA MEADEN

JOAN MEDILL

MRS M J MILES

MARIAN & DUDLEY MILLS

DAVID MILMAN

R A & K I MORGAN

ALEXANDER MORRISON

J P MOULTON

PETER MOUNTFIELD

IAN MYERS

ANGELA & GUY NEWEY

MRS J NEWEY

ANDREW NICHOLLS

LORNA NOBLE

GERALD M O'BRIEN

M O'DONOGHUE

STEPHEN, EMMA, KATHRYN & JENNY OSEI-MENSAH

MISS HELEN J T O'SULLIVAN

MIKE & MARGARET PARKER

A M PARKIN

TIM PEARCE

MRS MARION PONT

GUY J F POWELL

GRANT PROBERT

SIMON & CHRISTINE RAIKES

MR L V RAINEY

WILLIAM RANDALL

J E RANDLES

MR & MRS B RAYNOR

DAVID & BARBARA ROGERS

PETER & ADRIENNE ROGERS

EDWARD B RUBIE

DAVID RUSSELL

ROGER & MARION RUSSELL

DR CAROLINE SANDERS

R & P SAVAGE

DOUGLAS & MARIGOLD SEAL

VICTOR SEAL

BRIAN SENNITT

SEVENOAKS QUAKER MEETING

SEVENOAKS UNITED REFORMED CHURCH

BERNARD & MARGARET SHARP

SHOREHAM & DISTRICT HISTORICAL SOCIETY

DENISE & RICHARD SIMS

E JILL SMITH

LOUISE SPREYER

THE FRIENDS OF ST MARY'S CHURCH, SUNDRIDGE

JON & JO STEWART

HARRY TALBOT

SARAH TANNER

MRS AUDREY M J TAYLOR

IAIN TAYLOR

L C TAYLOR

WARREN & DIANA TAYLOR

MAJOR ALAN TAYLOR-SMITH

GEOFF & ADRIENNE THOMPSON

DR ANNE & DR ROBIN TONGE

ANDREA TREVENNA

NEILL & MYRTLE TRUEMAN

DR PETER TURNER

D R L VAUDREY

JOHN E VIGAR

MRS GRETEL WAKEHAM

DR ANTHONY J WALKER

BRUCE WALKER

IAN J B WALKER

ROGER & PAM WALSHE

MR & MRS C P WARD

JO WARD

THE REVD DR ROBIN WARD

PHIL WARN

ALEXANDER WATSON

JEAN WATSON

ROGER M WATSON

MRS LELA WEAVERS

JONATHAN WEBB

JOHN & JEAN WESTACOTT

MATTHEW & KATE WHITELEGG

CLARE & ANDREW WHITTAKER

JANE WILEY

ALAN & MARGARET WILKINSON

ALEXANDER WILLIAMS

CLAIRE & DAVID WILLIAMS

ELEANOR WILLIAMS

PAUL & HEATHER WILLIAMS

PAUL G & JANICE A WILLIAMS

MISS J E WOOD

MRS DULCIE WRIGHT

DR DUDLEY YARROW

MR & MRS P F YOUNG

Introduction

Modern Britain is by most measures a secular society. Firm Christian beliefs are held by a small number of people and church attendance, if indeed that is a mark of Christian belief and practice, continues to decline. However, the late 20th and early 21st centuries are the exception in English history. In previous centuries religion, most notably Christian belief, played a significant, if not dominant, part in the lives of large numbers of people and in the affairs of State. Indeed, in a recent book a distinguished historian has argued that from the 17th to the 19th centuries Protestantism helped to shape British identity.

Why look at religious belief and practice? Why does it interest historians? Firstly, the Christian church has a rich body of texts, recorded doctrines, rituals and buildings. Secondly, most people acknowledged some form of adherence to Christianity, if not to a specific church, until, perhaps, the 1950s. Thirdly, history is about change, and changes in the religious ideas and practices of individuals and communities provides a rich and varied tapestry for the historian attempting to understand what motivated and shaped people's beliefs in the past. Such a study does present serious problems. How can you understand why people thought and behaved as they did in a past age? It is not possible to interrogate them about their beliefs and behaviour. In Sevenoaks there are relatively few sources for a history of Christianity.[1] And even if the records were abundant we would still be faced with the challenge of interpreting what people in, say, the 16th or 17th centuries actually understood by various Christian terms and concepts such as, 'grace', 'salvation' and 'repentance', and in particular by 'hell', 'heaven', and 'toleration'.

We also have to grapple with 'the varieties of religious belief' including that tendency in most ages, not least our own, for people to fashion a personal set of beliefs in order to help them view more comfortably their place both in society and the wider cosmic order. In discussing religious belief it is also important not to ignore those who denied religion. Non-belief has always existed and became more widespread from the mid-18th century. Most 20th-century people have not read the writers of the Age of Enlightenment, or the works by the trinity of Darwin, Marx, and Freud, but our modern mindset has been profoundly shaped by their pervasive ideas. Christian and secular thought owes much to all of these factors.

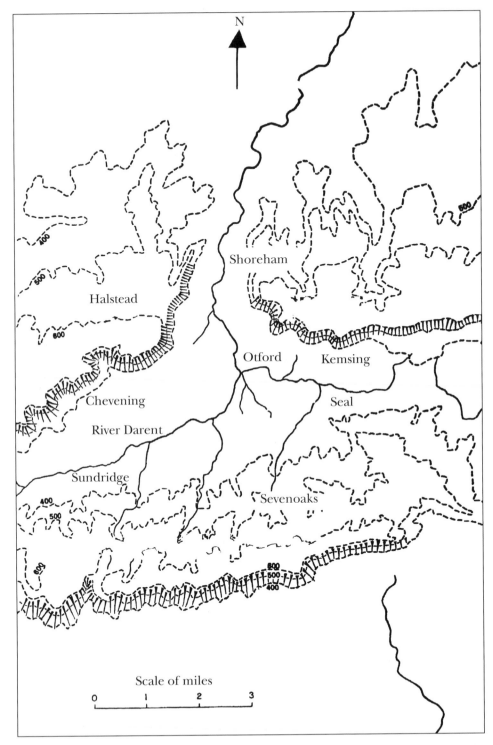

MAP 2   *The Landscape of the Sevenoaks Area.*
Sevenoaks is a hill town on the rising sandstone ridge. The River Darent flows east along the Vale of Holmesdale and then north through the gap in the chalk North Downs.

All books have a genesis. This edited collection of essays developed from an exhibition held to mark the second Christian millennium in 2000. The idea that local history societies should cooperate with churches to commemorate the millennium came from Gavin Reid, the then Bishop of Maidstone. The recently founded Sevenoaks Historical Society extended the original idea to embrace other religious groups and then set about organising the exhibition. The area chosen was the ancient hundred of Codsheath. Most of the churches, fellowships, and religious groups in Sevenoaks and the surrounding villages eagerly contributed. The resulting exhibition consisted of nearly one hundred A1 boards with mounted illustrations and accompanying captions and text. These were displayed on portable frames and managed by the secretary of the Sevenoaks Historical Society, Alan Wilkinson. The exhibition was first shown in the Stag Theatre in Sevenoaks, and then for several weeks toured the neighbouring villages. More than two thousand people visited the exhibition. It is largely due to visitors' comments and encouragement that the idea was born for a book on religious belief and practice in the area.

This volume of essays is arranged in two parts. Part I contains four essays that place the locality within the national picture. The second part consists of short essays on specific churches, fellowships and meetings, and on religious life and activities in the area. How should the contents in Part II of the book be ordered? Several ideas were considered as to how this should be done: chronological order based on when churches were founded, priority to Sevenoaks as the only town, or even a chronological order linked to denomination which would have put Anglicans (or perhaps Roman Catholics) first. In the end it seemed sensible to arrange Part II in such a way that it would be readily comprehensible to readers. The result is that the churches in Sevenoaks town are dealt with first, arranged roughly in chronological order of foundation, followed by the surrounding villages and hamlets in alphabetical order.

Relatively little research has been undertaken on the history of west Kent and consequently there are few serious published histories. Excellent histories of a number of villages – Otford, Shoreham, Chevening, and Halstead – exist, the last two published recently to mark the millennium. The town of Sevenoaks, which has a rich history, has been well served by John Dunlop's book published in the 1960s. But history is constantly changing and, inevitably, a new history of Sevenoaks is required, one that addresses the very different agendas, ideas, and interpretations promoted and argued over by numerous historians during the last forty years. This applies equally to religious and ecclesiastical history for which, in the past few decades, scholars have produced rich and exciting studies on all aspects of religious belief and activity.

Many churches and chapels have brief histories, usually written either to help visitors understand the building in its communal context, or to encourage fellow church members to take an interest in a history of which they are an integral modern part. Unlike many local institutions churches often have well-documented histories. Although many documents have been lost churches, and the denominations to which they belong, invariably hold primary records of their history and associations. These can be rich, although often scattered, sources that pose a daunting challenge to most non-historians. One consequence is that too often church histories are based solely on sources ready to hand, and focus heavily on architectural detail, certain clergy, and a few outstanding events. Beyond this narrow focus there is clearly a richer and more detailed history awaiting the skilled researcher, who is able to dissect and analyse the social relationships of parishioners and congregations, and the contribution that church or chapel has made to the social, economic and political life of the community. This is to get to the heart of what 'church' actually *is*: not the stones and bricks, timber and tiles, but the people themselves, the body of believers gathered together.

In this book a serious attempt has been made to focus primarily on the people who have constituted the various churches. The history of their beliefs and practices has been diverse. It has ranged widely from personal piety and purpose to casual adherence to a set of religious ideas endorsed by State or community. There were also those who from within the church questioned its teachings and others, in more recent times, who turned away from its doctrines and ministry altogether. This provides a fascinating insight not only to varieties of religious belief and practice, but also to cultural attitudes and economic relationships within the social history of rural west Kent. It is hoped that this brief attempt to place on record the history of religious belief and practice in Sevenoaks will encourage others to take this study further and to write more detailed histories of both the area and its religious life and experience.

Finally, a personal word as editor. I have tried to be even-handed and objective in editing a book that has relied on the goodwill of so many other people. Undoubtedly in places my own views have intruded, so it is only fair that I announce my own biases. I am a credal Christian acknowledging Jesus Christ as Lord. In the last 60 years I have been a member of Baptist, Christian Brethren, and Anglican fellowships in both the United Kingdom and in Africa. My first involvement with Christians in the Sevenoaks area was in the mid-1950s when I accompanied a friend who was preaching at the small Baptist chapel in Shoreham. For the last 30 or more years I have been a member of St Nicholas parish church in Sevenoaks, where once I served as a churchwarden. In my time in the town and area, I have come to value greatly the warmth and friendship of so many people in the wider Christian community.

Part One

LOCALITY AND NATION

Kentish Faith and Belief in the First Millennium

Joy Saynor[*]

Celtic Paganism and Early Roman Christianity

The varied landscape of river, valley land, high hills and forest which characterised the hundred of Codsheath in the past can, uniquely for Kent, claim that here Christian worship began in the last decades of the fourth century and continued to the present time. The hundred contained the settlements of Sevenoaks, Otford, Shoreham, Woodlands, Kemsing, Seal, Sundridge and part of Chevening. Although the hundred as an administrative unit belongs to the ninth century, Codsheath was 'one of the few Kentish hundreds based on a Jutish estate' in the mid-fifth century.[1] It is accepted that its earliest spelling, 'Godehede' (meaning 'God's Heath'), refers to one of the pagan gods of the Jutes. Wallenberg finds it first so written in 1178.[2] The hundred meeting place is unknown but three suggested sites are found on the wooded ridgeway where Sevenoaks later developed, on the hillock upon which Riverhead Church stands and on a raised piece of land between Twitton and the bottom of Polhill.

The first millennium of the Christian era in Kent as a whole, and in Codsheath Hundred in particular, can be categorised in the secular sphere as a period of upheaval in the social and economic life of the community. As far as religion is concerned, the picture shows the early paganism of the indigenous Celtic population, to which was first added the pagan gods of Imperial Rome. During the Roman occupation Christianity was twice introduced and its teachings accepted alongside pagan beliefs. After the Roman withdrawal in the early fifth century, it would appear that Christianity continued in the Darent Valley while pagan settlers established themselves. Bede's simplistic account of the origins of the invaders should be tempered with the qualification that he was writing in distant Northumbria describing events about which little reliable written evidence has survived, and which may or may not have occurred in Kent three hundred years earlier. His assertion that 'from the Jutes are descended the people of Kent' should be questioned in the light of recent archaeological evidence that 'it is not possible to confirm on archaeological grounds a Jutish folk migration arriving in Kent in the mid- or late fifth century'.[3] Instead the evidence of the East Kent invasion period cemeteries at Eastry, Finglesham and Woodnesborough appears to suggest that the settlers originated in Southern Scandinavia. From their homeland,

* Co-author of *Shoreham, a village in Kent* (Shoreham, 1989)

1

they introduced gold-foil pendants (bracteates) engraved with the image of Odin/Woden, king of their pagan gods. Furthermore the Kentish royal house was alone among early English royal dynasties in insisting on tracing its origin back to its 'ancestor', Woden. The church and the heathen gods marched hand in hand until, in the early seventh century, missioners from Canterbury established their primary mother church at Preston in Shoreham. The ninth- and tenth-century Viking attacks failed to dislodge the area's strong Christianity, but perhaps the host under Canute could have destroyed Preston's settlement of priests at the time of the second battle of Otford in 1016. Canute's conversion and his peace may have led to the rebuilding in stone of several of the hundred's small parish churches which would be continued by William and Lanfranc after 1066.

The valley of the Darent was particularly suited to the pagan Celtic deities of the period of Roman occupation; its very name, deriving from the Welsh 'derw' (oak trees), described the sacred oaks which grew along its banks. Tacitus described 'The religious groves dedicated to superstition and barbarous rites',[4] but the river waters were home to gentler beliefs; in the deep room of the Lullingstone Roman villa (some half a mile to the north of the boundary of Codsheath Hundred) three water nymphs were painted. Colonel G.W. Meates, the archaeologist responsible for the excavation of the greater part of the villa, believed that, although the probable Roman owner was influenced by Italian designs, there was possibly cross fertilisation with native Darent water spirits. The deep room was a carefully prepared place of worship within the villa, with tiled stairs leading down to it, and with plastered walls in red, green and orange-yellow surrounding a niche in which the three nymphs were depicted with arms entwined.[5] Further up the Darent at Otford, a similar water deity was identified.

Still further evidence of pagan worship was discovered at Lullingstone; on higher ground to the west of the villa, a Romano-Celtic temple mausoleum was constructed in the early fourth century over a tomb chamber containing the young man and woman owners of the villa. The typical enclosed *cella* was surrounded by an ambulatory and had a pillared classical portico leading into it. Perhaps the best depiction of such a temple can be seen on one of the mosaics found at Brading on the Isle of Wight. Less than a century after its construction, the Lullingstone temple fell into decay: the villa owners had adopted Christianity.

In the recently excavated small Roman villa near the mouth of the Darent, south above Dartford, a room has been tentatively identified as the place of worship of a pagan priest. It should be emphasised that the Darent, during the four centuries of Roman occupation, was easily navigable as far as Otford. Settlements, created by the Roman conquerors, stood on its banks with little more than half a mile separating them. The largest unexplained gap between sites occurs at Shoreham, stretching from the excavated bath block at the bottom of Mill Lane to Wickham Field in Otford.

Thus, when Christianity became officially adopted by the Roman state, the valley settlements could include its teachings among those of their panoply of heathen deities. But this fourth-century Christianity did not represent the first

1 *Chi-Rho monogram from Lullingstone Roman villa. The Romans settled in the Darent valley. The villa at Lullingstone contained a Christian house church, dating from the late fourth century, positioned above the pagan place of worship of earlier villa owners. The Chi-Rho Christian monogram (the first two Greek letters in the name of Christ) is set in a wreath with fluted columns on either side. It occupied one sixth part of the south wall of the main room in the house church.*

time the Gospel had reached Britain, or even, perhaps, Codsheath, although no evidence of a second-century conversion there has been identified. Bede, writing in eighth-century Northumbria, consulted 'the writings of the ancients' and from them stated that Christianity had reached this outpost of the Roman Empire in AD156, and that 'Britons preserved the faith ... uncorrupted and entire' until the persecutions of the Emperor Diocletian in the early fourth century when, in 301, St Alban was martyred.[6]

Lullingstone and Later Roman Christianity

In the late fourth century, after three changes of ownership, the Lullingstone villa became a site of Christian worship, as was now officially imposed from Rome. The late first-century nympheum was still allowed its pagan rites, but above it a small house church was constructed within the heart of the villa. Thus begins the most significant part of the history of Christianity in the Codsheath area: 'The history of Christian worship begins here and has been practically continuous from the last decades of the fourth century to the present day'.[7] Yet this church remained in use as a place of worship for only thirty-five years or so. Farming at the villa ceased, but prayer continued until around AD 420 among the ruins of the buildings.

2　*Lullingstone Roman villa. One of six figures on the wall of the house church, this drawing shows a young man with arms outstretched in prayer. He has dark eyes, red hair, and wears an ochre dress and cloak with a blue sash.*

One of the great discoveries made during the excavation of the house church was that its walls had been decorated with Christian symbols, and figures in an attitude of veneration. It is accepted that these figures are likely to be portraits of the family occupying the villa in the late fourth century, dressed in the rich robes of the period and with their arms raised in the early attitude of prayer. Two Chi-Rho symbols, red on white, were painted on the walls, and a larger Chi-Rho was inscribed on the ante-chamber wall. It seems likely that there was also a Christian place of worship of this period at Otford: the centre of a Chi-Rho was found painted in red on white plaster, and of a similar size to that at Lullingstone. Even so, there is evidence of pagan beliefs continuing at Lullingstone until the end: an infant burial place was discovered, which had been inserted by cutting through the concrete floor, possibly placed there by a native pagan after the villa had ceased to be inhabited.[8]

Pagan English Settlement in the Darent Valley

In AD 410 the Roman legions were recalled to Rome, ostensibly taking Roman Christianity with them, and forty years later Hengist and Horsa, commanding their three long boats, landed on the Kentish coast bringing with them Thor, Woden and a considerable number of other ferocious pagan gods.[9] Bede, quoting from Gildas, paints a scene of the greatest devastation: 'These heathen conquerors devastated the surrounding cities and countryside … priests were slain at the altar, bishops and people alike', but this seems an unlikely scenario for Codsheath Hundred during this early Dark-Age period. Archaeology supports Bede's opinion that 'from the Jutes are descended the people of Kent' and, along the Darent, the primary Jutish settlement reached to Otford. 'The whole of the Darent valley has long been recognised as one of the earliest cradles of English settlement in Kent'.[10]

A good case can be made for Otford having become the centre of one of the Darent's earliest large Jutish estates; ancient trackways crossed each other there, and one route led to the woodland covering the hill where Sevenoaks would develop and then on, into the great Wealden forest.

It has been suggested that, having given access to the settlers, the Darent became partially blocked, even silting up in places, so that, for more than a century, Codsheath was left isolated from neighbouring parts of Kent. To some degree, Bede contradicts himself by following Gildas' account of the destruction of the Christian religion in the wake of the Saxon advance. For he also details at length how, at the same time, the two continental bishops, Germanus and Lupus, travelled to Britain at the invitation from the Christian community 'to confirm their belief in God's grace', with the result that 'Catholics everywhere were strengthened and heretics corrected'.[11]

Bede does not identify the part of Britain where this took place, but we know that during this time one of the most important burials of a Jutish settler had taken place very close to the Codsheath area. During the course of a rescue excavation carried out in 1978 by the Dartford District Archaeological Group close to Darenth Park Hospital, the grave of a forty-year-old male was identified. Over the left shoulder had been placed, inverted, 'a complete and undamaged glass cup/bowl of fifth century date'. Most importantly, the base was decorated with the Chi-Rho monogram: 'The only glass bowl of this date with a Christian monogram to be found in this country'.[12] It was of Frankish manufacture and dated from the first half of the fifth century. The cemetery in which it was found was otherwise pagan; the Jute's body had been aligned east-west so he could possibly have been a Christian. Or perhaps this was his most precious possession: seized from, or gained in trading with, the continuing Codsheath Christian community. Further evidence for such continuity is provided by the significance of Preston in Shoreham during the Augustinian reconversion period.

The Reconversion of Codsheath Hundred

When the mission of Augustine began in East Kent in 597 Ethelbert, the English ruler of all the land from his kingdom of Kent to the Humber, gave the forty monks a base in Canterbury for their teachings. Codsheath was far away across the river Medway, which effectively divided Kent into two halves, and so the reconversion of west Kent had to wait until the early to mid-seventh century. It is almost certain that Shoreham (Preston), was one of the 44 mother churches of Kent although, unlike most of the others, it was not the capital of a royal estate. Nearby Otford enjoyed that distinction, and this would cause confusion in the historical picture in the following centuries. Today the present Preston Farm still extends over a considerable part of the valley floor and up the eastern slope of the downs which is known as Preston Hill. Its first spelling was 'Preosta-tun', implying a settlement worked by, or in support of, priests.[13] From this establishment of worker-priests there grew a huge Deanery of 34 benefices, stretching from Bexley in the north east to beyond the Medway in the south. Furthermore, as a mark of its long-standing ecclesiastical importance, and at the same time as the great gift of Otford from King Cenulf of Mercia, to the Archbishop, Shoreham was created a Peculiar of the Archbishopric. This meant that Shoreham (Preston), was exempt from the jurisdiction of the bishop of Rochester in whose diocese it lay.

But in spite of many years of Christianity in Codsheath, and particularly in the Darent Valley area, paganism still had believers, but they followed the Jutish, rather than the old Celtic, gods. Even the early Kentish kings were not immune

3 *Early Christian community similar to Preston, Shoreham. This is a reconstruction of the Anglo-Saxon monastery at Jarrow in the 8th century. Although of timber construction, the 7th-century building at Preston, Shoreham, may have appeared similar.*

from the lure of the old religion: Eabald, King Ethelbert's successor, refused 'to accept the Faith of Christ' until, in around 616, Lawrence, the second archbishop, persuaded him to renounce his idolatry, be baptised and to 'promote the welfare of the Church with every means at his disposal'.[14] Evidence of the confusion felt by Codsheath's population was found in the late 1960s during the excavation of a cemetery containing more than a hundred graves on the headland above Polhill. Although the churls, freemen and smaller freeholders were buried with their most valuable possessions, it is considered that many of them were proto-Christians, newly converted by the Preston community, but still clinging to their old certainties. Their families would have brought them to the top of this prominent hill from their villages and hamlets below, not only from Otford and Shoreham. The priests sent to convert them initially allowed them to continue to follow their old customs. They knew that even converted rulers did not wholly abandon their paganism. Bede records that in AD 627 King Redwald, after baptism, renounced the faith and 'tried to serve both Christ and the ancient gods, and he had in the same temple an altar for the holy Sacrifice of Christ side by side with an altar on which victims were offered to devils'.[14] And on his death, Redwald was buried in the great pagan mound of Sutton Hoo. On Polhill, burials began a little before the mid-seventh century and continued, without a break, into the eighth.[15] The cemetery was within the boundary of the Otford royal estate, but its burials, especially those of the richer graves, were too late to provide evidence of bracteates paralleling the finds from the sixth-century Finglesham cemetery near Eastry in East Kent.

Early Churches and their Foundations

In due time, each village settlement in Codsheath Hundred came to have its own consecrated space for Christian burial, an area of land which hardly altered in size until the large population growth in the 19th century. At first not even wooden churches were built, and wooden crosses were simply set up to mark the place of prayer. In Kent a portion of one such cross, this time of stone, is preserved in the crypt of Canterbury Cathedral. It originally stood in the late Saxon, stone-built parish church of Reculver; after the church was destroyed nearly two hundred years ago, the cross was broken and used by East Kent farmers until its significance was recognised. Small wooden churches then began to replace the crosses in the churchyards, resembling the early medieval woodland church of Dode in size, which, since it was built after

1066, was of stone construction. However, it was similar in extent, consisting of a small nave and chancel. Further down the Darent a substantial part of a stone Saxon church remains as the nave of St Margaret's Darenth.

Although outside the hundred of Codsheath, St Margaret's should be briefly considered: not only for its late Saxon nave, but because it illustrates several features of that hundred's early religious foundations. It stands high above the Darent, the venerated pagan river; it is built less than a third of a mile from the immense Roman villa of Darenth, and contains several hundreds of pieces

4 *St Margaret's, Darenth. A substantial part of the nave of this church is Anglo-Saxon. The building stands north of Shoreham on the eastern side of the Darent valley.*

of Roman tile in its walls, while its dedication (St Margaret), is to one of the five non-local saints found in the valley. Together with St Margaret, the other four saints thus venerated are St Peter and St Paul (Farningham and Shoreham), St Martin (Otford and Eynsford), and St Mary (Kemsing). But closer to the hundred boundary, during the excavation of the Lullingstone Roman villa, Meates identified the remains of the medieval parish church of Lullingstane (not to be confused with the still existing Lullingstone church close to the Castle): 'overlying the western part of the temple-mausoleum was the exterior west wall and the remains of the north and south walls'. Meates suggested that written evidence indicated a Saxon origin for the church, and that its orientation could be an example 'of the early Augustinian practice of siting Christian churches upon buildings that had once been used for pagan worship'.[16]

No doubt to help persuade pagans to convert to Christianity, early missionaries deliberately chose existing pagan shrines as sites for their churchyards and churches. Two examples at Kemsing and Otford were also close to Roman sites. Kemsing, where the south wall 'seems to have a Saxon thinness',[17] was built close to the well venerated by celtic pagans, which, like the church, was dedicated to St Edith, a Christian scion of the Kentish royal line. Otford church, probably first built in the 10th century and rebuilt at the period of the Norman Conquest, shows evidence of Saxon work in the north and west walls of the nave: in the height of the nave, and in the absence of dressed stone blocks.[18] A nearby holy spring, close to Becket's well, had, like Kemsing's well, a pagan Celtic beginning. Both Kemsing and Otford were on the route of pilgrimages to Canterbury long before Becket's murder. Otford, whose church overlooked an important early crossroads, was also situated on the droveway that came from Shoreham and passed through Sevenoaks, the market-place of the hundred, on its passage into the Wealden forest. Its dedication to St Bartholomew reinforced the importance of the trackways: the saint was especially concerned with poor travellers (as well as with healing and fairs). Chevening, on the Pilgrims Way (a name only given to the great prehistoric east-west trackway by 18th-century antiquarians), had the only Celtic place-name in the hundred derived from 'cefn'-ridge, and was also associated with a spring near the trackway. Its territory originally covered some ten thousand acres and it had control over daughter churches at Sundridge and Chiddingstone. Its dedication, to St Botolph, was one restricted to 'an exceptionally limited number of early foundations'.[19]

It might have been thought that St Peter and St Paul, Shoreham, would have shown evidence of some early Anglo-Saxon flint/stone construction, particularly as Preston was one of the 26 mother churches of Kent, but the parish church should not be confused with the missionary centre. It can be assumed that, before 1066, it was a small timber building similar to its neighbours in the Hundred. However, its dedication may have been chosen as a reminder of the direct link with Canterbury and the archbishop: the monastery which Augustine founded between his first church, St Martin's and his cathedral was dedicated by him to St Peter and St Paul. It was only after his death that the dedication was changed to honour St Augustine himself.

Surviving sources record the early ecclesiastical sequence of minster, mother church, daughter church and chapelry. Although both the *Enham Code* (1006-7), and the *Domesday Monachorum* and *Textus Roffensis* are outside the period to be considered, their evidence refers back to the early organisation of the Codsheath churches. The *Enham Code*, drawn up in the stressful Danegeld era by Ethelred II's close adviser, Archbishop Wulfstan, when the church's wealth was depleted and the clergy feared a return to paganism, first described the sequence of control from head minsters to chapelries. The two cathedrals of Canterbury and Rochester were the head minsters followed by the secondary minsters which were the original mother churches, often of seventh-century date; then came a number of seventh-century churches which did not become minsters, also secondary mother churches which had daughters, followed by private churches built by landowners on their holdings and finally Wealden forest churches which had been established by distant minsters. The *Domesday Monachorum* of Christ Church, Canterbury, and the *Textus Roffensis* of Rochester, contemporary with *Domesday Book*, both identify the relationship between minster, mother church, daughter church and chapelry in their respective dioceses.[20]

Shoreham (Preston) was one of the 45 primary mother churches definitely identified, and was, like the rest, based on a royal ecclesiastical estate: in this case, close by at Otford. Kemsing, although a mother church, may have been dependent at some time. Chevening was an example of a secondary mother church, not itself a minster, not dependent on another minster, which had two daughters at Sundridge and Chiddingstone. (Chevening, with its position on the major prehistoric east-west route through Kent, would appear to have been of greater importance during the first millennium than in later centuries.)

Another aspect of the early organisation of the Christian church in the area was the status of individual places of worship. Not all had their individual priest or rector; a few had the lesser position of chapelries, although this could hardly be discerned from the small, one- or two-cell timber buildings common to all. Otford does not come into this category in the Anglo-Saxon period: it only lost its rectorial status around 1290, becoming a chapel of Shoreham, a position it held until 1868.[21] Two undoubted chapelries were Greatness (Sevenoaks) and, in its earliest beginnings, St Nicholas, Sevenoaks. Greatness was named in the second of the two charters concerning land boundaries issued when King Coelwulf of Mercia granted the Otford estate to Archbishop Wulfred in 822. Greatness was situated on the border of the archbishop's new lands and on an ancient droveway which led up into the fringes of the Wealden forest. Later, post-1066, a hospital and chapel would be built on the same site (the present Bat and Ball crossroads). A pagan cult site may also have existed at Greatness springs. It was clearly of some importance in the pre-Conquest period.

St Nicholas, Sevenoaks (a late dedication), may have had its beginning as a hill top or landmark chapel: a wayside shrine on the track as it entered the woodland towards Penshurst. Travellers, fearing the dangers of the wild wood, would pray for a safe journey there. The hunter in Aelfric's late 10th-century *Colloquy* describes catching 'harts, bears, does, goats ... and a boar' and how 'I stood against [the wild boar], and suddenly slew him' for 'a hunter must be very brave, since all kinds of beasts die in the woods'.[22] For the average, timorous merchant, who had brought his goods to the stalls set up close to the chapel, and was about to set off into the unknown, prayers would have been most heartfelt. Two further chapelries were Woodlands, associated with Shoreham, and Seal, linked to Kemsing.

Politics and Christianity in the First Millennium

The churches and their priests did not exist in isolation from the political events that changed the direction of the history of Kent in the 450 years between the Jutish conquest and AD 1000. By the late seventh century, the once great Kentish royal line was in terminal decline; Kent was to be fought over by the Midland power of Mercia and the West Country power of Wessex. In 686 and 687, Kent was twice laid waste by Wessex and retaliated by burning Mul of Wessex, for which crime the Kentishmen were forced to pay £40,000 'in friendship'. Five years later, the first English archbishop was elected: 'Before this time the archbishops had been Roman, and afterwards they were English'.[23] To Shoreham, with its close relationship with the archbishopric, this must have appeared to be of much greater importance than the death of Mul. But before 700, Kent had had to recognise the overlordship of Mercia, and it was during this rule that, both in 742 and 822, great synods of the church, attended by the great and good from both Mercia and Kent, took place at Clovesho – identified possibly wrongly as Cliffe at Hoo; the Mercian kings then had their cantonal capital at the present Hoo St Werburgh.

However, this overlordship was not yet direct rule; this was only to occur in 785 under the great Offa of Mercia, nine years after the apparently indecisive battle between his forces and the men of Kent at Otford. The churchmen of the hundred must have offered up many prayers for the souls of the slain on both sides; it was important enough to merit a line in the Anglo-Saxon

Chronicle: 'The Mercians and the Kentishmen fought at Otford, and strange adders were seen in Sussex'.[24] Yet the battle was merely a foretaste of worse to come; in the closing years of the eighth century there arrived at Portland 'the first ships of the Danes to come to England'.[25] In the new century the Viking raids established themselves and Mercian rule was in decline in Kent making way for the rise of Wessex: the men of Kent submitted to Wessex in 825.

In this twilight of Mercian rule, two of the last rulers granted to Archbishop Wulfred (805-32) certain named areas of land on the east bank of the Darent, which created the nucleus of the great medieval ecclesiastical manor of Otford. Kings Cenulf and Coelwulf recognised the estate boundaries: the first chapter names them as Shoreham on the north, the Darent on the west, and Kemsing on the east; the second charter mentions Greatness, Seal Chart and the Weald (Andredsweald).[26] And at Otford, probably on the site of the later Otford Palace, a modest timber hall was built for the administration of the estate and perhaps for the occasional use of the archbishop.

For the Hundred of Codsheath, the tenth century should have been a time of stability and growth in both the ecclesiastical and temporal spheres: three interweaving areas of control had now been consolidated. Spiritually Shoreham, still having the support of the large farm at the old missionary centre at Preston, was the chief force in the continuance of Christian belief; in the temporal field the archbishop, in his role as landholder, maintained an excellent group of clerkly administrators to farm his Otford lands; thirdly, at Sevenoaks, a thriving market had developed where the two roads (up from the Darent valley and from London) met, allowing travellers to provision themselves before the rigours of the Wealden forest. In the wider national sphere Athelstan, the grandson of Alfred, had established himself as the island's most powerful ruler since, perhaps, the Roman occupation: 'No one more just or learned administered the state'.[27] Twenty-four years after Athelstan's early death Dunstan, one of the greatest archbishops in Canterbury's history, was enthroned in the Saxon cathedral.

But at the very time of Dunstan's installation more intense Viking raids, from both Norway and Denmark, were carried out; towns and villages in Kent, and the other southern counties, were destroyed; in 992 'it was decided, for the first time to pay tribute to the Danes ... It amounted to £10,000.' Such an admission of weakness resulted in higher demands combined with fiercer attacks. As the tenth century drew to a close 'came Anlaf and Swein [in 994] ... with 94 ships ... Doing as much harm as any host was capable of doing in burning, harrying and slaughter both along the coast and in Essex, Kent, Sussex and Hampshire.'[28] The effect upon the stable Codsheath Hundred of an even more concentrated attack in 997 can be imagined: the Kentish levies 'all too quickly turned and fled, ... the Danes ... got horses and rode far and wide as they pleased, destroying and laying waste almost the whole of West Kent!' Thus, in the words of the Anglo-Saxon Chronicle, ended the tenth century for our area.[29]

THE DEVELOPMENT OF CHURCHES AND PARISHES IN THE MIDDLE AGES

Timothy Boyle[*]

This chapter sets the development of churches and parishes in the Sevenoaks area against the background of the local landscape, society and economy in the Middle Ages. The chart lands (or sandstone ridge) on which Sevenoaks stands were heavily wooded, as was the region to the south: the great forest that stretched across the clay soils of the Weald of Kent, Sussex, Surrey and Hampshire.[1] By the early Middle Ages probably only the Vale of Holmesdale and the Darent Valley, to the north of the chart lands, had been extensively cleared of trees.[2] The soils of the Sevenoaks area were generally poor and there was an agricultural economy based mainly on cattle and pigs, a small amount of oats and wheat, and the products of the forest. Typically the inhabitants lived in farmsteads and hamlets scattered across the landscape rather than in nucleated villages. The earliest villages around Sevenoaks developed in the well-watered and more fertile areas of the Darent Valley and Holmesdale such as Shoreham and Otford, which were important early ecclesiastical centres.

The Archbishop of Canterbury was a principal tenant-in-chief in this area, mentioned in the Domesday Survey which was completed by 1086.[3] The Darent Valley and Holmesdale would have had the highest levels of population in the area between the 11th and 13th centuries. However, taxation records of the 1330s indicate that the population of the area around Sevenoaks was generally low compared with other parts of Kent. The average wealth of local people was similarly low, although there was variation according to the different soil quality in some areas.[4] It has been estimated that at the time of the Norman Conquest the population of Kent was possibly between forty and fifty thousand people. The population may have doubled between the Conquest and the mid-14th century when the Black Death reduced it by a third or even a half. Whole settlements were abandoned, such as the village of Woodlands, near Shoreham, which had its own church.[5] Thereafter the population level slowly recovered until, by the Reformation, it was back to at least that of 1340-50.[6]

The 13th century was important in the development of market towns and villages as the population grew. Such markets were closely linked to the growth of churches. Many market charters were granted in this period, although some places such as Sevenoaks may have been marketing centres in earlier centuries.[7] Between 1225 and 1280 charters granting or confirming the right to hold a

* Timothy Boyle, formerly senior lecturer in history, Goldsmiths College London.

5   Ancient drove road descending the sandstone ridge into the clay weald, near Underriver. By the start of the first millennium animals were being driven from the North Downs up the chart lands and then down tracks like these on the sandstone ridge to the wooded wealden area. Many of these old roads survive as tracks.

market were given by the Crown for Kemsing, Brasted, Westerham, Seal, Eynsford, Shipbourne, Ightham and Sevenoaks. It is possible that Sevenoaks' charter of 1280 was confirmed by the Crown as the king sought, in the face of opposition by the archbishop, to obtain more taxation and exercise political patronage. Few of these trading centres survived for any length of time after the Black Death and the subsequent economic decline of the second half of the 14th century, but Sevenoaks did. Sevenoaks market was the only one of those aforementioned known to have been functioning in the 16th century, as trading patterns changed.[8]

Medieval markets were centres for the exchange of the goods of a rural economy: livestock, foodstuffs, wood, cloth, leather goods, and household utensils. By the 13th century, population increase and the consequent subdivision of land meant that many peasants had insufficient land to meet their needs, and a larger number of people were engaged in occupations other than food production. Increasing prosperity also created greater demand for luxuries from the small number of wealthy people in the Sevenoaks area. Sevenoaks was within the manor of Otford and trade there was closely controlled by the lord of the manor, the Archbishop of Canterbury, through his agent, the bailiff. The large 15th-century timber-framed Bailiff's House can still be seen at 63-65 High Street, on the corner of Rockdale Road.[9] The dues, taxes and fines for breaches of regulations levied on market traders were an important source of income for the manorial lord. This economic activity generated wealth which helped to support the Church.

Parishes, Churches and Palaces

From the seventh century, the population of the area was gradually taught, and became accustomed to, the beliefs and practices of medieval Christianity.[10] There were important early churches known as minsters in east and north Kent which fulfilled both preaching and monastic functions. King Wihtrid's charter, dated 696-719, states that Kent had two cathedrals and eight other minsters.[11] As settlement spread, the minsters promoted daughter churches, some of which in turn founded new churches. The *Textus Roffensis* (probably

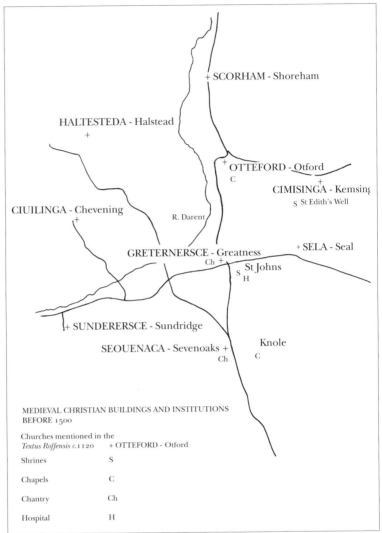

+ SCORHAM - Shoreham

HALTESTEDA - Halstead
+

+
OTTEFORD - Otford
C

+
CIMISINGA - Kemsing
S St Edith's Well

CIUILINGA - Chevening
+

R. Darent

GRETERNERSCE - Greatness
Ch +

+ SELA - Seal

S St Johns
H

+ SUNDERERSCE - Sundridge

SEOUENACA - Sevenoaks +
Ch

Knole
C

MAP 3 *The Jutish Parishes around Sevenoaks.*

MEDIEVAL CHRISTIAN BUILDINGS AND INSTITUTIONS
BEFORE 1500

Churches mentioned in the
Textus Roffensis c.1120   + OTTEFORD - Otford

Shrines   S

Chapels   C

Chantry   Ch

Hospital   H

compiled about 1120), Domesday Book of 1086 and the *Domesday Monachorum* of 1093-6 indicate that many churches and parishes existed in the diocese of Rochester, as well as in eastern Kent, by about 1000.[12] Shoreham, in the Darent Valley, was a minster. It was the only one in Kent not situated at the *caput*, that is the head or 'capital', of its estate, which was at Otford. Parishes were areas of land based on local communities, which provided sufficient income from the fees and tithes paid by all landholders to maintain their priest. In densely wooded areas of Kent, such as the High Weald, settlement was late and many churches were probably not founded until the 11th century or even later.

The initiative for founding new daughter churches and parishes came from the Crown, ecclesiastical houses and bishops, and lay lords, who wanted places of worship at a convenient distance for families and tenants. According to Alan Everitt, Otford, Sevenoaks, Kemsing, Chevening and Brasted churches

6 *A page of the Textus Roffensis showing the entry for 'Seouenaca': Sevenoaks. This is the earliest record of a parish church at Sevenoaks, c.1120.*

were founded by Shoreham, Seal by Kemsing, and Sundridge by Chevening. In many respects Otford became more important than Shoreham as it was the centre of an old estate which was held by the archbishops. The manor house at Otford became one of the archbishop's important palaces. The formation of parishes was related to existing settlement patterns, land holding, the terrain, and economic factors. Parishes such as Brasted, Sundridge, Chevening and, to some extent, Sevenoaks, were long in shape. This reflected the transhumance routes along which livestock were driven from the North Downs to the dens in the Weald. The first churches were undoubtedly of wood, with thatched roofs, the stone ones seen today not being built until the 12th or 13th centuries. There is often a pattern to where they were built: near sites of former Roman villas that had become manor houses, near to springs at the foot of the Downs or at 'holy' wells (often with a pre-Christian religious tradition), or beside roads and droves such as the ancient track through Holmesdale, later known as the Pilgrims' Way, and the parallel Greensand track. On the drove through Sevenoaks a wayside shrine was probably established, which later developed into St Nicholas' Church. The close proximity of the east end of the building to the road seems to indicate that this was so.

The Church: Jurisdiction and Administration

Sevenoaks has always been within the diocese of Rochester and a subdivision of the Deanery of Shoreham. However, in the Middle Ages, Shoreham was a 'Peculiar' of the Archbishop of Canterbury. This meant that it was subject to the jurisdiction of the archbishop, not the bishop. The former appointed the dean, who acted for him in all ecclesiastical matters. Before the Conquest, Kentish monarchs and nobles had made many gifts, principally of land, to the Church, and this practice continued throughout the Middle Ages. Thus the archbishop held much land in the area through both his secular and ecclesiastical roles. Indeed the two positions – lord of the manor of Otford and head of the Deanery – were almost certainly interconnected. The archbishop was able, as patron, to appoint most of the parish priests in the district.

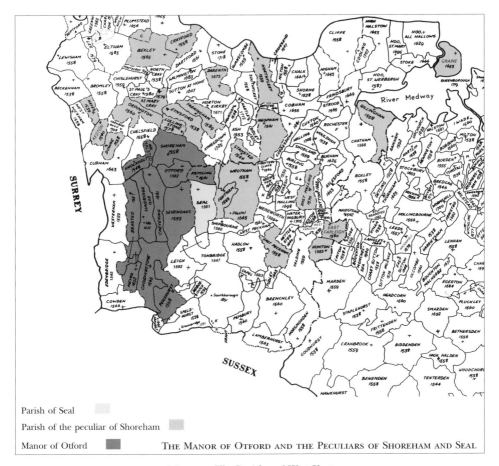

Parish of Seal

Parish of the peculiar of Shoreham

Manor of Otford

THE MANOR OF OTFORD AND THE PECULIARS OF SHOREHAM AND SEAL

MAP 4 *The Parishes of West Kent.*

The Peculiar of Shoreham, known in its secular context as the Bailiwick of Otford, comprised about thirty parishes in west and north Kent, including all those in Codsheath, although Seal, a daughter of Kemsing, was not in the Peculiar. The area immediately around Sevenoaks, the manor of Otford, was a consolidated piece of territory, in which the parishes were contiguous and, indeed, extended southward to include Somerden, and northward to Ruxley and Axtane. By the time of the Conquest, Sundridge was already a separate manor, and Sevenoaks and Shoreham were to follow, but they all remained held by the archbishop and part of the Peculiar.

St Peter and St Paul, Shoreham, was originally the minster for the whole Peculiar. One of its features in the medieval period was the number of distinguished churchmen who were rectors. These included Cardinal Hugo Vickers from 1293, Cardinal William de Testa from 1316, William Warham, Archbishop of Canterbury in 1526, and others. Pluralism, whereby clerics were appointed to many offices and drew several incomes, was common in the medieval Church and it must be doubtful that these men lived at Shoreham, at least for any lengh of time, and exercised their office. That function would have been performed by an ill-paid curate, while the legal incumbent received the emoluments.

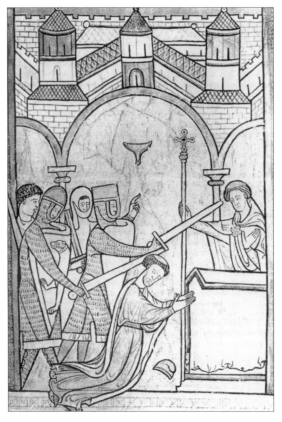

7 *The murder of Thomas Becket. Becket was appointed Archbishop of Canterbury in 1162. Within a few months he resigned as the king's chancellor and began to oppose the king. It was a conflict of personalities but the main issue was the division of authority between church and state. The rivalry between Becket and Henry became bitter. In late December 1170 four knights loyal to Henry murdered the archbishop in his cathedral at Canterbury. Within three years of his death Becket had been canonised as a saint of the Church. His tomb became a shrine visited by pilgrims. Pilgrimages to the shrine are perhaps best known from Geoffrey Chaucer's great poem,* The Canterbury Tales, *completed in the late 14th century.*

On account of its proximity to the archbishop's palace and its centrality as head of the Manor, St Bartholomew, Otford, became more important than Shoreham. It has been suggested that the church was founded by Dunstan, Archbishop of Canterbury 959-88, but the idea that Otford was older than Shoreham must be attributed to excessive local patriotism.[13] Thomas Becket, Archbishop of Canterbury 1162-70, lived for long periods at Otford. Later, pilgrims, en route to the shrine of Thomas at Canterbury, stopped at the east end of the church where there was a spring which became known as St Thomas's, or Becket's, Well. A legend grew that Becket had struck the ground with his staff and water had flowed which, it was said, was especially effective for healing grazes.[14]

Archbishops of Canterbury possessed palaces all over the country: usually at a day's ride from each other. Otford was conveniently situated between Canterbury and the palace at Lambeth, or other palaces at Charing, Maidstone, Mayfield, and Croydon. The Otford palace, originally a Saxon manor house, was substantially rebuilt in the 11th and 12th centuries. It is often assumed that the initiator of this reconstruction was Lanfranc of Pavia, Archbishop of Canterbury 1070-89, appointed after the Conqueror had engineered the deposition of the Anglo-Saxon Archbishop Stigand. The dimensions of 'Lanfranc's' palace are unknown, but it must have been impressive. All the medieval archbishops would have known the palace, including Becket who, it is said, banned nightingales from the palace gardens because one interrupted his prayers. Kings were not infrequent visitors. Otford Palace was totally transformed by William Warham, who was archbishop from 1504-31, as well as Lord Chancellor from 1503-5. Archaeological investigation has revealed the great extent of Warham's palace and that it contained a chapel separate from the parish church.[15] Warham was not to be outdone by his contemporary

8 *St Nicholas' parish church, facing south. The east end of the building is very close to the road indicating that it probably originated as a wayside shrine in early medieval times.*

at Hampton Court, Cardinal Wolsey, so he constructed his new palace at Otford in the same style and just as large. Monarchs and distinguished foreign visitors came to the palace: Cardinal Campeggio in 1518, and Henry VIII and Queen Catherine, on their way to the Field of the Cloth of Gold, in 1520. Thomas Cranmer, archbishop from 1533, drew up the 39 Articles of the Church of England here. Henry VIII sequestrated the palace for his own use, but soon decided that he preferred Knole. Consequently Otford quickly fell into disrepair and was pillaged for its materials, leaving little to be seen today.

Knole, overlooking Sevenoaks, also became an archbishop's palace. The house was originally a sub-manor house of the Otford estate. Thomas Bourchier, archbishop between 1454 and 1486, turned Knole from a medieval farm house into a grand palace, and lived there for long periods. It contained a chapel on the south-east corner of the house.[16] At the Reformation Archbishop Cranmer

9 *William Warham (c.1456-1532), Archbishop of Canterbury 1503-32. Warham served as archbishop for much of the reign of King Henry VIII. He rebuilt the manor at Otford into a splendid palace, completed in 1518, at the reputed cost of £33,000. Warham also owned the great house at Knole. Henry VIII took both Otford Palace and Knole from Cranmer, Warham's successor as archbishop.*

10 *An 18th-century engraving of Otford Palace. By the late 18th century little of the once splendid Otford Palace remained. Hasted, in 1797, wrote that 'there is nothing left of the mansion itself, but vast heaps of rubbish and foundations, which cover near an acre of ground'.*

was forced by the king to surrender Knole to him and it remained Crown property until sold in the early 17th century to the Sackvilles, who had previously leased it.

The Church: Practice and Belief

Religion and the Church permeated the thoughts and lives of medieval people and were integral to the community. Religion was not a private and personal matter, and the church was hierarchical and subject to the authority of deans, bishops, archbishops and, ultimately, the Pope. The parish priest was a most important person in the community and had invariably received some formal education. Frequently the parish priest or a chantry chaplain would provide education for the children of the parish. At St Nicholas church, Sevenoaks, the schoolroom in the 15th century was probably the 'parvise room' over the south porch, where there are small windows and a fireplace. Glebe land, held or leased by the Church, provided the priest with land that he could rent out to supplement his income from tithes.

The laity, rich and poor alike, were expected to attend church to hear and see the Mass, during which the priest celebrated Christ's death on the cross. The idea of purgatory, a place of suffering which dead souls endured before they could enter heaven, was especially significant. It underpinned both the need to seek pardon and the foundation of chantries, where prayers were offered to assist the salvation of souls. Christians were required to make confession, receive the sacraments, be baptised, and buried in the church or graveyard; the Church also assumed control over the celebration of marriages. In addition it had a social and welfare role: there were outdoor processions, Passion plays, and pilgrimages; alms aided the poor, and hospitals provided for lepers, the sick and the old.

Although the basic structure of the liturgy was uniform throughout western Christendom, practice varied from place to place. The Salisbury rite, known as 'Old Sarum', prevailed throughout England, but was not universal. The Church provided a series of services throughout the day, which were conducted in Latin, beginning with Matins and Vespers, also including Compline and celebration of the Mass. In an ordinary parish church the Mass was the most important rite, and it was supposed to be said by the priest each day, even when nobody else was present. Mass became increasingly important following the proclamation of the doctrine of transubstantiation by the Fourth Lateran Council in 1215. High Mass on Sunday was the principal religious event of the week for the laity, but, as time proceeded, because communion was supposed to be taken after confession, many Christians only did so as little as once a year, despite admonitions from the clergy to attend more frequently.

11 *Otford village showing the site of the former archbishop's palace. The palace was surrounded by a crenellated wall built of local ragstone and brick. Three-storey towers stood at regular intervals and also at the main gate, which gave entry to the Great Inner Court measuring 82m by 72.5m. The palace was larger than Hampton Court, and surrounded by extensive parkland. All that remains today is a single tower on the north west of what was the Great Court.*

Originally, communion was given as both wine and bread, but increasingly from the 12th century it became usual for only the bread to be offered. This was both for reasons of hygiene and out of growing respect for the Host; the argument for the latter being that as it constituted *both* the flesh and the blood of Christ the communicant would receive the blood of Christ in the bread. Other sacraments included baptism (conventionally of babies soon after birth), confirmation of the laity, marriage, the ordination of priests and the burial of the dead. Frequently burial was within the church, as was demonstrated by the recent discovery under the chancel of St Nicholas, Sevenoaks, of the remains of more than six hundred people.[17]

The interiors of churches were generally much more decorated and colourful than they are today. Murals depicted biblical scenes, saints' lives and didactic messages (often concerning death). Some windows contained stained glass. Statues of the Virgin and other saints were common, and the Stations of the Cross would be visited at Easter. The interior space was filled with the light, and smells, from many candles. Incense and holy water took a prominent place in ceremony and ritual. The Sanctuary, with the altar at the east end of the church and where the Host and a perpetual light were kept and the Mass was celebrated, was separated from the main body of the church by an ornate stone or wooden rood screen, creating a sense of mystery and sanctity. A medieval example survives at Shoreham.

There were few seats or benches and many of the congregation had to stand during services. Crucifixes were highly esteemed as a reminder of Christ's sacrifice, and also for their supposed ability to ward off the devil and other evil spirits. Saints' days, and other important events in the Church's calendar, such as the Feast of Corpus Christi or Rogationtide, a sort of Harvest Supper, were given special celebration with Masses and processions. Some medieval parishes possessed Missals or Mass books, codices of Gospels and Epistles, Psalters, office chants and saints' Lives. Christians were also expected to fast occasionally and, because Christ's crucifixion was on a Friday, to abstain from eating meat on that day and to eat fish instead. Finally, Christians were urged to go on pilgrimages to holy places such as Rome, Santiago de Compostela, Jerusalem or, in England, to Walsingham or Becket's shrine at Canterbury. This last was important for the Sevenoaks area as one of the major routes to Canterbury passed through Brasted, Sundridge, Chevening, Otford, and Kemsing.

Wills and testaments can reveal a great deal about the nature of late medieval piety and practice. A typical testament is that of John Speham of Shoreham, dated 1431, who asserted that his 'primary imperative was to commit his soul to Almighty God, the Blessed Mary and All the Saints'.[18] Medieval people were willing to bequeath wealth to the church, not least in the hope of eternal benefits. In 1371, for example, William Steel left 20 shillings for the fabric of Chevening church; in 1475 William Rogers left 40 shillings for the repair of the steeple at Otford; in 1485 Katherine Mercer, a widow, left 6s. 8d. for church works at Shoreham; in 1510 Clemens Broke, another widow, left 40 shillings for a cope, 20 shillings for a silver censer and ten shillings for a silver cross for Sevenoaks church.[19]

Chantries and Hospitals

From the 13th century, chantries became a common form of endowment of churches and chapels in England by the gentry and merchants. Chantries were thus particularly associated with towns, where merchants lived and operated. Chantry foundations became numerous again after the Black Death when the large number of deaths in frequent outbreaks of plague focused minds on death and eternity. By the 1530s when, during the Reformation, chantries were suppressed along with monasteries and hospitals, there were more than three thousand chantries in England.

The southern part of the Peculiar of Shoreham contained five chantries, two of which were in Sevenoaks. In 1257 the rector of Sevenoaks, Henry of Ghent, endowed a chantry which was dedicated to the Virgin Mary. An altar was erected in St Nicholas', where Mass was said to the Virgin on three days each week. A chantry house for the chantry priest, although not the present building, stood to the north of the churchyard. An endowment of land to support the chantry was provided at Otford and on Romney Marsh. Mass was said for Henry and all Christian souls. In 1298 a chantry for saying Mass for the sick was founded at St John's, or Greatness, Chapel, probably located near the north-west quarter of the Bat and Ball crossroads and close to Greatness

Springs. One medieval text refers to it as Riverhead Chapel, although it was probably some way from there. It had a pre-Conquest origin, as the *Textus Roffensis* indicates, as a chapel of ease of Halstead. A likely explanation is that a Saxon thegn who held land at Halstead also held land at Greatness and founded a chapel there. This chapel was probably linked to the Hospital of St John the Baptist when that institution was founded at the bottom of St John's Hill. This was a hospital for the poor, aged and sick, and the tax registers of Pope Nicholas III show that it was in existence by 1292. There were no monasteries, priories or nunneries in Sevenoaks. However, it is probable that the Hospital of St John was served by monks or canons, although it was not an enclosed house.[20]

The Church: Personnel

It is thought that during some periods of the Middle Ages in England the clergy constituted at least 10 per cent of the population. The clergy was entirely male and (supposedly) celibate. From about 1000 the papacy tried to enforce celibacy on the clergy, but it was not until about 1150 that all bishops were unmarried, and not until 1200 that parish priests were. Inevitably many priests had sexual liaisons, fathered children and, in some cases, kept concubines. Most parish priests were secular (non-monastic) clergy. There were five degrees of holy orders, of which priest was the highest. It is estimated that there were about 23,000 seculars at the time of the Conquest and about 26,500 by 1500. The process of entry to the priesthood was ordination by bishops, but it would seem that in the Middle Ages it was unusual for ordinations to occur in the cathedrals at Rochester and Canterbury. The usual venue was a parish church and, for example, we find archbishops ordaining many men at Sevenoaks in 1283 and 1295, and at Otford in 1299 and March and December 1367.[21] From the 12th or 13th centuries most of the parishes in the area have lists of incumbent priests, rectors or vicars. For example, the first rector of Sevenoaks is recorded in 1217, of Kemsing in 1265 and of Halstead in 1282. Retiring priests were sometimes provided with a pension, paid out of parish funds, as was the case in July 1480 when Sevenoaks was obliged by Archbishop Bourchier to pay nine marks per annum to Richard Clerk. Similarly, on retiring as vicar of Chevening in 1493, John Potter was awarded a pension of five marks per annum plus victuals.[22]

Pluralism was widespread, and the practice often attracted a great deal of opprobrium. In the 13th century William de Testa, Rector of Shoreham, was granted dispensation by Pope Gregory X also to be Prebend of Wingham and a canon of Canterbury. John Ixworth, Rector of Sevenoaks in 1395, was allowed by Pope Boniface IX to hold canonries at Salisbury, London, Westbury, Beverley, Southwell and another parish in Norfolk.[23]

Although medieval women could not be ordained into holy orders as clergy, there were many ways in which they could participate actively in religious practice. Many women became nuns, and by becoming abbesses or prioresses they acquired a degree of authority in the wider community, especially when they were from the royal or aristocratic families. Women were expected to be pious and generous to the Church; they frequently founded religious houses, almshouses and chantries. They also went on pilgrimage; a few women went with husbands on Crusade. Some widowed women took a vow of chastity. Books, and benefactions of gentry and aristocratic women, indicate that the Blessed Virgin Mary was highly venerated in the later Middle Ages. The Church's view that male and female roles were largely separate, especially with regard to ordination, was challenged by some who held the unorthodox religious views generally known as Lollardy. It is possible that some Lollard women claimed to be priests on the grounds that 'all holy men and women members of Christ are priests'.[24]

The Church: Finances

Through landholding, tithes, fees and gifts, the Church became a wealthy institution although many individual parishes and clergy were poor. The Church accumulated much land and in many areas became the largest landholder. Out of 150 identified manors held in Kent at the time of Domesday, 83 were held by lay lords, nine by the Crown and 62 by the Church. After the Conquest much land was sequestrated by the Crown, by the king's half-brother Odo, Bishop of Bayeux, and by others. Archbishop Lanfranc sought to establish which land had belonged to St Augustine's Abbey, Canterbury, of which he was *ex officio* Prior, and which land was held by the archbishop in virtue of his office. He eventually recovered all the land held before 1066, and thus the archbishop continued to hold the manors of Otford, Sundridge, Eynsford and, indeed, the whole of the Bailiwick of Otford, for which in 1161 he owed the Crown 60 knights' fees. Du Boulay has calculated that the average net annual value of the archbishop's lands, though not just in Otford, was £1,345 for the period 1086-1200, £2,128 for the period 1200-95 and £3,178 for the period 1295-1535. Unfortunately no records seem to have survived of the income of individual parishes, although the register of Cardinal John Morton, Archbishop of Canterbury 1486-1500, gives us valuations and tithes for some parishes, including Sevenoaks, which totalled £40 and £2 respectively.[25]

The fiscal and property power of the Church increasingly worried the Crown and caused much general hostility. Edward I's response was the Statute of Mortmain in 1279 that forbade further acquisitions of land by the Church. It had little effect because the Church had already acquired so much, including in the Peculiar of Shoreham. One consequence of so much Church land ownership in Kent was that deforestation was slower than elsewhere because the Church discouraged wholesale felling of trees and preferred to manage its woods rather than destroy them.[26] It is said that by the Reformation the Church owned about 40 per cent of the land in Kent, which may have helped kindle popular resentment of the Church and anticlericalism.[27]

The Church and Unorthodox Beliefs

It would seem that the English population remained doctrinally orthodox for most of the Middle Ages, although there may have been a deep vein of anticlericalism. Many of the heresies prevalent in Europe did not appear in England. However, in the late 14th century, Lollard ideas did. These were associated with the Oxford theologian John Wycliffe (1329-84) and his followers. Wycliffe attacked many Catholic fundamentals such as papal authority, confession, transubstantiation and monasticism. His major proposition was that reliance on the Bible was the main source of religious authority, and therefore the Bible must be translated from Latin (the Vulgate) into English, which he proceeded to do. Some Lollards came to regard the Pope as the Antichrist.

Unaccustomed to heresy the English Church was slow to react, but a counter-attack against Wycliffe and his followers at Oxford was led by William Courtenay, Archbishop of Canterbury, 1381-96. Thereafter, throughout the 15th century, the Church battled with Wycliffe's followers. In the 1420s and 1430s many Lollards were found in the Weald of Kent. Heretics were discovered in West Malling in 1425, in Tenterden in 1428, when 30 people were arrested, and again in 1438, when five were executed. They were found in Hadlow and Brenchley in 1431 and Tonbridge in 1496. The Church's final assault on heresy culminated in the early 16th century, on the initiative of Archbishop Warham, with trials held in 1510-12 in London, Lincoln and Coventry. At the same time a large number of trials were held at Canterbury, Otford, and Sevenoaks, both in the parish church and at Knole. Fifty-three people were tried, including 12 from Tenterden, eight from Staplehurst, seven from Cranbrook and four each from Boxley and Canterbury, but none from Sevenoaks. Five were delivered to the civil authorities for burning as unrepentant heretics. The rest were given penances to perform. The most common penance was carrying a faggot of wood on public occasions (to represent burning), confinement to a parish or locality, and being forced to inform on others who had unorthodox beliefs or books.[28]

Conclusion: the Later Middle Ages and the Reformation

In the years following 1348, repeated outbreaks of bubonic plague (the Black Death) swept England, ultimately reducing the population by as much as one half. The economic effects were profound. The number of peasants and thus agricultural labourers fell, and land under cultivation contracted. For example, in the manor of Otford there was a marked decline in arable land between 1350 and 1450.[29] Throughout the country the balance of power shifted between lords, tenants and peasants, with the latter groups challenging both lay and ecclesiastical authority. The Church's income decreased; the number of clergy to serve the people was reduced, not only by death, but because many priests fled the plague in the belief that they could escape it. One archbishop of Canterbury, Thomas Bradwardine, originally from Cowden, died of plague in August 1349, and it has been suggested that as many as half the secular clergy perished from the Black Death. The aged bishop of Rochester, Hamo Hethe, retired to Trottiscliffe where, although he survived, he lost from his household four priests, five squires, 10 servants, six clerks and six pages.[30]

Serious civil disturbances occurred in the late 14th and 15th centuries: the Peasants' Revolt of 1381, Cade's Rebellion of 1450 and Fauconberg's Kentish Rising of 1471. Many people from the Sevenoaks area joined in Cade's Rebellion and in the victory won by the rebels at the battle of Solefields on 18 June 1450, a few hundred metres south of St Nicholas' Church. One consequence of this widespread discontent was that automatic deference towards the Church, and also to secular authority, declined, thus preparing the ground for the major changes in the Church in England known as the Reformation. Lollardy had also anticipated many of the changes of the Reformation and prepared the way for it.[31] When the Reformation came contemporaries would initially have recognised continuity as well as change in religious belief and practice. Henry VIII, whatever others desired, wanted the rituals of the Catholic Church to continue, but within a Church where ultimate authority lay inside England. A key issue therefore was where final secular authority lay in a Christian society. Nevertheless, doctrine, liturgy, and church discipline inevitably came to be questioned. An uninhibited national sovereignty was encouraged, and this helped to increase English nationalism and an intense dislike of foreign (papal) influence in both secular and ecclesiastical matters.

For a long time English folk memory, culture and historiography has been generally hostile to late medieval English Catholicism. Recently some scholars have taken a more favourable view, although not always convincingly. In 1995, for example, one historian wrote: 'I continue to believe that the late medieval church, in England at least, was in a state that satisfied the spiritual and social aspirations of the vast majority of the English people'.[32] Yet there can be no doubt that profound religious change happened in English society in the decades either side of 1530. When in 1534 the clergy in the Sevenoaks area were required to renounce papal authority the order was accepted, whatever the reasons, without apparent demur by the clergy in Brasted, Chevening, Halstead, Kemsing, Otford, Seal, Sevenoaks, Shoreham and Sundridge, as well as in other parishes throughout the Peculiar of Shoreham.[33]

REFORMATION

Alexander Morrison[*]

The title of this chapter uses familiar and convenient historical language, but most historians would nowadays take issue with the idea that the English Reformation was a single, datable event, sparked by Luther's 95 theses of 1517, and accomplished by the break with Rome and the sweeping legislation and expropriations of Henry VIII's reign. The changes of the 16th and 17th centuries had intellectual roots that in England went back as least as far as the teachings of John Wycliffe at the end of the 14th century. Not only did the turbulent reigns of Edward VI and Mary significantly alter the legacy of their father, but the tensions within the fledgling Church of England were by no means resolved by the Elizabethan religious settlement of 1559. The struggle was not simply between the Protestant Church of England and the Counter-Reformation, it was also an internal one between radicals and conservatives for the soul of the national church, that was carried on throughout the Great Rebellion and Civil War. By 1660 Presbyterianism and nonconformity were tainted with rebellion, and the chief perceived threat to the Anglican settlement would come once again from Catholicism. Whilst this was often illusory, it took very concrete form with James II and his designs to legalise nonconformity. If the Glorious Revolution which ousted him undermined the principle of passive obedience to the monarch that had been so vociferously promoted by the Church of England after 1660, it is fair to say that it ushered in a period of religious stability or, some might say, stagnation. The doctrinal and ritual questions that had plagued the Church in the 16th and 17th centuries ceased to be a major source of debate as the Church sank into a comfortable Erastian passivity. The radical Anabaptist and Catholic threats receded, apart from the Jacobite uprisings of 1715 and 1745, whose inspiration was far from being wholly religious. The Reformation was thus a lengthy, though not a constant, process, and altogether 1688 is a fairly satisfying concluding date for the most turbulent period in English religious history since the arrival of Augustine. Where the process can be said to have begun is more complicated.

The Particular Nature of the Reformation in Kent

The peculiarities of Kent are manifold: its British (that is, Celtic) name, so unusual in an eastern county, its Jutish customs and laws, and the practice of gavelkind, or partible inheritance, rather than the primogeniture prevalent

[*] Alexander Morrison is a Fellow of All Souls' College, Oxford.

elsewhere in England. The county's proximity to London meant that the will of the centre could never be entirely ignored, but notoriously bad roads and local solidarity mitigated this somewhat. As Alan Everitt has shown, even by the time of the Great Rebellion, there were relatively few 'outsiders' to be found amongst the Kentish gentry: a mere eighth of about a thousand families.[1] The newly rich lawyers and court officials of the Tudor world, who flocked to buy land in Essex, Hertfordshire and the other Home Counties, were less frequent in Kent, which, owing to gavelkind and early, small-scale enclosures, had very few of the large estates that attracted incomers. Because of its proximity to London, Sevenoaks represents an important exception to this pattern, as the Bosvilles, Lambardes and Sackvilles who purchased, or were given, estates surrounding the town all owed their fortunes to the law.

If the prevalence of traditional gentry families and poor communications encouraged religious conservatism, the economic dynamism of the cloth towns of the Weald (such as Cranbrook and Tenterden), with their relatively large concentration of wealthy, literate bourgeois families, made them much more fertile sites for the growth of religious radicalism. They were joined by a strong anti-clerical tradition in Canterbury itself, where the municipality resented the dominance of the cathedral, and the relatively cosmopolitan ports, such as Folkestone, Dover, Sandwich and Chatham, also harboured a fair number of heretics. This was less true of west Kent, but towns such as Sevenoaks which, though dominated by large estates, had good communications with London and a strong ecclesiastical and, later, royal presence could not remain impervious to the currents of change at the centre. The single most important fact about Kent was the presence there of the Primate of the English Church at Canterbury. The county was always the first to feel the impact of changes in archiepiscopal policy, whether that meant the destruction of the trappings and rituals of Catholic worship or their reinstatement. Within Kent, Sevenoaks thus represents a town with little real independence from outside interference, whether that came from the great estates, from London, from Canterbury, or a combination of the three. The turbulent events of the Reformation and Great Rebellion could not pass the town by.

The Causes and Progress of the English Reformation

The assumption underlying much scholarship on this period, notably A.G. Dickens' elegant work *The English Reformation*, is that late medieval English Catholicism was spiritually bankrupt, and had already lost the support and faith of 'ordinary people'. As he put it:

> English Catholicism, despite its gilded decorations, was an old, unseaworthy
> and ill-commanded galleon, scarcely able to continue its voyage without
> the new seamen and shipwrights produced (but produced far too late
> in the day) by the Counter-Reformation.[2]

The monasteries abused their endowments; priests terrified their congregations with the spurious doctrine of purgatory, threatening them with ages of torment if they did not leave money for *diriges* and prayers to be

offered up for their souls in chantries; the laity were kept in ignorance and
superstition owing to the retention of Latin as the sole vehicle for Scripture.
The twin corrosive influences of Lollardy and humanist learning were held to
blame for beginning the destruction of this tottering structure. Almost the only
Protestant doctrine not anticipated by John Wycliffe at the end of the 14th
century was justification by faith alone, and there is no doubt that Lollardy,
in the form of small, largely urban 'cells', survived into the Tudor period.
Lollard martyrs are well attested to by John Foxe, in the *Acts and Monuments*
or *Book of Martyrs* (1554-63); to give a Kentish example, several Lollard groups
in the vicinity of Cranbrook, Benenden and Tenterden were denounced to
Archbishop Warham from which, in 1511-12, 50 people abjured heresy and
and five were burned.[3] The humanist tradition is exemplified by the great
Dutch scholar Erasmus, who became the first teacher of Greek at Cambridge
in 1511, and in 1516 published a new and accurate Latin translation of the
New Testament, and also by John Colet, who delivered a famous series of
lectures on St Paul's Epistles at Oxford in 1496-9 which were among the
first to point out the differences between the apostle Paul's vision of how
the Church should be organised and the Catholic reality. It was upon this
tradition of dissent and enquiry, as much as upon the Lutheran model, that
the doctrinal edifice of the English Reformation would be built.

In east Kent and the Weald the indigenous Protestant tradition seems
to have been stronger than in other counties; it also came under Lutheran
influence from across the Channel very early. Michael Zell thus argues that 'in
Kent the Reformation thus began before the English State broke its institutional
ties with the "universal" Catholic Church'.[4] This statement may well be true
of east Kent, from which most of his examples are drawn, but it is less so of
the Sevenoaks area. The early 16th century saw a flurry of religious building
activity here and elsewhere, which belies the image of a Church on the verge
of collapse. The towers at Seal and Sevenoaks date from this period, as do
the north aisle and Easter Sepulchre at Otford. Here we find that in 1532
Robert Multon stated in his will that 'I will that myn executour shall cause
the image of our Ladye of Petye to be made and sett in the North Side of the
newe Ile',[5] and as late as 1537 John Rogers left money for the maintenance
of tapers before the image of the Virgin Mary and St Thomas.

The rhythm of life in late medieval England was closely bound up with the
calendar and ritual of the Catholic Church. The mystery plays and processions
at Corpus Christi, the beating of the bounds on Rogation Sunday, the Lent
and Easter symbols of ashes and palms, and the frequent saints' days provided
opportunities for a display of local wealth and pride, as well as popular
entertainments. The idea that a particular saint would personally intercede
with God for the benefit of a soul suffering in purgatory was deeply comforting
to many people. The austerity of scriptural Christianity could be extremely
alienating: it is worth remembering that the cult of the saints had played a
crucial role in the original conversion of Europe to Christianity by providing
monotheism with a human face, so that pagan worshippers could retain
the personal and specific intercessors they had been used to. Even the self-
consciously godly William Lambarde, who railed against 'innumerable such

toyes false priestes have devised, and fonde people (alas) have believed'[6] (referring to the 'Rood of Grace' at Boxley Abbey, revealed as a piece of mechanical trickery in 1538), took care to describe the various saints' cults and superstitions obtaining in pre-Reformation Kent in great detail, betraying, perhaps, a certain nostalgia for some of them.

However appealing they are to intellectuals, past and present, there is little evidence to suggest that either Lollardy or humanism had much popular appeal, certainly in comparison with the colourful ceremonies and comprehensive ritual calendar of the Catholic Church. It would be entirely anachronistic to suggest that 16th-century Englishmen all felt that the Church's authority depended solely on its adherence to the letter of scripture, rather than the weight of tradition and precedent, and the important social role it played. As Collinson puts it: 'There is no reason to believe that an intellectually demanding and morally rigorous religion transmitted by the spoken word had a broad, natural appeal'.[7]

Christopher Haigh and Eamon Duffy are the chief proponents of the view that late medieval English Christianity was vibrant and popular, and that the Reformation constituted not the inevitable collapse of a rotting structure, but a deeply unsettling disruption of the order of life and death.[8] Churches were stripped of images, furniture and fittings that represented not only cherished local cults, but also generations of donations and memorials. As Duffy puts it, the dead, for whom prayers and remembrances had formerly been constant, were utterly cast out of the company of the living when the chantries were dissolved, as that of St Peter in Sevenoaks parish church was in 1536, together with the hospital of St John at Greatness. In Otford, in 1537, Roger Multon's son caused the most holy local image, that of St Bartholomew (who granted favours in return for chickens), to be taken down, an event described with much relish and self-righteousness by Lambarde (Multon was his wife's grandfather).

> Assuredly, throughe the fraude of this foxe, the countrie people (as wise
> as capons) were many yeeres together robbed of their Hens and Cocks:
> till at length it chaunced King Henrie the eight … to have conference
> with some of the towne, about the enlarging of his Park there; Amongst
> the which, one, called Maister Robert Multon (a man, whom for the
> honest memorie of his godly zeale and vertuous life, I stick not to
> name) detesting the abuse, and espying the Prince inclined to hear
> him, unfolded the whole packe of the idolatrie and prevailed so far in
> favour, that shortly after, the King commaunded Saint Bartholomew to
> be taken downe and to be delivered unto him.[9]

This incident took place a year before Cranmer's notorious 'deed of exchange' with the king, whereby he surrendered Knole and the manor of Otford, together with the new palace there, to the Crown, in return for land of lesser value. This marked the end of the archiepiscopal presence at Knole. As is fairly clear from the anecdote, when the Reformation came to west Kent, and arguably to England in general, it was far more as an act of State

12 *Protestant martyrs of Mary's reign. Religious intolerance and persecution was pursued by all factions during the Reformation. In England the Protestant cleric John Foxe wrote* Actes and Monuments *or* Book of Martyrs *(1554-63) which became a bestseller. In this illustration Archbishop Cranmer and other bishops are being burned to death for heresy in 1556.*

than as a popular measure. Henry VIII was doctrinally conservative, and it was Papal encroachments on newly established Tudor national sovereignty, rather than abuses prevalent in the unreformed Church, or scepticism about the scriptural basis for the primacy of Rome, which prompted him to kick against Catholicism. In 1521, after all, a bonfire of Luther's books was held at Cambridge by royal command, and Henry produced a book entitled *An Assertion of the Seven Sacraments*, refuting Luther's contention that only two, baptism and communion, were scripturally sanctioned. For this the Pope gave him the title Defender of the Faith, which the monarchs of England have borne ever since. The occasion for the break with Rome was Pope Clement VII's refusal, under intense Habsburg pressure, to annul Henry's marriage to Catherine of Aragon. The first Act of Supremacy was duly passed in November 1534. Thomas Cromwell's injunctions to Deaneries that followed provided only for the abrogation of 'superfluous' holy days and 'restraint' in pilgrimages and the worship of images. The 'Bishop's Book' of 1537 envisioned greater reform, and injunctions were sent out forbidding lights before images, and denouncing 'good works' as superstition, rather than the path to salvation. However, the six articles in 1539 represented, if anything, a reversion to earlier norms: transubstantiation, and thus the Mass, was upheld, and the spiritual benefits of private masses affirmed, together with the need for clerical celibacy. What is beyond dispute, however, is that the Church, whether in the form of monastic or other religious endowments, was stripped of a very large part of its wealth under Henry, which found its way into secular hands. This led to a chronic under-funding of the majority of Church livings that persisted until well into the 19th century.

The path to reforms of doctrine, practice and belief in the Henrician years, other than the destruction of religious endowments and the establishment of the Royal Supremacy, is not, however, to be found in the tentative steps recorded in the statute book. Far more significant was the appearance of numerous English translations of the Bible and New Testament, beginning with William Tyndale's in 1526 (itself a translation from Erasmus's Latin version), in which he had received considerable assistance from Kentishman John Fryth, who was later martyred for his pains. The impact of this circulation of the scriptures amongst the small, largely urban literate classes is difficult to assess. There is plenty of anecdotal evidence for parish hecklers disrupting services because they did not accord with biblical provisions, but perhaps the most compelling evidence for official disquiet at the religious and social consequences of the spread of lay interpretation is the Act of Parliament of 1543, which attempted to restrict readership to the clergy and gentry by forbidding lower-class laymen from reading the scriptures themselves, and instead insisting that they receive the word of God through the medium of a priest, albeit in their own language. It seems highly unlikely that this can have been very effective, as the Tudor State did not have the resources to police people's reading habits, and could not attempt to censor, or ban, the Bible as it did with other Protestant and Lollard texts.

With the accession of Edward VI in 1547, or more precisely the ascendancy of an extreme Protestant clique at court under Protector Somerset, religious legislation moved far beyond the conservative confines of the Henrician Reformation. It is in this short reign that, according to Duffy, the most traumatic episode of the Reformation can be found. The cult of the saints was systematically attacked and destroyed, the Mass ceased to be celebrated, ritual was simplified or disappeared altogether, and the State appropriated the material spoils. Images, reliquaries, chalices, roods, thuribles – the rich legacy of generations of bequests for Catholic worship – all but the bare minimum were requisitioned from the Church by the Treasury, and melted down for the value of the bullion. Stone altars were ordered to be destroyed and replaced with wooden 'holy tables' that would only be moved into the chancel for the 'Lord's Supper', as the sacrifice of Mass had now become. In 1544-5 Cranmer composed the English Prayer Book to replace Latin, and orders were given in 1549 for its purchase and adoption by all English churches.

Archbishop Cranmer ensured that Kent received unusually large numbers of Reformist, or 'Puritan' clergy for whom, the sources make fairly clear, their congregations were not always ready (no fewer than 210 presentations were made to benefices in the county between 1541 and 1553).[10] The county also suffered heavily when the process was thrown into reverse with Bloody Mary's accession in 1553, when 101 incumbents were ousted.[11] All Edward's religious legislation was repealed, together with the Act of Supremacy, and Catholic worship restored, at least in theory, in every particular, leaving churches with the knotty problem of replacing the roods, chalices, and other trappings which had only just been removed. If the initial impact of Protestantism was traumatising, this was perhaps still more true of the Catholic restoration under Mary; the purge of Kent's clergy on her accession was particularly

thorough, with Sevenoaks losing its rector, Walter Darkenold. Although Duffy
contends that Mary's reign saw a very effective restoration of Catholic rites
and doctrine, enthusiastically welcomed by a populace weary of Protestant
bigotry and austerity, most of his examples are drawn from the religiously
conservative west and north of the country. There was certainly no attempt
to restore the financial base of the Church by reappropriating endowments
from their secular purchasers, no doubt partly because it would have provoked
far too much opposition from the gentry, but also because even a Catholic
monarch might have a preference for a Church too poor to be independent
of her authority. Notoriously, Mary's reign also saw the beginning of religious
persecution. This was hardly unprecedented, as Henry had cheerfully burnt
recalcitrant monks and 'dangerous Anabaptists' alike (it was he, after all, who
ordered Fryth's execution in 1533), and Edward VI's reign had not been free
of bonfires at Smithfield either. The executions were, however, on a larger
scale than in either of the previous reigns, and suspicions were voiced that
the religious agenda was being set entirely by the Spanish presence at Court.
Cranmer, Latimer and Ridley, burnt at Oxford, are the most famous martyrs,
but Kent alone suffered a total of 54 burnings between 1554 and 1558, more
than any area other than London.[12] There seems little doubt that in the long
term Catholicism suffered from its association with Spain and specifically with
the house of Habsburg, represented by Mary's husband, Philip II.

The Elizabethan Religious Settlement

With the accession of Elizabeth came a period of relative, if deceptive, peace.
Burnings and martyrdoms ceased and were replaced with fines for recusancy[13]
and other less violent measures. The character of the English Church would
be determined to a great extent by the doctrines of Calvin and Bucer, rather
than Luther; many of the Marian exiles who returned with Elizabeth's accession
had taken refuge in Geneva, Strasbourg, Basel and other European cities.
Under Calvin Geneva was then at the cutting edge of Reformation thinking;
justification by faith alone and predestination were the most important
orthodoxies, together with a rejection both of the traditional hierarchy of the
church, and of secular control: a council of religious elders, or Presbyters, was
the highest ideal of church government. Whilst the latter tendency would not be
allowed to raise its head until the most turbulent years of the Great Rebellion,
the Presbyterian ideal, and attacks on episcopacy, became a characteristic of
the 'Puritan' tendency within the Elizabethan Church.

The rebellion of the northern earls, followed by the execution of the
Duke of Norfolk, the last remaining Catholic grandee, marked the end of
Catholicism as a serious political force until after the Restoration. It was over
the following 40 years that the 'Protestantisation' of Kent and other counties
would be accomplished. The publication of an English edition of Foxes's *Book
of Martyrs* in 1563 was one landmark in this process: probably the most effective
weapon the proponents of Protestantism possessed, apart from the English
Bible, it was a superb piece of propaganda which did much to paint Catholicism
in those bloody, superstitious and, above all, foreign colours in which it
would continue to be seen by most Englishmen well into the 19th century.

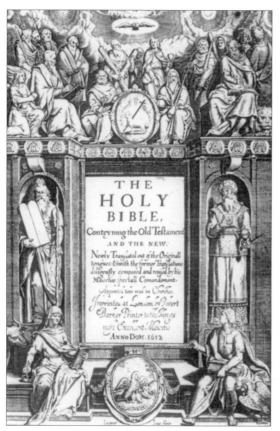

13 *Title page of the Authorised Version of the Bible. Various English translations of the Bible were available in the 16th century: by Tyndale (1526) and Coverdale (1535), and the Geneva Bible of 1557 dedicated to Queen Elizabeth I. At the Hampton Court conference, 1604, James I commissioned 54 scholars to produce a new translation. The result was the publication of the Authorised Version, or the King James Bible, in 1611, which surpassed other versions and remained the standard translation until the 20th century. The Bible was central to Protestantism and copies were placed in every English church by 1540.*

The form of Protestantism practised under Elizabeth, defined by the 'Thirty-nine Articles' of Anglican doctrine and practice, was considerably more moderate than that which had existed during Edward VI's reign. The Prayer Book maintained a reassuringly familiar liturgy, differing from the Mass substantially in its doctrinal significance, but not in its ritual form. Surplices and the making of the sign of the cross were enjoined on all clergy (these were the two 'popish practices' which particularly enraged reformers) and Elizabeth forbade preaching on contentious subjects, and above all on the Calvinist doctrine of predestination, which she rightly realised was repellent to all but the most zealous. The realisation that the Papacy was little more than a tool in the hands of the house of Habsburg, England's greatest enemy, probably reconciled people to the new status quo. After the Papal Bull excommunicating Elizabeth in 1572 it became, at least in theory, impossible to be both a Catholic and a loyal subject of the Crown, though many recusants did attempt this.

We really know very little about popular religious belief and how it changed in this period. The technique, pioneered by Dickens, of examining the preambles to the tens of thousands of surviving Tudor wills for 'Protestant' or 'Catholic' sentiments has been shown to be flawed.[14] Very often the preamble can only have reflected the opinions of the clerk or priest who drafted the will. Furthermore, as it was a public, legal document, one would have to be very foolish indeed to draw up a will expressing belief in doctrines proscribed by law. All wills really show is that people did pay close attention to legislation, and whether under Henry, Edward, Mary or Elizabeth, did their best to ensure that their publicly expressed and recorded religious sentiments did not go beyond the bounds of what was permitted. There are indications, however, that radical Protestantism was on the rise. Under the relatively tolerant archiepiscopate of Matthew Parker, Puritan 'conferences' became common in the towns of east Kent, such as

Sandwich, Ashford and Faversham, where the godly could meet to discuss ideas that were proscribed at the parish church.[15] Recusants never entirely disappeared; indeed Dickens argued that their numbers grew considerably between the 1570s and '90s as the Counter-Reformation missionary effort, spearheaded by the Jesuits, began to have some effect, especially in Yorkshire and other northern counties. The Armada, however, represented the only really serious threat of a Counter-Reformation.

If the threat from Catholicism had receded, the apparently peaceful and consensual condition of the Church during Elizabeth's long reign was extremely deceptive. Traditionalists were dissatisfied with the inadequate observance of the prescribed rituals by the more reform-minded clergy, whilst they in turn chafed against these 'survivals of Popery' and called for a completion of the English Reformation on the presbyterian model, shorn of episcopacy. The circulation of an English translation of Calvin's *Institutes* in the 1570s only sharpened their demands. The pressure became all the greater once Scotland, under the leadership of the formidable John Knox, embarked on a much more thorough Reformation after 1568 and abolished episcopacy. However, by the 1590s there were signs of dissent from the 'Calvinist Consensus' within the Church of England, and some theologians at the universities, notably Peter Baro, Professor of Divinity at Cambridge, publicly rejected the doctrine of predestination. At the same time, a ritualist movement can be identified amongst the clergy, later to be given the title 'Arminianism', after a Dutch theologian who rejected strict predestinarian theology. Whilst they at first confined themselves to an insistence on the practices prescribed in the Prayer Book, which were often ignored by more Presbyterian-minded clergy, William Laud, at Oxford, later initiated a movement for the beautification of churches that included the restoration of stone altars smashed under Edward VI, new stained glass and even statuary. Their activities were a cause of intense disquiet to those who thought that the English Reformation was half-baked even without further preservation of such 'popish baubles'.

When James VI of Scotland succeeded Elizabeth in 1603 there were Puritan hopes that he would enforce further ecclesiastical reform in England based on the Scottish model, but these were dashed at the Hampton Court Conference in 1604, which upheld the status quo. James' conservative sympathies should have been clear to all, as he had already restored bishops to the Scottish Church, albeit in truncated form, and he is famous for coining the phrase 'No Bishop, no King, no Nobility', which neatly sums up contemporary attitudes to the interdependence of the secular and religious hierarchies. Should the authority of bishops, guardians of the ecclesiastical hierarchical order, be destroyed, as many zealous religious reformers urged, it was feared that the divinely ordained 'golden chain of being' which linked society together in its proper order, from the king down to his poorest subject, would also be snapped. The events of the Great Rebellion and the Commonwealth, which began with ecclesiastical reform and ended with the disruption of fraternal war and the execution of the monarch, were to bear this out (and it was during the Commonwealth, indeed, that the above phrase was recalled). Apart from commissioning the Authorised Version of the Bible, one of the great monuments of English literature, James did succeed in preserving the ecclesiastical peace whilst he revelled in the wealth of his new kingdom. His 'reforms' of the Church of Scotland, which now had an uneasy episcopal-Presbyterian form of government, would, however, have extremely serious long-term consequences. On a local level, James presented John Donne to the rich living of Sevenoaks (which was in the royal advowson) in 1616, a position he held until 1631, although he was very much an absentee incumbent.[16] The fragile consensus within the Church of England became ever more strained during James' reign, largely owing to concern about what would happen on the accession of his son.

Charles I and the Great Rebellion

There were numerous signs when Charles was still Prince of Wales that his religious tastes were 'formalist' or 'Arminian'. He chose chaplains of the latter persuasion to accompany him to Madrid during his mad dash there with the Duke of Buckingham in 1622-3, which was intended to arrange a marriage with the leading Catholic power of Europe, and is supposed to have given Charles a dangerous insight into the grandeur and sophistication of an absolutist, Catholic court. Although the idea of the 'Spanish Match' mooted by Buckingham was eventually given up, the prince's marriage to Henrietta Maria of France, a zealous Catholic, was no less religiously suspect. Her chapel at Whitehall, together with those of the French and Spanish ambassadors, became a haunt of English recusants, and the opulence and openness of services there scandalised Puritan opinion. When Charles dissolved the bellicose Parliament of 1629, after its refusal to vote him the usual royal income from Tonnage & Poundage and subsidies, a series of hurried resolutions were passed in its final session; the first of which, reflecting gentry concern about the King's religious proclivities, was that 'Whosoever shall bring in innovation of religion or by favour or countenance seek to extend or introduce Popery or Arminianism ... shall be reputed as a capital enemy to the Kingdom and Commonwealth'.

It was no surprise when Charles made William Laud, the leading 'Arminian', Archbishop of Canterbury in 1633. This was followed by a period of intense disruption in the national Church as Laud, with Charles' full support, attempted to apply to the whole country the ideas he had developed at Oxford. Kevin Sharpe has suggested that some of his measures for the restoration of church fabric and ecclesiastical dignity were not wholly unpopular, but because they were not accompanied by any measures to restore the Church's endowment they placed considerable financial burdens on ordinary parishioners for 'beautification' and ritual purposes of which they frequently disapproved. Despite Laud's assertion that 'the standing of the table either way was a matter of indifference', the restoration of 'popish' stone altars with rails could easily be seen as the prelude to a restoration of the Mass. Laud might plead that communion rails were needed to prevent instances such as one in Dorset where a dog stole the communion loaf, but the Calvinist majority of the clergy were appalled by what they considered to be a creeping Counter-Reformation which mirrored the more violent process on the Continent. Religious passions were accordingly running high amongst the gentry and clergy in 1640, when Charles made the fateful decision to call the first Parliament in over 10 years to raise funds to counter a rebellion north of the border.

Events in Scotland and Ireland played a crucial role in bringing about the Great Rebellion. Charles' religious policy in Scotland had been even less circumspect than in England, as he tried to impose Anglican practice on a Presbyterian system, causing the Scots to renew their National Covenant with God in 1638, repudiating the power of the bishops. The introduction of a prayer book on the English model was the final straw that provoked rebellion, well before such a course was thought of in England. Charles' trusted lieutenant in Ireland, Lord Strafford, then suggested that an Irish, Catholic army, raised by the King and outside the control of Parliament, might be used to suppress this Presbyterian uprising, which added fuel to the flames. Catholic rebellion in Ireland swiftly followed, darkly (and quite falsely) suspected by MPs to be in support of the king, which led to Strafford's indictment for treason. He was sacrificed by Charles to a vindictive and by now openly rebellious House of Commons, whilst Laud was also imprisoned in the Tower, and later executed.[17]

The question of who fought on which side and why in the English Civil War has attracted a good deal of research, and if this is still inconclusive it is because the traditional political division between Parliamentarians

THE SERMON AND PROPHECIE
OF
Mr. JAMES HVNT
of the County of *Kent*.

Who profeffeth himfelfe a Prophet,
Which hee hath endeavoured to deliver in moſt Churches in
and about *London*, but ſince delivered in the *Old-Baily.*
Octob. 9. 1641.

Written with his owne hand.

Printed for *Thomas Bates*, 1641.

14 The Sermon and Prophecie of Mr James Hunt. *Hunt came from Sevenoaks. He was an unscholarly layman and extreme Puritan who favoured independent congregations. Described as 'a fanatic and frantic preacher', his various pamphlets led to his trial and imprisonment in London in 1641.*

and Royalists makes very little sense. The generally accepted chronology of events leading up to the Civil War runs thus: Sir Edward Coke's 'discovery' of the Magna Carta as the founding document of English liberty, the beginning of Charles I's personal rule without Parliament in 1629, the forced loans, Ship Money, Hampden's case, and the attempt on the five members. In recent years, however, this has been overlaid with an understanding of the deeper reasons which caused a substantial proportion of the English gentry to take up arms against their anointed monarch, thus threatening a hierarchy upon which they themselves depended. These reasons were above all religious; the overwhelming majority of the petitions from the counties which flooded into Westminster in 1640-1, often with thousands of signatories, were complaining of abuses in the Church, notably pluralism,[18] rather than Charles's dubious methods of raising money; of the hundreds of political pamphlets produced before January 1642, four times as many were devoted to the impeachment of the bishops as to the

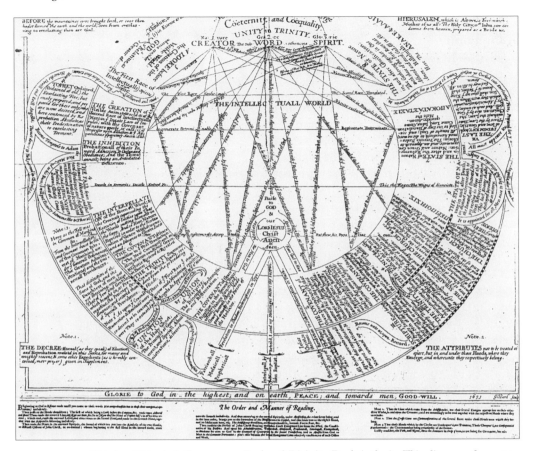

15 *Nicholas Gibbon's* A Summe or Body of Divinity Real (*1653*). *This diagram, from one of Gibbon's books attempts to show the ways in which the various truths of religion are connected. Gibbon became Rector of Sevenoaks in 1631. He was a learned man and, like his vicar William Turner (1614-44), moderate in his religious views and eager to reconcile people of different views where possible. However, he had little sympathy for Puritan ideas and there appear to have been few people in the Sevenoaks area in the 1630s and 1740s who adhered to such beliefs. After his ejection during the Civil War, Gibbon was briefly restored to the living at St Nicholas in 1660-1.*

attempt on the five members. Seventy-five per cent of published parliamentary speeches were also concerned with religion. As Sir Edward Dering, the most prominent Kentish MP and chairman of the Parliamentary Committee for religion, wrote: 'Neither Star-Chamber, nor High Commission, nor Ship Money, nor Strafford's death … are … equivalent to the settling of the Church[19].'

Many gentlemen who had vehemently refused to pay Ship Money became Royalists, but there were none of known Presbyterian sympathies on the King's side. Catholics, and those who believed that the episcopal hierarchy was essential to the maintenance of social order, almost without exception fought for the King, though given the strong 17th-century horror of rebellion and the belief in the need to maintain the natural hierarchy, less explanation is required to show why people became Royalists. On the Parliamentary side, the rebellion was not intended to overthrow the King, still less to execute him, but merely to bring him to his senses and, above all, bring about a 'Godly

Commonwealth' in England; the core of the Parliamentary party wanted to abolish episcopacy, the Prayer Book and other popish survivals, and introduce Presbyterian government for the Church of England. The story of the Great Rebellion is that of the overwhelming of these fairly modest aims by far more radical social and religious movements, followed later, under Cromwell, by a conservative political (though not religious) backlash. It was the bill to abolish episcopacy in 1641, followed quickly by the Grand Remonstrance (which passed by the narrow margin of 159 votes to 148) that seems to have decided many gentlemen, previously hostile to the King, to throw in their lot with him: Hyde, Falkland, Digby and Sir Edward Dering, went over to the King at this stage despite having little enthusiasm for him personally.

During the Great Rebellion Kent's sympathies were largely royalist: the marsh drainage and enclosure schemes that radicalised social relations in East Anglia had little impact here. The Kentish petition to preserve episcopacy drawn up in 1641 by Dering and Culpeper, the knights of the shire, attracted thousands of signatories, and was followed in 1642 by another urging Parliament to reach a settlement with the King. However, the county's proximity to the capital, and the fact that it was cut off from the main centres of loyalty in the West Country and the North, determined its domination by the Parliamentarians.[20] A rising by Kentish conscripts to the New Model Army on Wrotham Heath in April 1645 was quickly crushed by reinforcements from the capital.[21] 1648 saw a massive rising against the parliamentary committee in Kent, which sparked off the second Civil War. In Sevenoaks the Parliamentarian Colonel Sir Edwin Sandys seized Sir John Sackville, a Royalist sympathiser; this was followed by widespread looting in Knole and around the town. Later the Parliamentary committee which governed the county would be accused of 'erecting to themselves a seraglio at Knole', a reference to expenditure of over £3,000 (the estate was sequestrated in 1645).[22] A brief rebellion against Parliament broke out in the Sevenoaks area in 1643 after the Rector of Ightham, John Grimes, not only refused the new oath swearing loyalty to Parliament but encouraged his parishioners to do the same. A rebel camp of about 2,000 men grew up on the Vine in Sevenoaks, but most fled when they heard that a Parliamentary force under Colonel Richard Browne was on its way, and the rump of about five hundred men was ignominiously scattered in a battle at Tonbridge. In 1644, shortly after yet another mutiny of over 4,000 Parliamentary soldiers from west Kent at Sevenoaks, the town's Royalist rector, Dr Nicholas Gibbon, a moderate and scholarly man with a strong belief in episcopacy, was ejected from his living. 'He and his 11 Children were forced to take Sanctuary in a poor Cottage, which, with some small Parcel of Land, he Rented at Four Pounds a Year. There he was obliged to throw aside his Canonical Habit and to drive the Plow himself.'[23] He was replaced by Thomas Kentish, a 'preaching minister', from London.[24] Gibbon urged parishioners not to pay tithes to Kentish and for this he was briefly imprisoned in 1645. However, Kentish preached against the execution of King Charles in 1649 and Parliament removed him, too, from the living at Sevenoaks.

Matters did not end with the introduction of Presbyterian church government, nor was the dynamic of religious change determined entirely by the gentry in

Parliament. Christopher Hill's work, though marred by Marxist blinkers which lead him to attribute an anachronistic class structure to 17th-century English society, is nonetheless extremely valuable in examining the radical religious ideas of the poor.[25] His emphasis is on how religious messianism and close reading of the Bible among groups such as the Ranters, Diggers, Levellers and, to some extent, the Quakers translated into a questioning of the existing social order, and a belief that the kingdom of heaven, the 'New Jerusalem', could in fact be attained on earth by a strict adherence to the dictates of scripture, and a radical redistribution of property. There could be no clearer evidence of the tremendous impact that over one hundred years of direct access to the English Bible had had upon the population, even though only a minority was literate. Adherents of these religious groups were largely to be found among the urban poor and cottagers from counties such as Essex that had been hard hit by the move to enclose commons. The most important force for religious radicalism was undoubtedly the New Model Army, whose heavily indoctrinated and often well-educated officers and men, having enabled the Parliamentary gentry to win the war, turned on their masters after Charles's death and introduced Britain to military dictatorship, with the destruction of the national Church and organised religion very high on the agenda.

Owing to repression by the Commonwealth regime under Cromwell the wilder independent religious sects were suppressed, and of the groups that emerged in these years only the Baptists, Presbyterians and Quakers maintained an organised existence after the Restoration; the latter's arrival in Kent can be dated to 1655,[26] when the preachers were William Caton and John Stubbs (who were put in the stocks and pelted at Maidstone). In 1664 Nathaniel Owen, a wealthy mercer and a Quaker, was renting a tenement in the centre of Sevenoaks.[27] The religious anarchy of the period 1641-59 bred a terror of nonconformism among the gentry, many of whom had been ousted from their positions as JPs, militia captains and sheriffs during the Commonwealth: to them an upsetting of the 'natural' order of society. This led to a reaction in favour of organised religion as the best guarantor of the social hierarchy, not just a return to the Presbyterianism of 1641 (which was probably what General Monck had in mind when he led his army south from Scotland in 1659 to break the New Model Army and remove the Rump Parliament) but to full-blooded, loyalist, episcopalian Anglicanism. When they were given the opportunity to express this feeling after Monck called elections to the Convention of 1659 a Restoration, not just of the monarchy, but of the Anglican Church, became inevitable.

The Anglican Restoration

The 'prayerbook' tendency within the Church of England returned with a vengeance after 1660. Robert Beddard has shown how, at Canterbury, Archbishop Gilbert Sheldon successfully revived all the cathedral's rights and privileges, together with its complete independence from the municipality.[28] There was a new emphasis on the sacred nature of the monarchy, and the duty of 'passive obedience' towards it as guarantor of the social and religious hierarchy. All office holders were required to swear an oath that it was 'unlawful, upon any pretence whatsoever, to take up arms against the King'. Yet a mere 28 years later a large section of the political elite, with considerable popular support, had deposed the monarch for a second time, forcing him to flee the country and replacing him with a foreigner who came at the head of an invading army. Once again religion, and specifically anti-Catholic paranoia, lay at the root of this volte-face. Signs of disagreement had manifested themselves very early, when Charles II famously promised 'Liberty to Tender Consciences' before his accession, and the 'Cavalier' parliament that he then called, ostentatiously loyal in all other respects, rejected out of hand any suggestion of tolerance of nonconformity; the Act of Uniformity of 1662 restored the Prayer Book, and deprived all clergy who would not accept both it and the Thirty-nine Articles of their livings. Subsequent attempts by the monarch, whose Catholic sympathies many suspected, to introduce a measure of toleration for religious dissent (the 'Declarations of Indulgence'), using the royal prerogative powers met with equally determined resistance. This new attachment to Anglican conformity by the gentry did not mean the established Church was placed on a sounder financial footing; there was no restoration of endowments, and most livings remained extremely poor. Sevenoaks was lucky, however: in 1677 Richard Bosse, the incumbent, left a library of 1,000 books valued at the very large sum of £73, showing that he was both wealthy and well-read.[29]

In 1678 Titus Oates' fabricated 'Popish Plot', alleging a Catholic conspiracy to return England to the Popish fold through the assassination of the King, revealed the depth of anti-Catholic feeling now prevalent at least among the urban population in England. London in particular was torn apart by hysteria and riot, but things were deceptively calm when Charles' openly Catholic brother, James, ascended the throne in 1685. So strong was the instinct of obedience to the monarch, and the dread of rebellion, among the gentry and clergy, that Parliament voted him an immensely generous subsidy that enabled him to dissolve it almost immediately, until he needed to pass religious legislation. Over the next three years James II, with a degree of stupidity that has probably never been equalled by a British monarch, succeeded in wholly alienating his natural supporters in the counties. In his desperation to drive through a toleration bill that would allow Catholics (and, incidentally, Protestant dissenters) to practise their religion freely, he ousted the Tory gentry from their positions as JPs, sheriffs, and MPs, and attempted to pack the House of Commons and the counties with dissenters, often of low birth. At the same time a standing army of 30,000 was raised with Parliament's subsidy, ostensibly for service in Ireland, prompting uneasy memories of the tyranny of the New Model.

The Glorious Revolution that ousted James and replaced him with his Protestant daughter and son-in-law was altogether a tidier and more aristocratic affair than the Great Rebellion, and it saw little social upheaval and few lives lost. The oligarchic, firmly Protestant settlement it introduced lasted, with little alteration, until 1832. However, it did see one last religious twitch within the Anglican establishment, in the form of the Nonjuror bishops, notably Archbishop Sancroft, who, vehemently as they had opposed James, were not willing to see the doctrine of passive obedience flouted, or the sacred nature

Clergy
The Rector (or Vicar) was
in charge of the parish and
responsible for church services.
From the Reformation onwards
most clergy in the established
church were well-educated men
who had studied at either the
University of Oxford or of
Cambridge.

Churchwardens
Two churchwardens were
responsible for the parish church,
one chosen by the parishioners
and the other by the incumbent.

The Vestry
This was the room attached to the
chancel of the church. The Vestry
meeting composed of incumbent,
churchwardens, and ratepayers,
was a general assembly of
parishioners that administered the
parish. Often it met in the Vestry,
although it might meet in a local
public house. The Vestry meeting
in Otford often gathered in The
Bull Inn.

Tithes
These were paid in kind or money
to support the parish church and
the minister.

Law and Order
An elected parish constable was responsible for petty
law and order with in each parish. He summoned
parishioners, collected the county rate, and national taxes
such as the land tax, kept the gaol, supervised weights
and measures, and issued ale licences.

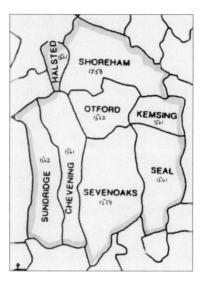

Parish Registers
The registers, made compulsory in 1538, recorded
baptisms, marriages, and burials within the parish.
The map shows dates when registers are extant for
each parish.

The Poor
From the 1590s to 1834 the parish
was directly responsible for the poor
within the parish. Elected overseers,
responsible to the parish and the
Justices of the Peace, administered
the poor rate and allocated relief
to those in need. Relief was given
in various forms – clothing, coals,
bread, and money. The parish
workhouse (it was on St John's Hill
in Sevenoaks) provided shelter for
some of the poor in exchange for
work. The workhouse also afforded
a last resort for the elderly poor and
sick, and orphaned children. People
not born within the parish were
ineligible for relief and could be
removed to their parish of origin if
they became a burden on the poor
rate. The Settlement Act of 1662
set out ways in which a person
could claim to be legally settled in
another parish.

Roads
By an Act of 1555 parishes were
required to elect every Easter a
'Surveyor of the Highways'. The
surveyor was responsible to the
Justices of the Peace. He was
empowered to raise a local rate
in order to maintain the roads
within the parish, and also to
supervise statute labour by which
every householder (or those paid
to take their place) worked for
four (later six) days each year
repairing and maintaining local
highways. The system lasted
until 1835.

MAP 5 *The Parish as a Unit of Civil Administration. Tudor government gave parishes responsibility
for the poor, the highways, and for petty law and order. Baptisms, marriages and burials were also
recorded. A civil parish often coincided with an ecclesiastical parish. The parish of Sevenoaks, with
boundaries probably agreed by 1200, stretched from the River Darent, south up the chart hills to the
sandstone ridge, and then down in to the Weald of Kent.*

of the monarch as head of the Church called into question. Their refusal to
acknowledge William III's legitimacy was the last challenge to the political and
religious consensus to emerge from within the established Church until the
rise of Methodism at the end of the 18th century. Nonconformity remained
commonplace, but became increasingly respectable, as even the Quakers, seen
as dangerous radicals 40 years previously for their refusal to acknowledge
the social hierarchy by doffing their hats, sank into a prosperous anonymity.
Britain had seen almost two hundred years of religious passion tear society
and the state apart. Queen Anne's reign continued to see bitter disputes
between Anglicans and Protestant dissenters over issues such as 'occasional
conformity' on the part of the latter to avoid the penalties of the law, but the
keynote of the 18th century would be Erastianism: that is, a subordination
of organised religion to secular purposes. The volatile mixture of political
radicalism and religious nonconformity that had characterised the 17th century
did not disappear entirely in the 18th, but it would represent little threat to
the established order until after the American Revolution.

Churches in the Modern Age

David Killingray[*]

The last 300 years were centuries of great economic, social, and political change. Population increase, industrialisation, urban growth, and new forms of transport and communication gradually transformed the face of Britain and the ways in which people lived. By 1860 more people in Britain lived and worked in towns than in rural areas. The franchise had been gradually extended and by 1930 all adults over the age of 21 had the vote. With the increase in democratic liberties came a stronger sense of individuality. Old religious restrictions that had penalised nonconformist Dissenters and Roman Catholics were slowly removed and religious belief became more a personal and private matter. Churches, particularly nonconformist ones, enjoyed great increase in the 19th century although early in the next century they began to decline in both members and influence. Throughout the 20th century the Church of England remained the established church with many official roles at both national and local level, but from the middle of the previous century Britain had become an increasingly secular society. By 2000 few people went to a church regularly although many continued to have some form of belief in a divine being. And since 1950 immigrants from Asia and Africa have brought new religious ideas and practices to many British towns.[1]

In the mid-19th century Sevenoaks was a small market town with an economic life mainly dependent upon the rural area. Until 1828 the only 'factory' industry was silk spinning at Greatness which employed mainly women and children.[2] The advent of the railways connecting Sevenoaks to London in the 1860s resulted in a slow increase in population, urban growth, and more rapid social change. A century later Sevenoaks was a prosperous town with light and tertiary industries and many people commuting to London and other towns to work. By then the motor car was rapidly transforming the town and the way in which many people lived. Up to the 1830s the parish provided the major institution of local government. The parish, or more specifically the vestry, presided over by the incumbent collected local taxes, maintained certain roads, upheld law and order, and provided education and relief for the poor.[3] The parish church was also the major source of private charity for the poor. This local system based on the church might have been adequate for a rural society but it could not meet the new demands of the rapidly changing economic and social order. From the 1830s onwards new institutions of central

* David Killingray, Emeritus Professor of Modern History, Goldsmiths College London.

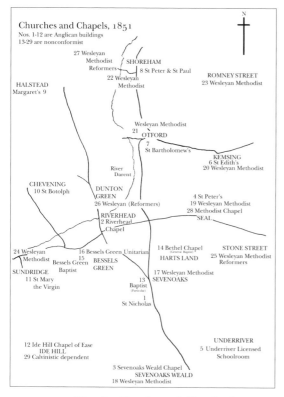

Churches and Chapels, 1851
Nos. 1-12 are Anglican buildings
13-29 are nonconformist

27 Wesleyan
Methodist
Reformers
SHOREHAM
8 St Peter & St Paul
22 Wesleyan
Methodist
ROMNEY STREET
23 Wesleyan Methodist
HALSTEAD
Margaret's 9

Wesleyan Methodist
21 OTFORD
7
St Bartholomew's
KEMSING
6 St Edith's
20 Wesleyan Methodist
River
Darent
CHEVENING
10 St Botolph
DUNTON
GREEN
26 Wesleyan (Reformers)
4 St Peter's
19 Wesleyan Methodist
28 Methodist Chapel
RIVERHEAD
2 Riverhead
Chapel
SEAL

24 Wesleyan
Methodist
Bessels Green
SUNDRIDGE
11 St Mary
the Virgin
15
Baptist
16 Bessels Green Unitarian
BESSELS
GREEN
14 Bethel Chapel
(General Baptist)
HARTS LAND
17 Wesleyan Methodist
SEVENOAKS
13
Baptist
(Particular)
1
St Nicholas
STONE STREET
25 Wesleyan Methodist
Reformers

12 Ide Hill Chapel of Ease
IDE HILL
29 Calvinistic dependent
UNDERRIVER
5 Underriver Licensed
Schoolroom
3 Sevenoaks Weald Chapel
SEVENOAKS WEALD
18 Wesleyan Methodist

MAP 6   *Churches and Chapels 1851.*

and local government were created and the role of the parish declined, although in 1894 parish councils became the smallest unit of secular local government.

The 18th Century: Parish and Dissent in a Protestant Nation

England in the 18th century was avowedly a Protestant nation ruled by a Protestant monarch.[4] Moreover, that Protestantism was episcopal and determined by Acts of Parliament which at the same time discriminated against both other Protestants (such as Congregationalists, Quakers, and Baptists), and Roman Catholics.[5] The privileges of the Church of England permeated the political fabric of the country and in a small town such as Sevenoaks the clergy, closely allied to landowners, promoted social order from the pulpit. Dissenters in the Sevenoaks area were thin on the ground. The not very accurate Compton census of 1676 recorded only 174 dissenters in west Kent and 46 Roman Catholics (or those 'Suspected or Reported such'). Forty years later, Dr John Evans listed a total of 55 dissenting congregations in the whole of Kent: some 11,150 people who constituted a mere 1.25 per cent of the total population.[6]

St Nicholas' was the sole public church building in Sevenoaks in 1700. Knole had a private chapel and there was another at Bradbourne that is now a private house. The small gathering of General Baptists at Bradbourne probably met in a home; their first Meeting House was erected at Bessels Green in 1716 and is now the Unitarian church. Theological differences over the Trinity led to a split and a group of Particular Baptists seceded in 1769 to establish what is now the present Baptist chapel in Bessels Green. Methodism, springing from the preaching of George Whitefield, and John and Charles Wesley, developed out of the Church of England in the mid-18th century. The Wesleys' aim was spiritual revival, not the founding of a new denomination. Their idea that God was intimately concerned with everybody had a popular appeal. John Wesley's first visit to Sevenoaks was in October 1745 when he preached by the 'Free School' 'to a large, wild company' on 'for all have sinned'.[7] Wesley's revivalist and populist outdoor preaching was not welcomed by many clergy in the Church of England although the itinerant evangelist found a warm supporter in Vincent Perronet, the evangelically-minded vicar

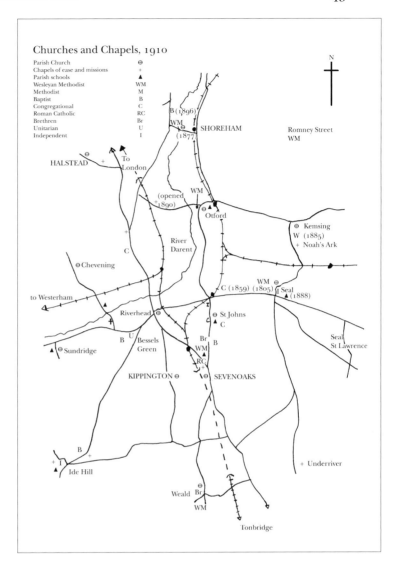

Churches and Chapels, 1910

Parish Church	⊕
Chapels of ease and missions	+
Parish schools	▲
Wesleyan Methodist	WM
Methodist	M
Baptist	B
Congregational	C
Roman Catholic	RC
Brethren	Br
Unitarian	U
Independent	I

B (1896)
WM
(1877)   SHOREHAM   Romney Street
                              WM

HALSTEAD   +   To
                 London

WM
(opened
+1890)
                 Otford
                              ⊕ Kemsing
                              W (1885)
                              + Noah's Ark
River
Darent
⊕ Chevening
                 WM ⊕
           C (1859) (1805) ﬁ Seal
                        ▲ (1888)
to Westerham
           Riverhead ⊕
                 ⊕ St Johns
                 ▲ C
                              Seal
                              St Lawrence
           B U
              Bessels   Br B
              Green   WM
           ▲ ⊕ Sundridge   ▲
                        RC
                        +
KIPPINGTON ⊕   ⊕   SEVENOAKS

                              + Underriver
        B   +
     + I   +
     ▲ Ide Hill

                 ⊕
           Weald Br
                 WM
                 Tonbridge

MAP 7 *Churches and Chapels 1910.*

of Shoreham.[8] By the last quarter of the 18th century, a Wesleyan Methodist meeting place had been opened in the centre of Sevenoaks.

There is little solid evidence from the Sevenoaks area to support the once popular idea of a factionalised Church of England and local clerical neglect during the18th century. Nor is there evidence of deep discord between the established Church and dissenters. Rather, as William Gibson has recently written, there was a 'widespread and profound commitment to peace and tranquillity among both the clergy and the laity', and 'the same applied to divisions between Anglicans and Dissenters; not only did most live in peace with one another, but in many ways they did not see themselves as separate and discrete.'[9] Certainly pluralism was widespread and underpaid curates ministered in many parishes, and at times theological disputes assumed bitter forms, but for the most part a good deal of tolerance prevailed. The advowson

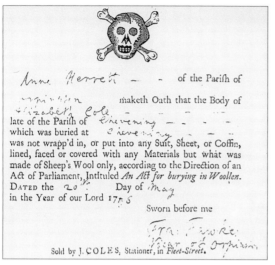

Anne Herret — - of the Parish of
\.\.\.\.\.\. maketh Oath that the Body of
Elizabeth Cole — - - - -
late of the Parish of Evening — - - -
which was buried at Evening - - - -
was not wrapp'd in, or put into any Suit, Sheet, or Coffin,
lined, faced or covered with any Materials but what was
made of Sheep's Wool only, according to the Direction of an
Act of Parliament, Intituled *An Act for burying in Woollen*.
DATED the 20th Day of May
in the Year of our Lord 1756
                                         Sworn before me

                                         Fra: Fawke
                                         Vicar of Orpining
Sold by J. COLES, Stationer, in *Fleet-Street*.

16 *Affidavit for burial in wool, Sundridge,
1756. The Sundridge burial registers contain
numerous affidavits for burial in wool, which
were required by an Act of Parliament 1678,
that was not repealed until 1814.*

of St Nicholas came into the hands of the Curteis family in 1716, and for the next 200 years they provided a dynasty of rectors.[10] The Sevenoaks living was well endowed. A regular church income came from tithes and pew rents. Other established churches also received tithes and most churches and chapels derived income from pew rents. Nonconformist ministers received modest wages.

The Curteises, as prosperous landowners, had a private income and at various times they served as Justices of the Peace. Since the Reformation most Church of England clergy had received a university education, but relatively few nonconformist ministers did so until the 20th century. Thomas Curteis, the first of the dynasty and a graduate in physics from Cambridge, also had the living at Wrotham. He had been brought up as a Presbyterian and was a Low Churchman tolerant of dissenters, as was William, his son and successor. He was thus strongly anti-Jacobin and determined that his curates should not promote High Church views. Thomas Curteis, who appears to have been an attentive and charitable minister, was also a Whig, campaigning for Whig parliamentary candidates put forward by the Duke of Dorset at Knole, and pressuring his tenants to give their vote to that cause.[11]

By the early 18th century, Sevenoaks parish church had box pews and a gallery on three sides of the nave. The nave lacked clerestory windows and the building was gloomy, and in winter probably very cold. Sermons were preached twice on Sundays from a three-tiered pulpit that stood on the south side of the nave, although few sermons have survived from that century.[12] The liturgy of the established Church rested on the Book of Common Prayer, itself grounded on the Bible, which provided the basis of belief and practice. Music to accompany psalms came from the church band in the west gallery; an organ was only installed in 1798. By the end of the 18th century many new hymns had been written. Some of the finest hymns, in terms of poetry and theology, were written by the Congregationalist Isaac Watts and the Methodist Charles Wesley, and were widely adopted by churches of various persuasions in the 19th century.

It is not known how many people regularly attended Sunday services in the area. In outlying areas of large parishes such as Sevenoaks, Sundridge, and Seal, people were reluctant to attend when the weather was wet or cold and the roads difficult to use. The level of functional literacy is also unknown although both the Apostles' Creed and the catechism, widely used in charity schools, contained a summary of faith that was usually learned by heart. The

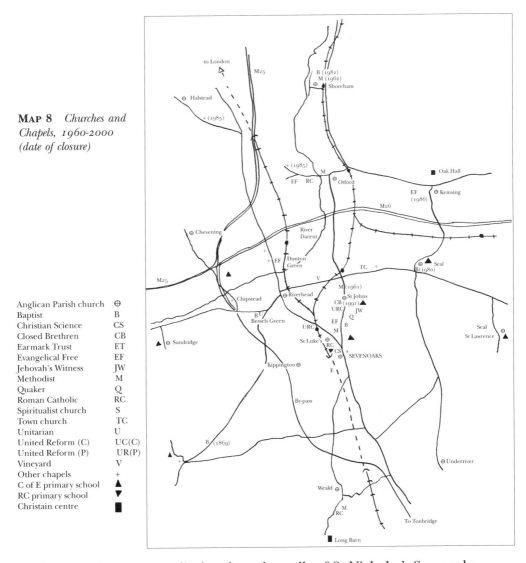

MAP 8 *Churches and Chapels, 1960-2000 (date of closure)*

Anglican Parish church   ⊕
Baptist   B
Christian Science   CS
Closed Brethren   CB
Earmark Trust   ET
Evangelical Free   EF
Jehovah's Witness   JW
Methodist   M
Quaker   Q
Roman Catholic   RC
Spiritualist church   S
Town church   TC
Unitarian   U
United Reform (C)   UC(C)
United Reform (P)   UR(P)
Vineyard   V
Other chapels   +
C of E primary school   ▲
RC primary school   ▼
Christain centre   ■

Ten Commandments were displayed on the walls of St Nicholas', Sevenoaks, as rules to be observed and obeyed. Communion occurred infrequently, probably four times a year, and communicants knelt at the rail outside the chancel, the area of the church building which was reserved for, and under the authority of, the incumbent. It is difficult to know what 18th-century people in the locality believed and understood about Christian doctrine. Undoubtedly many had firm convictions about life after death. The practice of burying people in the churchyard facing towards the east in expectation of the return of Christ and the resurrection continued into the 20th century. Parish churches offered important social *rites de passage* to parishioners: baptism of infants, marriage and burial were dutifully entered in the parish registers kept in the vestry. Within the Church of England a practice that had become more popular since the previous century was the confirmation of youngsters to mark their formal entry into the church as adults.

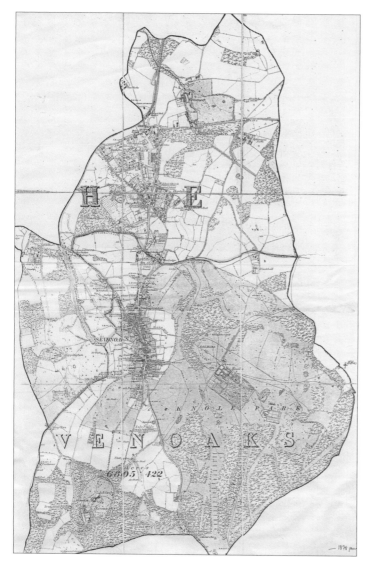

MAP 9   *The Parish of St Nicholas, Sevenoaks, 1870. The original parish of Sevenoaks covered nearly 7,000 acres and was five miles long, stretching from the southern banks of the River Darent, south up the chart lands and down the scarp of the sandstone ridge into the forested clay lands of the Weald. Sevenoaks, at the junction of roads from London and Dartford to Rye, was a small market town largely reliant on local agriculture. The coming of the railways in the 1860s resulted in further growth in population. St Nicholas was the sole Anglican church within the parish until the 1820s and, other than Knole House, the largest building in the town. New parishes for Sevenoaks Weald, St John's, and Kippington were created in the 19th century. This map shows the boundaries of St Nicholas' parish in 1870. The present ecclesiastical parish of St Nicholas is shown by the line across the map. The south-west area of the parish has largely been developed for houses since 1945.*

In discussing Christian belief in the area it is also important to consider the continuation of folk belief as well as non-belief. Some people believed in magic while others moulded their own religious ideas from a thin knowledge of Christianity. Rationalist ideas also increased in the second half of the 18th century and it would be surprising if they had not circulated among certain freethinkers in an area so close to London. This did not necessarily mean that people stopped going to church or ceased to regard themselves as Christian. Throughout time, people's Christian beliefs and ideas have been shaped and altered by pressures from secular culture.[13]

Church Growth in an Age of Toleration

Periods of the 19th century have been dubbed as 'ages': of democracy, reform, steam, tolerance, and so on. It was certainly an age when religious belief

17 *St Nicholas' church, Sevenoaks, south elevation, 1809. Recently discovered architectural drawings by George Byfield, presumably drawn up in a competition to restore St Nicholas, shed new light on both the exterior and interior of the building in the early 19th century. These plans had apparently lain in a Midlands attic for many years until the owner kindly sent them in 1998 to Canon Miles Thomson, then rector of St Nicholas'. Byfield's drawings include plans of the building as it was in 1809. An elevation of the south side of St Nicholas' 'in its present state' shows four dormer windows towards the west end of the nave roof that gave light to the galleries. Presumably there was a similar number of windows on the north side. The pulpit stood against a pillar on the south aisle. There were four entrances, to the north of the east wall, on the north and south walls (the present porches), and through the west door below the tower. Access to the gallery was by stairs in the south-west corner of the building. Byfield's scheme proposed the demolition of the 15th-century south porch and parvis room, relocating the vestry, a centrally placed pulpit near the east end, and new doorways. The original drawings by Byfield have been deposited in the Victoria and Albert Museum. Excellent copies have been made for St Nicholas' Parish Church, and other copies deposited in the Centre for Kentish Studies in Maidstone.*

was important and in which official religious tolerance increased. In 1791 Roman Catholics, who probably numbered 80-90,000 throughout the country, were permitted to have registered places of worship and to be admitted to the professions. Nearly forty years later more sweeping reforms took place. In 1828 the Test and Corporation Acts were repealed thus removing the final legal disabilities from all dissenters. The next year Roman Catholics were recognised by law as full citizens. This was not accomplished without considerable hostility. Anti-Roman Catholic feeling was very strong, particularly in southern counties, demonstrated by the tens of thousands of people who turned out on Penenden Heath, near Maidstone, in October 1828 to protest at Roman Catholic emancipation. The number of Catholics in west Kent was small and those who acknowledged the Pope, who was also a foreign secular ruler, were popularly suspected of being un-British. Through the 19th century Roman Catholics grew in number helped by Irish immigration. In 1850 the hierarchy was re-established although that, and other activities which appeared to strengthen the position of Catholics, was strongly opposed by Protestants of different theological persuasions. Anti-Catholic sentiments were frequently expressed in the Sevenoaks press throughout the 19th century, and also at a national level. For example, in 1901 William Cunningham, the Roman Catholic priest of Sevenoaks, joined with other Catholics in protesting at the declaration made by Edward VII at the opening of Parliament, in accordance with the 1689 Bill of Rights, that denounced various central Catholic doctrines as superstitious.[14]

At the start of the 19th century Methodists, Congregationalists, and Baptists were relatively weak and lacked a sense of national coherence. The established Church dominated much of English official public life throughout the century. However dissent, or nonconformity, grew in both numbers and influence, and by the middle of the century there were nationally slightly more adherents of nonconformist than established churches, although not in Sevenoaks and the surrounding villages. Church-going probably increased; new churches were built or reordered.[15] For example, the tower of St Nicholas parish church was reconstructed and clerestory windows were inserted in the nave in 1811-13 at the cost of £12,000. Further minor changes were made throughout the century, and major internal alterations took place in the 1870s when the mid-17th-century galleries and pews were removed and new bench pews and stained glass windows installed. Other local Anglican churches were greatly altered by Victorian clergy who thought that they were improving and modernising the buildings. At Halstead the local squire pulled down the Saxon building and built a new church nearby.

New Church of England chapels of ease were built in peripheral areas of parishes to make it more convenient for parishioners to attend services. In Sevenoaks parish new churches opened at Weald in 1822, Riverhead in 1831, and St John's in 1858; the same happened in Sundridge parish at Ide Hill in 1807, and in the parish of Seal at Underriver by 1875. In remote areas of parishes mission halls were built, as was the case at Twitton and also on Goathurst Common. But there were also new parish churches. The main one was at Kippington, just to the west of Sevenoaks town, where William Thompson, a wealthy tea merchant, alienated by the ritualism at St Nicholas, was permitted to build a church on his estate and to create a new parish in 1878. Part of the new parish was separated by the railway, and a temporary 'Iron Church' was erected in Granville Road in 1878; 120 years later it became the separate parish of St Luke's.

As nonconformist congregations grew they, too, built churches. Many of the nonconformist churches in the area date from the 19th century: some simple functional buildings, such as the Baptist chapel in Hartslands opened in 1842, and other more imposing structures. The Congregational church on St John's Hill, Sevenoaks, was built in Gothic style in 1867, complete with a spire and a seating capacity of 500, in the misplaced optimism that the population of the area would rapidly grow. Finance for these new churches came from local congregations and the help of denominational organisations. Occasionally money came from wealthy Christian philanthropists. The most notable were

Sir Samuel Morley, the reformist Liberal MP and Congregationalist, who lived at Leigh, Henry Swaffield, a Methodist stockbroker, who came to live in Sevenoaks in the 1870s, and Mrs Rycroft, who endowed both the chapel and chaplain at the mission hall on Goathurst Common. By contrast the few Roman Catholics in the area continued to celebrate Mass in private homes; from 1880 they met in an iron church in Gordon Road that is now the site of St Thomas' church, opened in 1896.

Church Attendance and Social Class

The population of Sevenoaks and the surrounding area grew steadily through the 19th century. How many people regularly attended church is not known. Church of England clergy regarded all those living within the parish as members and rarely kept records of attendance. On the other hand many nonconformist churches required members to formally join the church and so membership figures are more accurate. Only once, on a rather dreary Sunday in late March 1851, was an official census taken of attendance at all places of religious worship.[16] The returns shocked many in the established Church because it showed the growing strength of the nonconformist churches as well as the small percentage of the working-class population who bothered to attend church in the growing industrial cities and towns. However, in rural west Kent the Church of England retained its dominance and attendance for all denominations was relatively high. However, there was a sizeable part of the local population for whom church attendance appears not to have been a matter of great importance (see Table 2, p.65).

Many prominent people in 19th-century society placed great emphasis on the influence of the church as a force for moral and social good. Even those who were not very devout, like the high Tory Robert Herries of St Julians, thought that attendance at church set a good example to their servants. Writing to his cousin in 1837, he said: 'I think you will agree with me that if the church is to be upheld, now is the time to show our adherence to it in every possible way'.[17] This sense of moral purpose continued through the Victorian years. As the century progressed churches of all denominations became bastions of the middle classes. The principal members of churches of all kinds tended to be drawn from the 'respectable' sections of society who dressed appropriately for Sunday services. These tended to be ratepayers who had a financial interest in a more closely regulated community and a strong sense of social class distinction. Private restrictive covenants on property within Sevenoaks town allowed for middle-class villas but excluded working-class housing. As a result a new working-class 'village' was built north of the town on a green field site at Hartslands from 1841 onwards; within five years it had become a community of over three hundred people. The social class divisions of Sevenoaks and the surrounding villages were in many respects reflected by the church that people attended and the pews in which they sat.

Social class consciousness pervaded most congregations, irrespective of denomination; for example, at the Congregational church on St John's Hill in 1888, a wealthy woman benefactor demanded separate services for working-class Sunday school children.[18] Christianity, especially in its evangelical form,

18 *Late 19th-century confirmation card from Hildenborough parish, immediately south of Sevenoaks. Until the late 19th century a majority of infants were probably baptised in a parish church. Confirmation of the young person of vows made on their behalf by parents and godparents usually occurred between 14 and 17 years of age. To qualify for confirmation the candidate had to be baptised and to be able to adequately say the catechism, the creed, the Lord's prayer and the Ten Commandments. Confirmation was meant to qualify a person to take Holy Communion but many did not. Until the 1850s feasts and festivities accompanied confirmation services. Some times these became riotous. By the 1890s fewer young people were being confirmed and there were more girls than boys going through the ritual.*

might proclaim that all were 'one in Christ Jesus' but social class distinctions were all too often buttressed by 19th-century Bible interpretations that explained why such differences existed. And churchmen were ready to disclaim responsibility for uncongenial groups of people who moved into a parish, such as nomadic workmen or gypsies. The rector of Sevenoaks rejected any spiritual responsibility for the navvies building the railway to Tonbridge in the 1860s. Gangs of navvies were often involved in drunken brawls at weekends and their spiritual welfare was left first to an unreliable visiting chaplain with a temporary tin chapel erected on Tubs Hill, and then to a London City Missioner.

Evangelical Revival, Social Reform and Politics

The evangelical revival, which originated with George Whitefield and Methodism in the second half of the 18th century, emphasised human sinfulness and the need for personal salvation. Evangelical preaching emphasised personal conversion through Christ's saving work on the cross, and a high view of the Bible as the word of God leading to activism in spreading the gospel.[19] Christian action and adherence to a set of rules involved a close observance of the Sabbath, mission at home and overseas, and attempts to redress social ills. By the late 18th and early 19th centuries the most prominent evangelicals were within the Church of England. They led the campaigns to abolish the slave trade and emancipate slaves and the great social reform movements directed to improving the working and living conditions of the poor and the exploited. Evangelicals' primary concern was people's spiritual condition rather than social action for its own sake. Predominantly politically conservative, they reacted strongly to the French Revolution with its violent, atheistic, and anticlerical doctrines that threatened the religious and social order. Evangelicals preached moral reform but they also wanted an orderly and disciplined society where people respected government, worked hard and knew their social place.

There were relatively few evangelicals in the established Church in west Kent in the 19th century. Vincent Perronet, vicar of Shoreham from 1728-85, and his sons were evangelicals, and John Rogers' wife, Harriet (of Riverhill House), was the daughter of John Thornton, a member of the 'Clapham sect' whose most prominent member was William Wilberforce. Many local Methodists, Baptists and Congregationalists were avowedly evangelical as is evident from the emphasis on Biblical preaching in their churches, the nature of their services, and their involvement with mission. This 'holy zeal for the salvation of souls' is well demonstrated by the life and activities of Catherine Martin, a Wesleyan, in mid-century Sevenoaks. She taught Sunday school, collected missionary subscriptions, visited the aged and sick, distributed tracts house to house, engaged in a town mission, regularly attended prayer meetings and services on Sundays and several weekdays, while also caring for her six children.[20] Most established churches in the area during the 19th century were not evangelical, although St Nicholas', Sevenoaks, became so following a change of rector in 1907.

Due to the official position of the established Church, and the great significance attached to Christian ideas in the 19th century, religion was central to politics at both national and local levels of government. We have already seen this with the struggle to achieve Roman Catholic emancipation. Religious questions figured prominently in the major debates on social reform. The Poor Law Amendment Act of 1834 removed individual parish responsibility for poor relief and passed it to new Poor Law Unions, which were administered by an elected board of guardians, although these included representatives of local Church of England clergy. The new law was strongly opposed by Thomas Curteis, the rector of Sevenoaks, who claimed in a pamphlet addressed to the prime minister that the old system worked adequately.[21] In Sevenoaks the poor suffered under both systems; the old workhouse on St John's Hill was overcrowded and pest-ridden, while the new Union workhouse, eventually built at Sundridge in 1843, not only labelled the poor as second-class citizens but its strict regime deterred all but the desperate. However, despite its often harsh provisions the new poor law did provide relief for the aged, the sick, and the orphaned when families were unable to do so.

More contentious were the questions of church rates, tithes and education. Rates and tithes were levied on all and, not unreasonably, opposed by aggrieved dissenters. Until 1868, churchwardens could impose a rate on all householders in the parish, irrespective of whether they were members of the Church of England, for the upkeep of the parish church and churchyard. Those who refused to pay could have their goods distrained. This happened in Riverhead in 1833 when Nicholas Chatfield, a dissenter, had his pig taken in lieu of the rate. When attempts were made to auction the animal a small riot occurred. Those involved were taken to court but acquitted.[22] The tithe was a tax on property whereby all those within a parish contributed to the support of the established Church. Dissenters naturally objected to this unfair imposition and campaigned to change the law, sometimes refusing to pay it. Originally paid in kind this had largely been commuted to money by the late 18th century; the Tithe Commutation Act of 1836 reformed the system and tithes became a rent charge based on the current price of grain.

Religion and political party affiliation were often closely intertwined in the 19th century. Anglicans, as members of the established Church, often identified with Conservative ideas and principles. Thomas Curteis, rector of St Nicholas' from 1874-1907, was chairman of the local Conservative association. Nonconformity attracted Whigs and Liberals, although such allegiance was far from rigid. For example James German, a leading radical Liberal in the 1880s and 1890s, was a member of the High Church on St John's Hill, in Sevenoaks, where his daughter taught in the Sunday school and married the curate. Some nonconformist ministers played a prominent role in local political affairs. John Jackson, the former Baptist minister, was active in Liberal politics and became deputy chairman of the Urban District Council when it was created in 1894. By the end of the First World War John Rooker, rector of Sevenoaks, wrote to the local newspaper endorsing Lloyd-George in the 'coupon' election; he stood as a Liberal Party candidate in the Urban District Council elections of 1920.

Education

Such formal education as existed in the 18th and early 19th centuries was mainly in the hands of the parishes. The limited school curriculum focused on basic literacy and numeracy. Lady Boswell's School was founded as a parish charity in 1692; today it is the St Nicholas church school. Other parishes around Sevenoaks also had small parish schools: for example, a National School was established in 1818, at Dry Hill Lane, serving the three parishes of Chevening, Sundridge and Brasted.[23] The Union workhouse also had a school for its youthful inmates. At the same time the number of private schools increased and by the middle of the century there were 28 in Sevenoaks, of which no fewer than 25 were supported by religious bodies, mostly by the Church of England. John Felkin, minister of the Baptist chapel in Hartslands, set up a school there in the 1840s, while John Jackson, a former Baptist minister, ran a school with his wife near the Vine. By 1870, when the Education Act of that year stipulated that elected school boards should provide education where it was not offered by church schools, probably well over half the children in the Sevenoaks area were receiving some kind of formal education: most of it provided by Christians. Until the 20th century the area had a single secondary school, the Queen Elizabeth Grammar School (the present Sevenoaks School), available to local children. It was seen as a Christian foundation and throughout the 19th century was closely identified with St Nicholas' parish church where students sat in the School House gallery for services. From 1770-1874 all the headmasters were ordained in the Church of England. The School continues to have an ordained chaplain.

The Education Act of 1870 was the response of the State to the rapid increase in the population, and the failure of the churches and the charitable system to meet the need for schooling. The Act created a national system of elementary education with local rates funding both Church of England schools and the newly founded Board schools, such as Cobden Road School, Sevenoaks. Many Anglicans objected to their loss of control over education, while nonconformists resented paying rates to support Church schools. Education became a religious and political issue, hotly contested at both local and national levels. Nonconformists objected to the 1902 Elementary Education Act that extended rate aid to denominational schools. Local 'passive resisters' were led by the Revd Charles Rudge, Baptist minister at the Vine, and Albert Bath, a farmer of Halstead, who were summoned for deducting from their rates the 'sectarian portion'.[24]

Ritualism

In the modern secular age it is often difficult to understand how people in the past could be so exercised over differences of religious belief and practice, although it is easier to understand why nonconformists objected to local taxation supporting schools of the established Church. One of the great controversies within the Church of England in the 19th century began with the Oxford Movement of the 1830s, a protest at increasing State intervention in the affairs of the Church. This developed into Tractarianism, a High Church party which stressed the continuity of the Church of England with the pre-Reformation Church and emphasised the authority of the Church, the bishops and the sacraments. An early local Tractarian was the Revd William Hodge Mills, vicar of St Martin, Brasted, who introduced Tractarian forms of services from 1865 onwards. Most evangelicals in the Sevenoaks area were nonconformists.

The revival of pre-Reformation ritual by the Tractarians, or Anglo-Catholics, led to opposition from evangelicals of the Low Church who objected to the introduction of new forms of clerical dress, and Catholic liturgical practices, in Anglican churches. Differences were often deep and rancorous. When Thomas Samuel Curteis became Rector of St Nicholas', Sevenoaks, in 1874 he set about introducing ritualist forms of worship that the parish clerk denounced as 'bad, strange and startling'. It seems that church attendance declined. William J. Thompson, one of the churchwardens and of evangelical persuasion, disapproved of ritualism and he petitioned the Archbishop of Canterbury for a new parish and church on his estate at Kippington. St Mary's, built at considerable expense, was opened in 1880.[25]

Some High Church practices, although less commonly their theological interpretations, were absorbed even by low Anglican and nonconformist churches. By the early 20th century most Anglican clergy had adopted clerical collars and robes, and embraced the practice of regular communion services. Robed choirs were introduced and flowers increasingly adorned services even in some evangelical and nonconformist churches. Gothic styles of architecture were also closely associated with the Oxford Movement, and ritualists built new churches, and adapted interiors, to accord with what became known as ecclesiological principles. Within a short time the same Gothic style was being adopted for new nonconformist churches. Elements of 'nonconformist

19 *Hop-pickers in west Kent hop gardens (1890s). Every autumn until the 1970s thousands of families from the poorer parts of East London would spend one or two weeks in Kent picking hops. The pickers camped or lived in rough shelters near the hop gardens. In the Sevenoaks area there were several hop gardens and the pickers became an added responsibility to local clergy. Some clergy did not regard them, or other groups of itinerant labourers such as railway navvies, as 'their' parishioners and refused to attend to them. Special missions with travelling evangelists were formed specifically to reach hop-pickers and navvies.*

Gothic' can be seen in the Congregationalist church on St John's Hill (1865), the Baptist church on the Vine (1886), and the Wesleyan Methodist church in the Drive (1904).

Music

Hymns were rarely sung in the established churches at the start of the 19th century; services included chanted psalms and canticles, usually led by the parish clerk. Most nonconformists used hymns and this practice gradually extended to the Church of England. High Churchmen compiled *Hymns Ancient & Modern*, first published in 1861, and this became a standard hymn book for use in Anglican churches. In the 1850s and 1860s over 400 collections of hymns were published in England alone. Much sacred music was also written for performance in churches and became widely popular. It was not uncommon for concerts at the *Royal Crown Hotel* in Sevenoaks (the site of the present Stag Theatre) to include sacred solos and arias. By the late 19th century many churches, of all denominations, had installed an organ to provide music. An organ was placed in St Nicholas', Sevenoaks, in 1797; by the mid-19th century the organist was an elected position organised by the vestry. A woman organist was elected in 1846 and two women contested the position in 1860.

Churches in the 19th century adopted special forms of service for Easter and Christmas. Christmas carols became commonly sung, and harvest thanksgiving services began in the 1840s. Major crises in the 18th century often occasioned special services on officially endorsed fast days. In the 19th century national crises were increasingly met by days of prayer, as was seen during the cholera epidemics of 1832 and 1853, the Crimean War in April 1854, and, when during the Indian Rebellion of 1857 Wednesday 7 October was observed as a day of solemn fast, humiliation and prayer. These activities were most prominent in Anglican churches but were also followed in nonconformist ones. Such days continued during the First World War, and in the Second there was a special day of prayer on 26 May 1940 as the British army faced defeat in France.

Mission at Home and Overseas

Sevenoaks people reading overseas news in the local and national newspapers were increasingly made aware of the wider world including foreign wars, emigration schemes, and imperial activities such as the Indian Rebellion. Many Christians were actively concerned with missions to spread the gospel both at home and overseas. Denominational missionary societies, formed from the 1790s onwards, sent missionaries abroad and also brought them home to visit churches to solicit interest and funds. By the late 19th century missionary fairs and exhibitions were a regular feature of many churches' activities, and news was also carried in parish magazines and the national ecclesiastical press. Parallel with this foreign interest was a concern for home mission: among railway navvies, in the locality and seasonal hop-pickers from London's East End on local farms. The Salvation Army, which used public band music to aid its street evangelism, engaged in social work among people that the regular churches often ignored. In its early days, in southern English towns, the Salvation Army was met by abusive crowds, whose hostility was often enouraged by brewers and publicans. When the Salvation Army began services in Sevenoaks in 1887 it received a rowdy reception.[26]

One of the most successful forms of home mission were Sunday schools, which began in the late 18th century. By 1910 more than six million children attended them up and down the country where they learned not only Bible stories, but also literacy and numeracy. Most Sevenoaks churches had Sunday schools, particularly the nonconformist ones, and children who regularly attended were rewarded with prizes, summer outings, treats and Christmas parties. Other evangelistic organisations in Sevenoaks included the Young Men's (and Women's) Christian Association (nearly a hundred and seventy members meeting in 1895 for Bible study, as well as social activities, in Sevenoaks old market hall),[27] Christian Endeavour at Sevenoaks Baptist church, and, by 1910, a Scouts Bible class at Kippington church. Nonconformist churches played a prominent part in temperance movements, but there was also a Roman Catholic temperance group in Sevenoaks in 1881. By the end of the century local churches were also active in providing venues for leisure activities by sponsoring football clubs and leagues, athletics, cycling, and rambles.

Assaults on Christian Orthodoxy

Although church-going remained important for many, particularly middle-class people, throughout the 19th century, there were growing challenges to religious belief. New scientific ideas, such as Darwinism, that seemed to question the inerrancy of the Bible threatened the faith of some, or challenged them to modify their beliefs. Some assaults came from liberal theological ideas within Christianity itself, spurred on by German critical scholars, which challenged literal interpretations of the Bible. At the same time there were Christians who welcomed new, and often uncomfortable, ideas and yet whose faith remained firmly rooted and orthodox. John Rogers of Riverhill House, for example, a biologist, fellow of the Royal Society and friend of Darwin, remained a convinced Christian in the face of new scholarship. Of course, there were those who were agnostics or atheists (probably an increasing number in the area by the early 20th century), and probably even more who were either indifferent to the churches or were outspokenly hostile to Christian beliefs and activities. In any study of religious belief that large part of the population who showed no interest in it should not be ignored.

Faced with assaults on their beliefs in the early decades of the 20th century the tendency of many Christians in Sevenoaks, as elsewhere, was to close ranks and hide behind a defensive wall of traditional assumptions. This emphasised a pietistic position that demanded close observance of Sunday rest, and condemned various old and new social activities and practices such as dancing, playing cards, going to public houses, smoking, attending the cinema, and even listening to the wireless. It provided good copy for satirists who helped promote the image of narrow-minded, joyless, and self-righteous people. Like all stereotypes it contained an element of truth. The cultural baggage of the Victorian age began to be discarded as patterns of religious social behaviour changed steadily, particularly after the 1960s, and increasingly many social activities frowned on in an earlier age became generally accepted. The moral imperatives remained, at least in principle, but Christians, along with the rest of society, were subjected to the pervasive pressures of a modern popular culture that promoted ideas of licence in human relationships, particularly in sexual matters. In some cases church leaders and lay people fell into line with prevailing behaviour to the consternation of those who looked to maintain traditional beliefs and practices.

Twentieth-century Church Decline

In the 19th century religion played a central part in national and local life; large numbers of people identified with a church or a chapel in one way or another, although the influence of the 'nonconformist conscience' steadily declined from the 1880s. By the 20th century formal religion became increasingly meaningless to many people in England. Church attendance continued to fall, although many people attended services for anniversaries and festivals at Christmas, New Year, and Easter, and also during the two World Wars. Nevertheless, the carnage of the First World War hastened that decline. Religious language and ritual continued to play a prominent part in national

20 *Wedding party at Shoreham c.1910. Marriages brought together family and friends. Most of the people in this photograph have not been identified although the seated children belonged to Daisy and James Bolton; he was a sign writer and painter who lived in Sevenoaks. The custom of the bride dressing in white dates from late Victorian times. Sunday was often a popular day for weddings in the 19th century. Lord Hardwicke's Marriage Act, 1754, required all marriages (except for Quaker and Jewish marriages) to take place in an Anglican church or chapel. Banns, which indicated intention to marry, were read on three successive Sundays in the parish church of both the bride and the bridegroom. Marriages were recorded in the marriage registers of each parish. From 1836 marriages could take place in nonconformist churches, and civil registration was introduced in 1837. Well into the 20th century the majority of marriages took place in a place of Christian worship.*

life, but was increasingly detached from its religious roots. Membership of churches decreased more rapidly in the second half of the century, and the influences of a Christian heritage ceased to be so obvious in family and social life. Moral and social pronouncements made by clergy at local and national levels had marginal impact. Sunday schools rapidly declined in number after 1960. In contrast to the national picture Roman Catholic churches tended to see an increase in number of members, helped by continued immigration from Ireland and the Continent. Despite the decline in church membership and increased secularism, many people claimed to believe in 'God' after the 1960s, although they did not belong to, or regularly attend, a place of worship. Civil marriages increased in number in the late 20th century, although many people who rarely came to church still wished to use it for baptisms, marriages and, especially, funerals.[28] Inevitably the process, and reasons for, decline in religious belief and practice have been much debated by historians and sociologists. Grace Davie has referred to the desire of people to believe without belonging, and to 'vicarious belief': the need to be identified with something tangible but not to be directly involved.[29]

New Religious Movements

New religious movements, further encouraged by Enlightenment ideas of liberty of belief, flourished in the mid- and late 19th century. Many, with a loose base in Christianity, originated in the United States. Mormons campaigned for converts in Britain from the 1840s, and the movement's missionaries were still calling door-to-door in Sevenoaks over 100 years later although they did not have a local 'temple'. Christian Science, and the ever active Unitarian Jehovah's Witnesses, were more successful, and established meetings in Sevenoaks; the former have a building near the post office, and the latter's Kingdom Hall is the old Baptist chapel in Hartslands. Spiritualism, which enjoyed some popularity in the decade of grief after the First World War, continues to have a few adherents in Sevenoaks. The Bahá'í faith, which came from Islam and originated in Iran in the mid-19th century, also established a small gathering in the town. Even greater change has come to religious expression in Britain since the 1950s from immigrant communities, particularly people from the south-Asian continent, who have brought Islam and Hinduism to many cities and towns (although barely yet to Sevenoaks).

War and Memory

One occasion when local churches could be seen to play a significant role was during times of severe crisis, as in the two World Wars. Between 1914-18 and 1939-45, church services and ceremonies offered comfort, and purpose to the war effort. This role continued after the wars with rituals to remember the dead. Sevenoaks and the surrounding villages all have their war memorials, as do various institutions such as the main post office and Sevenoaks School. A common inscription was 'For God, For King, For Country'. Most memorials were dedicated in the years 1919-21, and were often paid for by public subscription.[30] The cross was a common form of memorial, the largest being cut in the chalk hillside above Shoreham. Armistice Day, marking the truce on the Western Front on 11 November 1918, became a solemn annual day of remembrance with military parades and appropriate church services, a practice that continues. Services were held, usually in the parish church, for royal occasions, Empire Day, and annually to dedicate the civic authorities and various local bodies such as ex-servicemen's associations and the Boy Scouts.

High and Low, Content and Form

The differences between High and Low Church remained significant as did the difference in interpretation of Scripture between evangelicals and liberals. Under T.S. Curteis' ministry, St Nicholas', Sevenoaks, was firmly in the High Church camp.[31] In 1907 Curteis retired and sold the advowson. It was bought by an evangelical trust, which included the Thompsons of Kippington.[32] John Rooker, an evangelical minister, was appointed to the living, and thereafter St Nicholas' became a church of that persuasion. Earlier T.S. Curteis had arranged with the archbishop for the patronage of St John's to be switched from his right as rector to him personally. When he died, in 1913, his executors sold the patronage to the Guild of All Souls, thus ensuring that St John's still continues as an Anglo-Catholic church.

Such differences helped to shape liturgy. The services at St John's have been and are markedly different in ritual and form from those at St Nicholas'. Essentially evangelicals stressed the centrality of the Bible and the need for personal conversion. The High Churches did not necessarily disagree with this but placed greater emphasis on the sacraments and liturgy and the traditions of the Church. The greatest difference between conservative and liberal churches by the end of the 20th century was over some of the basic tenets of the Christian faith. Differences between churches continue despite local attempts at ecumenism through the Sevenoaks District Council of Churches. For example, most evangelical churches supported the Billy Graham Crusade in 1954, whereas they would not participate in a ritual such as the annual ceremony at St Edith's Well, Kemsing, or a pilgrimage to the shrine at Walsingham.

Clergy clearly influence the direction that a church takes. The Methodist system, until recently, of moving ministers every three to four years largely prevents this from happening but in many churches ministers may remain in office for a long time. At St John's, Sevenoaks, the much loved Father Edward Hawkes served from 1921 to 1957. Notwithstanding that a minister might have particular views, this does not necessarily mean that he is able to sway a congregation. Given the many hundreds of sermons preached it is surprising how few have survived; there is little way of knowing what was preached Sunday by Sunday although occasionally books based on sermons were published.[33] During the 1920s E.L. Langston, Rector of St Nicholas', Sevenoaks, was a leading light in the millennarian Advent Testimony Movement, but there is no evidence that his ideas gained adherents in Sevenoaks.[34] Clergy could hold ideas that, even, if trickled into sermons, might be ignored or simply not understood by members of the congregation, many of whom had a limited knowledge of theology and certainly of church history. Churches based on congregational principles could call the minister to account and also terminate his appointment; being minister of a Baptist or Congregational church could be an unstable position. Although Anglican ministers had clergy freehold, and could often rely on the support of the bishop, their position could become very uncomfortable if they lost the confidence of a sizeable part of the Parochial Church Council and of the congregation.

Church unity has been regularly discussed at national and local levels but the only fruit in England came in 1972 when Presbyterians and Congregationalists came together to form the United Reformed Church. Both churches of that persuasion in Sevenoaks accepted the union and they have become very tightly linked together. There is considerable local cooperation between churches, usually those theologically attuned to one another. Since the mid-1990s Campaigners, a uniformed young people's movement, has been run jointly at St Nicholas' and the United Reformed Church on St John's Hill. Churches also tend to align on certain issues; most nonconformists and evangelicals are opposed to gambling and some also find common ground with Methodists in demanding firmer regulation of the laws relating to the consumption of alcohol. Individual members of churches also met in a range of Christian and secular organisations such as aid organisations, Amnesty International, and the Campaign for Nuclear Disarmament.

Adapting Buildings

The decline in church membership has resulted in a fall in the number of clergy. A further consequence is that some churches have had to share a minister, such as Ide Hill and Sundridge. However, one new parish was created in Sevenoaks in 1996 when St Luke's finally separated from Kippington. Church buildings, once largely used only for Sunday services, took on a new life and social form by opening throughout the week to meet the needs of the community. Many nonconformist buildings were relatively new and unencumbered by an historic structure or location that inhibited adaptation and modernisation. The Anglicans were less fortunate although they often had prime sites. Old buildings were also costly to upkeep and often ill-suited to the needs of a church in the late 20th century.

The Baptists and the Unitarians at Bessels Green each sensitively extended their 18th-century buildings in the 1980s and 1990s, as did several other churches. By sacrificial effort in the 1990s the United Reformed congregation on St John's Hill, Sevenoaks, put a new floor in the lofty nave of their 19th-century building, thus providing a worship area above, and meeting rooms and facilities below. At the same time St Nicholas', Sevenoaks, having long been faced with a serious lack of space, partly solved this problem by excavating an undercroft beneath the nave, chancel and side aisles to provide for expanding needs.[35] Many of the Pentecostal or charismatic churches formed since the 1970s met in private homes and were thus often called 'house churches'; otherwise they often rented buildings such as schools. This was the pattern initially followed by the Town Church, until they decided to have their own building, by the Vineyard Church, and also by members of the Closed Brethren after they sold their small chapel in St John's Road.

New Patterns of Worship and Ministry

Patterns of worship have, like church buildings, changed. In the 19th and early 20th centuries some churches had services on Sunday afternoons. One or two even had separate services for working-class people in the belief that they would be more at ease apart from the company of the better clothed and better educated middle classes. By the 20th century the standard pattern in most churches of all denominations was for a single service in the morning and one in the evening, although the High Church practice of early morning communion was adopted by most Anglican parishes. Sunday schools were either held in the morning or in the afternoon. Many people were 'oncers', going to a single service, although a strong evangelical tradition was to attend twice. Growing material prosperity after 1950, with increased ownership of the television and the motor car, provided an alternative to church on Sundays and contributed to the decline in congregations. Parallel to this was the erosion of Sunday as a special day. Sabbatarian sensitivities, which had been strong and oppressive in the 19th century, slowly withered although many

21 *Modern evangelism. Sharing the good news of Jesus Christ has been a principal aim of the church since New Testament times. By the end of the 20th century evangelistic rallies and missions had been largely replaced by smaller and more informal gatherings, often in a home and involving a meal, with people invited to discuss Christianity. Both the 'Alpha' course that originated at Holy Trinity Brompton, London, and 'Christianity Explored', from All Soul's Langham Place, London, have this purpose. They have been used nationally and internationally by churches of all denominations, and by several churches in Sevenoaks. Both provide an introduction to Christian beliefs, but the 'Alpha' course has a more charismatic emphasis than 'Christianity Explored'.*

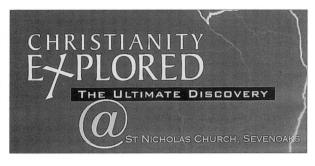

laws restricting commercial activities on Sundays remained on the statute books. By 1994 most of these laws had been repealed or amended and an increasing number of shops opened in Sevenoaks on a Sunday.

Church became a more informal affair from the mid-1960s. A decreasing number of people dressed in their 'Sunday best' for church services. In Sevenoaks many commuters who were required to wear a suit during the week were happy to go to services in casual clothing. Across the denominational spectrum church services were conducted with greater informality and involved more lay people. From the 1950s to the 1970s new translations of the Bible became available in place of the *Authorised* or *King James Version* of 1611 which, with its archaic language, had been the standard text read publicly in churches and privately by Christians. First there was the *Revised Standard Version* in 1952 which was followed by the *New English Bible* in 1961, and the *New International Version* in 1979. The Roman Catholic *Jerusalem Bible* was published in 1966 which, following the Vatican Council of 1962-5, Catholics were increasingly encouraged to read for themselves. One noticeable change in the language of the Bible, and of worship and prayer, was that the use of the second person singular, for example 'thee' and 'thou', and archaic verb forms such as 'doeth' and 'listeth', were steadily abandoned both publicly and privately. In 1980 the Anglicans modernised their liturgy by introducing an Alternative Service Book that could be used alongside the Book of Common Prayer, which remained as the doctrinal standard for the Church of England. Lay participation increased in Anglican services; Roman Catholic services abandoned Latin for English in the 1960s.

The late 20th century also saw great changes to music in churches. This had been an ongoing process with the Anglican *Songs of Praise* increasingly used since its publication in 1926. The organ was often replaced or supplemented by other musical instruments; new hymns and music for a wide range of tastes were written and used by congregations and choirs. As a result some churches appeared to be more lively and colourful places, less hidebound and open to new forms of worship that included drama and dance. Change, and sometimes the lack of change, to both buildings and forms of worship, was difficult for some people. There has always been a movement in and out of individual churches and that process continued in the late 20th century. Many of the newly formed independent churches in Sevenoaks were founded by those who wanted a more vibrant or charismatic style of worship. The Town Church and the Vineyard were both charismatic fellowships, part of that national movement since the 1970s to place the work and power of the Holy Spirit at the centre of worship and Christian life. An earlier charismatic group known as the Earmark Trust, formed by people breaking away from several churches in the late 1960s and meeting in a private home, soon bore some of the marks of a sect and became mired in damaging acrimony.[36]

One change worrying to some Christians was the ordination of women. Certain nonconformist churches had ordained women as ministers since the 1920s, although the practice did not spread widely. A prominent woman preacher was Maude Royden who is commemorated by a plaque in Weald parish church. The Church of England was slow to change although deaconesses could carry out most ministerial tasks, participating in, but not conducting, the communion service. In 1992 General Synod voted to allow the ordination of women to the consternation of many Anglo-Catholics and some evangelicals. By 2003 women clergy were a common part of the local ecclesiastical scene, running churches in Otford (both Methodist and Anglican), and at Brasted. Until that year the Revd Judith Rose was the Archdeacon of Tonbridge with oversight of the Sevenoaks Anglican churches. However, the Roman Catholic church remained firmly set against any change to its principle of a celibate male priesthood.

Continued Social and Educational Roles

The modern state has taken over many of the social and welfare roles that were once largely performed by the family, the Church, and other private charities. However, much educational, social, and charitable work is still carried out by churches at both local and national level. The 19th-century system of church schools has continued into the 21st century. These are mainly primary schools run by the Board of Education Anglican diocese. Many children from the area attend the diocesan Bennett Memorial secondary school in Tunbridge Wells. The oldest church school in the area is Lady Boswell's in Sevenoaks, which dates from the 17th century; there are others in several of the villages. St Thomas' Roman Catholic church also had an elementary school, established in Hartslands in 1881, a precursor to the present primary school in Granville Road opened in 1977. Two relatively recent initiatives by combined churches in the town were a Christian counselling service, originating in St Nicholas' but now operating from the URC church in the London Road, and the employment of detached youth workers. But Christian involvement extended

22 *African missionaries in Sevenoaks, 1999. While belief in Christianity has steadily declined in Britain, it has grown rapidly in sub-Saharan Africa. Africa now sends missionaries all over the world. Most are from mainstream churches. A few come from African independent churches, some of which have prophet leaders who make expansive, and often non-Christian, claims. This leaflet, promoting a Nigerian independent church, was handed out in Sevenoaks High Street on a Sunday morning in 1999. The Brotherhood of the Cross & Star claims that its leader knows all, can raise the dead to life, can heal the sick, understands all human languages, and is 'The Sole Spiritual Head of the Universe'.*

Brotherhood of the Cross & Star

THE PROMISED KINGDOM OF GOD IS FULFILLED

Leader Olumba Olumba Obu
The Sole Spiritual Head
Brotherhood of the Cross & Star

"In the days of these kings shall the God of heaven set up a kingdom which shall never be destroyed..."(Daniel 2.44).

to most of the voluntary charities in the district. A number of the churches operated schemes to aid the elderly, the unemployed, single parents, the housebound, and also various overseas development charities such as Christian Aid, Tear Fund, and Cafod. Harvest Festivals and annual gift or toy services provided an opportunity for church members to distribute food and toys to those in need. An early form of local aid to the poor, that also raised money for church activities, was the jumble sale first started in the late 19th century. Well into the 20th century several local churches ran coal, clothing and shoe clubs for poorer members.[37]

Historically churches in Sevenoaks, as elsewhere throughout the country, have always been linked into the wider Christian network through the diocesan structures of the Anglican Communion, the Roman Catholic Church, and the denominational, and confessional bodies of the free churches. Most churches were also associated with one or more of both home and overseas missions. The Church Mission Society and the Society for the Propagation of the Gospel appealed to different wings of Anglicanism; the Baptist Missionary Society and the Methodist Missionary Society were denominational bodies; the Roman Catholic churches had regular visits from missionary orders. All of these missions had their local agents who solicited funds, arranged missionary meetings, and encouraged active involvement in the business of mission. An increasing trend after the 1970s was for young people, in a 'gap' year between school and higher education, to volunteer to work for a Christian mission agency at home or abroad.

As church membership and attendance through the 20th century became more a measure of personal Christian commitment, so church activities increasingly focused on the identity of the church as a fellowship or family. Holidays and camps had long been part of church youth work, with Boys' (and Girls') Brigade and young people's camps, but less so for adult church members. In the late 20th century church holidays increased: some focused on inter-denominational gatherings, such as the annual Spring Harvest meetings at holiday camps, and some sponsored by charismatic groupings of churches.

Holidays were also organised by individual churches. Since the 1970s, for example, St Nicholas' parish church has regularly run annual house parties for up to a hundred and fifty people, as do a number of other churches. Hildenborough Hall, south of Sevenoaks, began as a Christian conference centre founded by Tom Rees, who had been an evangelist at St Nicholas' parish church in the 1930s. In the 1960s the centre moved to Shorehill, a large house above Kemsing; today the house is owned by another Christian organisation, Oak Hall, which runs overseas holidays. Just outside Weald village, at Hall's Green, is a Christian activity centre for young people, part of the evangelical trust that runs the Carroty Wood centre near Shipbourne.

Conclusion

During the late 1990s church membership continued to decline nationally and locally. The call by the Archbishop of Canterbury in 1990 for a Decade of Evangelism failed to arrest the slide. In the middle of the century approximately fifteen per cent of the population of Britain attended church; according to Callum Brown 'what made Britain a Christian nation before 1950 was not the minority with a strong faith, but the majority with some faith'.[38] A majority of those going to church were women. By 1989 the number of people attending church in Sevenoaks had dropped to 9.5 per cent, certainly a higher percentage than the national average and of the county generally but nevertheless a steep fall since the 1950s. Not all churches declined at a similar rate. On average evangelical churches held up better in membership than did churches of a more liberal persuasion. Indeed, certain Sevenoaks churches have bucked the trend by continuing to attract young families, and having flourishing Sunday schools, large youth groups and even a second morning service. There are few statistics to show whether this healthy pattern of membership results from attracting the middle classes, the 'unchurched', or people from other churches. For some Christians, especially those with children, there is considerable appeal in a large and active church with facilities for a wide range of young people. At the same time there are those for whom religious belief is a private matter and who prefer to worship in a more traditional environment.

The overall picture at the end of the second millennium was of a society largely indifferent to organised Christianity. The minority that attended church were probably marked by a greater degree of commitment than had been seen formerly. At the same time there were some people who, although they rarely attended a place of worship, nevertheless continued to have an interest in spirituality. In the last decades of the 20th century this was often directed towards eastern and mystical religions and the occult. Some people turned to 'New Age' ideas that were an amalgam of aspects of eastern mysticism and a reverential view of mother nature that also embraced Yoga, alternative medicines and certain ecological issues. This, often merely lip service to spirituality, now seems to have waned. A recent report on attitudes to religion in England highlights a widespread suspicion of Christian institutions and belief, albeit often based on misunderstanding and a lack of knowledge of Christianity.[39] For some this was combined with a wistful regret that belief was no longer possible.

Table 1: **Population of the Sevenoaks area**

(a) Sevenoaks town	
1695	891
1801	2,640
1841	5,061
1901	9,741
1951	16,059
2001	20,059

Note: figures before 1901 include
Sevenoaks Weald; figures for 1951
and 2001 include Riverhead and Dunton Green.

(b) Sevenoaks district					
	1801	1841	1901	1961	2001*
Chevening	756	1,003	1,074	2,113	2,720
Halstead	145	289	595	1,582	1,700
Kemsing	320	376	644	3,709	4,014
Otford	497	798	1,698	3,179	3,300
Seal	993	1,618	1,688	2,687	4,073
Shoreham	828	1,021	1,515	1,863	1,900
Sundridge	715	1,254	1,724	2,248	2,300
			* estimates		

Table 2: Religious census of 1851
[Total population of area 15,013]

Church/chapel	Seats	Adults	Children
Anglicans			
St Nicholas', Sevenoaks	1400 -	1020	-
Riverhead Chapel	600 (400)	525	150
Sevenoaks Weald Chapel	300 (180)	166	112
St Peter's, Seal	430 (220)	268	153
Underriver Licensed Schoolroom	80 (80)	50	30
St Edith's, Kemsing 150 (60)	76	75	
St Bartholomew's, Otford	200 (200)	185	93
St Peter & St Paul, Shoreham	350 (350)	190	139
St Margaret's, Halstead	[150] -	139	86
St Botolph, Chevening	220 (118)	229	93
St Mary the Virgin, Sundridge	410 (182)	215	137
Ide Hill Chapel of Ease 160 (160)	114	129	
Subtotal	4,450 (1,950)	3,177	1,197
Nonconformists			
Baptist (Particular) Sevenoaks	390 (130)	203	73
Bethel Chapel, Hartslands			
General Baptist	196 (30)	110	85
Bessels Green Baptist	160 (60)	116	75
Bessels Green Unitarian	120 (123)	55	31
Wesleyan Methodist, Sevenoaks	266 (93)	261	73
Wesleyan Methodist, Weald	80 (80)	51	-
Wesleyan Methodist, Seal	70 (70)	19	-
Wesleyan Methodist , Kemsing	80 (60)	35	-
Wesleyan Methodist, Otford	120 (110)	30	-
Wesleyan Methodists, Shoreham	146 (84)	132	43
Wesleyan Methodist, Romney Street	92 (86)	24	4
Wesleyan Methodist, Sundridge	102 (70)	66	21
Wesleyan Methodist Reformers, Stone St	[40] (40)	30	-
Wesleyan (Reformers), Dunton Green	70 (70)	33	46
Wesleyan Methodist Reformers Shoreham	80 (80)	-	-
Methodist Chapel, Seal	100 (100)	50	119
Calvinistic Independent, Ide Hill	120 (120)	115	-
Subtotal	2,232 (1,406)	1,330	570
TOTAL	6,682 (3,356)	4,634	2,934

Notes
1. Seating. Where the number of actual seats is unknown the estimated number has been placed in square brackets. Numbers of free seats have been set in *italic* and placed in round brackets.
2. Attendance. The numbers given are those reported for Census Sunday, 30 March 1851. Where there were two services half the smaller attendance figure has been added to the larger one; where there were three, one third of the smallest figure has also been added. Average attendance figures, provided by some churches and chapels, have not been included in the table.

Part Two

CHURCHES AND CHAPELS, MISSIONS AND MEETINGS

I

St Nicholas Parish Church, Sevenoaks

David Killingray

Sevenoaks began as a small market centre. It is not mentioned in the Domesday Survey as it was subordinate to the more important ecclesiastical centres at Shoreham and Otford. However, there is evidence that a church building of some kind stood on the site of St Nicholas' before the Conquest. This was probably a wayside shrine used by drovers involved in transhumance, moving cattle and swine from the chalk Downs up the sandstone ridge and into the forested area of the Weald. This is indicated both by the proximity of the east end of the present building to the High Street and the dedication of the church to St Nicholas, the patron saint of travellers.[1]

The earliest known record of Sevenoaks as a parish is in the *Textus Roffensis* of around 1120. Little is known of the early church buildings. The first was probably of timber with a thatched roof. Dunlop has suggested, by a series of drawings, the possible evolution of the building to the present perpendicular building as it might have appeared in 1520.[2] By then the settlement had been a market centre, although without a charter, for many decades. Local ragstone provided material for a more substantial building. This may have been in the mid-13th century when Henri de Gand, the Rector, also built a chantry chapel at St Nicholas for Masses to be said for the souls of his parents. By the mid-15th century Thomas Bouchier, the Archbishop of Canterbury, had bought the manor of Knole which he then developed as a major palace. He may also have been responsible for the expansion of the perpendicular building that is the present St Nicholas.

Reformation Changes

Little primary research on Sevenoaks in the 16th century has been done. How the ideas of the Reformation came to the town is unknown. Being on the main road from Rye, the town was on a possible conduit for new religious ideas and books coming from the Low Countries and Germany. Equally little is known of the interior furnishings of St Nicholas and the undoubted changes brought to fabric and fittings in the mid- and late 16th century. The registers of baptisms, marriages and deaths are extant from 1565. It is safe to assume, given Sevenoaks' proximity to London, that by the middle of the reign of Elizabeth the clergy at St Nicholas were Protestant in theology, and that the Bible and Prayer Book were central to worship. Preaching also became more important.[3]

23   *The possible evolution of St Nicholas, Sevenoaks. This series of drawings by Bernard Fenner suggests how St Nicholas church may have gradually changed from a wayside chapel to the present late 15th-century perpendicular building. Other early church buildings in the area may have developed in similar ways.*

The Archbishop of Canterbury was the patron of St Nicholas until the Reformation, when it passed to the Crown. The poet John Donne was rector, but as far as is known he preached only one sermon in the church, in July 1617. None of the rectors or vicars in this period appear to have been influenced by Puritan ideas. Dr Nicholas Gibbon, a scholarly man of moderate views appointed rector in 1631, clashed with certain of his parishioners when he built a wall around the spring on his glebe land. Following the rising of July 1643, he was accused of encouraging anti-parliamentary feeling. Ejected from his living, he had to support his 11 children by manual labour.[4] He was replaced by Thomas Kentish, a 'preaching minister', but he in turn fell foul of Parliament, which removed him in 1650 for preaching a sermon denouncing regicide. Gibbon was briefly restored to St Nicholas in 1660.

During the years of the Commonwealth, the interior of St Nicholas was remodelled. Box pews were installed and a gallery was constructed which ran above the south aisles, under the tower and part of the way over the north aisle. By then, or at a later date, the church had a three-decker pulpit positioned adjacent to one of the central pillars on the south of the nave.

In all probability the windows were of clear glass, but nevertheless the heavy oak woodwork and gallery would have made the interior dark and gloomy. Several monuments within the building date from the 17th and 18th centuries: dedicated to William Lambarde, the author of *A Perambulation of Kent* (1576), to Lady Margaret Boswell, by whose will was founded the Lady Boswell school (now the St Nicholas primary school), and to Jeffrey, Lord Amherst, the conqueror of Canada.

The Curteis Dynasty

The advowson of St Nicholas, having passed from the Archbishop of Canterbury to the Crown, was bought in 1716 by the Curteis family. For nearly the next two hundred years Curteises, or close members of the family, were rectors

24 *A monthly family service led by the curate at St Nicholas, 1986. The congregation, then numbering between three and four hundred people, is at prayer facing the communion table at the east end of the chancel. The pipes of the original organ, dating from 1797, can be seen on the left. Superseded by an electronic organ, the old pipes were merely decorative. The monthly family service brought together adults and the children of Junior Worship. Because of lack of space the one hundred or more children in Junior Worship met on other Sundays in the church school, which was nearly a kilometre away from St Nicholas. Services, morning at 10.30 and evening at 6.30, followed the Alternative Service Book, in temporary use from 1980. It was replaced in 2000 by Common Worship. The Book of Common Prayer was used at the eight o'clock morning communion service, which was attended by between twenty and thirty people. Evening services usually had a congregation of 250 including many teenagers who were members of the Contact youth group that had another meeting at eight o'clock. A copy of the New International Version of the Bible was in most pews although some members brought their own bibles. The pulpit is to the right of the curate. The sermon, between twenty and thirty minutes in duration, was based on a Bible text or passage. House groups and a midweek prayer meeting were held during the week. The practice of clergy robing at St Nicholas' has since declined, while the alterations made in the mid-1990s enabled the communion table at the east end to be moved to a more central position in the building. St Nicholas, along with many other churches, both Anglican and nonconformist, had pew rents until the early 20th century in order to meet the expenses of the building and minister.*

25 *The choir at a Harvest Festival service in St Nicholas, 1986. Harvest Festivals gradually became common in both Anglican and other churches from the 1840s. Robed male choirs in parish churches largely date from the mid- 19th century. Women and girls were accepted in many choirs in the 20th century. Since 1995 St Nicholas has had a mixed choir, without robes, to lead worship from the gallery in the west end of the building.*

of the parish.[5] It was a fairly prosperous living. Despite having a number of fine houses and being termed by a contemporary writer 'a pleasant town', parts of Sevenoaks were dirty and unkempt, particularly among the closely built houses around the market square at the junction of the London and Dartford roads. Traffic through the town had increased after the Farnborough to Tonbridge road had been turnpiked between 1709 and 1750, and with the growth of Tunbridge Wells as an elite resort.

By the first decade of the 19th century the structure of St Nicholas, particularly the tower, was in 'ruinous condition … and dangerous for the inhabitants to attend Divine services therein'. An Act of Parliament was required to levy a local rate to raise the money to replace the roof, and to rebuild and make safe the upper part of the tower. This was done in 1812-13, but at great cost. In the process clerestory windows were put in the nave and battlements added. Successive Curteises varied in their theology. None

26 *Excavating the undercroft at St Nicholas, Sevenoaks, 1994. Most churches have undergone some form of structural change. This has been the case with St Nicholas, which was built in the late 15th century. Until the 19th century the building was candlelit with minimal heating in winter. By 1980 it was inadequate for the many needs of the church family. After much prayer and consultation it was agreed that the only way to enlarge the building was to dig beneath it. This was expensive and involved delicate engineering. Robert Potter of the Sarum Partnership, who had experience of similar work, was the architect, while Ove Arup acted as structural engineers. In this picture the columns of the nave are on temporary supports awaiting the insertion of the main pillars. The work was completed on schedule and the church family moved back into a building better equipped for worship and communal activity.*

27 *Living as the people of God. The annual house party, begun in the 1970s, has become an institution at St Nicholas. Up to a hundred and fifty people of all ages go away on holiday to enjoy each other's company and to learn more about how to apply the Christian Gospel individually and communally. There are also many activities for smaller groups, such as a men's walking group shown here on the South Downs Way at Whitsun 1993.*

were inclined to take extreme positions until 1874 when the Tractarian-minded Thomas Samuel Curteis succeeded to the living. Curteis 'restored' the building by removing galleries, replacing box pews with open ones, moving the organ and installing new stained glass; he also introduced many features of Anglo-Catholic worship to St Nicholas. His actions antagonised many parishioners including one of his churchwardens, a wealthy evangelically-minded merchant, who withdrew to build a church on his estate at Kippington.

The Twentieth Century

When Curteis resigned in 1907 he sold the advowson, which was bought by an evangelical trust. An evangelical minister was appointed to St Nicholas and since then the church has remained within that theological tradition. Various changes were made to the building, including a new vestry and north porch, while the plaster ceiling of the nave, damaged by fire in 1947, was replaced by a timber-framed one in the mid-1950s. However, the most important changes to the shape of St Nicholas occurred in the mid-1990s. The congregation had grown, as had the Sunday school and young people's work, and ideas of worship and fellowship had also changed; the physical plant was inadequate for all those needs. One major problem was how to adapt St Nicholas in a way that would be sensitive to the architectural riches of a listed building standing in a conservation area. For the congregation there were also questions of cost and whether it was right to invest scarce financial resources in stones and mortar. Inevitably there was opposition from various local and national interests cautious about any change to the building.

The eventual solution, endorsed by most of the congregation, was to build an undercroft, and at the same time to raise a proportionate sum of money for mission at home and overseas. This scheme, entitled 'Building for the Gospel',

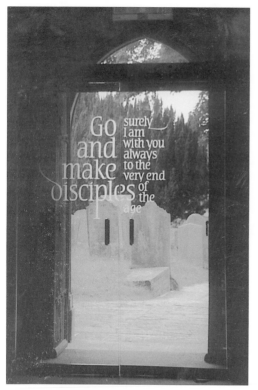

Go and make disciples surely I am with you always to the very end of the age

28 *The new west doors, St Nicholas, 1996. The new glass doors at the west end of St Nicholas are inscribed with Jesus' final words and promise to his disciples, in Matt. 28:19.*

involved the delicate task of building a suite of rooms below St Nicholas. By 1995 the work was finished; within two years the fellowship had paid the costs. The new undercroft provided meeting rooms, catering facilities, a book shop, a coffee shop, and lavatories, all neatly hidden below the original building. A new choir and organ gallery were constructed beneath the tower. Chairs replaced fixed pews thus making the building more flexible.[6] Even with the increased space, however, the pressure on the undercroft facilities from the number of young people made it necessary to start a second morning service.

St Nicholas parish church recognises the Bible as the Word of God, acknowledges the Cross of Christ as the only way to salvation, and is committed to mission both locally and globally. The building provides an open and user-friendly environment for regular Sunday worship and also for use by the wider community. Within the fellowship at St Nicholas the aim is to build relationships in a family atmosphere, both within the church building and in smaller groups based on homes. The Gospel (the good news) is presented in a variety of ways that cater for a wide range of people and interest groups, and includes lunches for retired people, baby and toddler groups, music and art evenings, as well as the regular times of worship.

2

St Mary the Virgin, Riverhead

L.P. Best

The local architectural historian John Newman has described St Mary the Virgin, Riverhead, as 'A naive little building by Decimus Burton, 1831, in a lancet style. The view of the w front from the road down below is indeed rather sweet, a short tower pinched between steep roofs.'[1] The building is distinguished by its green copper spire.

In 1760 General Jeffrey Amherst (later Lord Amherst) led a military expedition up the St Lawrence River in Canada and took Mont Real from the French. It was reported that along the river he found 'farms, well cultivated land, villages with schools and churches set on the hills with tapering spires, and all were dedicated to Saint Mary the Virgin'. Lord Amherst and his successor rebuilt the hamlet of Riverhead and their estate was called Montreal. In 1811, in conjunction with Multon Lambarde, he gave land and money for the building of a school, a vicarage and a church. The need for the church was 'to save their households and the villagers the long uphill walk to St Nicholas Church in the town'.

The architect of St Mary was Decimus Burton. His original building comprised only the nave. The Incorporated Society for Building and Enlargement of Churches made a grant of £700 towards the building costs. The church was consecrated by the Archbishop of Canterbury in August 1831, as a chapel of ease to St Nicholas, Sevenoaks.[2] When it opened there were nearly six hundred places, four-fifths of them free. The minister was a perpetual curate. In 1976 the parish of St John, Dunton Green, was combined with that of Riverhead.

29 *St Mary the Virgin, Riverhead, 2000, designed as a chapel of ease by Decimus Burton and built in 1831.*

75

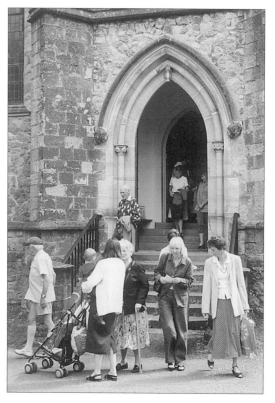

30 *Worshippers leaving St Mary, Riverhead, 2003. The formal Sunday 'best' clothes began to disappear for many worshippers in all churches in the late 20th century. Many people began to come to church in informal clothes better suited for comfort and ease rather than for appearance.*

The first vicar, appointed in 1864, was Canon James Burn-Murdoch. He was wealthy and little concerned that the stipend was very small, although subsequent incumbents had great difficulty in meeting the costs of running the large vicarage. In 1904 the vicar stayed for less than one year because he could not afford the costs. Canon George Bell (1905-47) occasionally let the vicarage and lived elsewhere because he could not afford to maintain the large house. This state of affairs existed even though, in the 1870s, Burn-Murdoch had persuaded the Ecclesiastical Commissioners to transfer some 42 acres (17 ha) from the intended parish of Kippington to that of Riverhead. This land had some large houses standing upon it that would have added to the income of the parish of Riverhead. How this came about is obscure, but there was some animosity between James Burn-Murdoch and William Thompson, then a churchwarden of St Nicholas, Sevenoaks, not least because some of this land was owned by Thompson. However, the affair was settled amicably by 1876.[3] George Bell described Riverhead as a poor village with a very large vicarage needing many servants. The church, he noted, was a gloomy barn-like place where bats used to circle at Evensong.

James Burn-Murdoch (1863-1904) was not only prosperous, but also a great benefactor to St Mary. In 1882, during his incumbency, the chancel was built in Early English style, the architect being Sir Arthur Blomfield. The Incorporated Society for Building of Churches made a grant of £40 towards the enlargement on condition that all the sittings were to be free. The Salviati glass mosaic over the altar, Christ in Majesty (1894), was his gift in memory of a son who had died aged 16 months. As an indication of changing tastes it is interesting to note that at one time the mosaic was painted blue and had to be restored at a later date. The east window, by C.E. Kempe, is to the memory of James Burn-Murdoch and was dedicated in July 1905. The high altar was designed by J.N. Comper. A sacristy was added in 1924. An adjoining parish room was opened in 1885: a large wooden building behind the church, it was eventually demolished in the early 1980s. After many years' delay, caused by financial and planning problems, a new hall was built to the north of the church, designed by local architect Christopher Rayner and opened in May 1999.

The Battle of Britain was, literally, fought in the sky over Riverhead. As there was no air-raid shelter for the school children the vicar, George Bell, asked the Amherst family if they would consent to empty the family vault under the nave so that it could be used as a shelter. The family agreed and afterwards the vicar is reported to have said: 'I have done something no one else has done! I have just buried several Earls and Countesses in a few minutes in the churchyard'.

After 170 years St Mary is still the centre of a thriving community with a loyal congregation. The new hall has widened the scope of Church activities: there are regular meetings organised for young children and for teenagers, the hall is also used by the Sunday school, the Mothers' Union and for meetings of other societies in the parish. We live in changing times and the Church is not immune. As the structure of St Mary has seen changes and developments over the years, so now the very nature of its ministry is changing. There is greater emphasis on teams of parishioners working together with the incumbent providing ministry. With the decline in the number of full-time parish clergy, questions are being asked about how much longer each parish can expect to have its own parish priest. Whatever the future holds we can be assured that St Mary will continue to be a focus for worship and ministry and remain a sign of God's presence in the community.

3
St Mary, Kippington, Sevenoaks
Diana Atkinson

The Victorian church of St Mary, Kippington, consecrated in 1880, was founded and endowed by William James Thompson, who in 1864 had bought the Kippington Estate, previously owned by generations of Farnabys, from the Austen family (relations of Jane Austen). He had made his fortune in the family firm of tea-brokers with the steadily increasing demand for Indian and Ceylon tea. William Thompson was a prominent public figure and benefactor in Sevenoaks: he was founder and chairman of the Sevenoaks Water Company; he helped found the Cottage Hospital; and he donated the Drill Hall in Argyle Road. Thompson was also a Justice of the Peace and High Sheriff of Kent, but his outstanding contribution to Sevenoaks was the beautiful church built on his estate.[1]

William Thompson was a man of deep Christian convictions. He had been a church warden at St Nicholas' church, but in the mid-1870s 'his somewhat evangelical views' were at variance with those of the rector, the Revd Thomas Curteis. Thompson successfully applied to the Archbishop of Canterbury for permission to endow and build his own church in Kippington, which, unlike the daughter churches of St Nicholas, was to be an independent parish from the start. The rector seems to have agreed amicably to this proposal for a new parish to be carved out of St Nicholas, saying that 'there is room in the dear Church of England for both'.

The new parish of Kippington extended across the main part of Thompson's estate, bounded by Oak Lane and Brittain's Lane (with a rather odd northern boundary due to a difference of opinion with the parish of Riverhead), but it also included the area bounded by the London Road and Tubs Hill on the other side of the deep railway cutting. The advent of the railway had brought increased prosperity to Sevenoaks and this part of the parish would have been the most densely populated at that time, as indeed it is now. While St Mary's was being built, a small edifice known as 'the Iron Church' was put up in Granville Road, this area also belonging to William Thompson. This continued to be used for prayer meetings and (somewhat extended) as a parish centre until it was destroyed by a bomb in 1944. St Luke's was meanwhile being built as a daughter church of St Mary's; the foundation stone was laid in 1903. The two churches functioned closely together for the first 40 years, having the same vicar and sharing many of the activities, and St Luke's did not technically become a separate parish until 1996, despite effectively operating as a separate church since about 1942. The Kippington Parish Magazine in 1957 was in fact called *The Cutting*, the cover featuring a tunnel set in a deep cutting with a picture of St Mary's on one side and St Luke's on the other.

Despite being effectively cut in two, the new church of St Mary seems to have been well-attended from the start. At that time it had a seating capacity of about four hundred and fifty, Thompson's endowment being augmented by pew rents. The parish magazines up to 1916 attest to an astonishing number of church-based activities: Bible classes (separate sessions for men and ladies), Lads' Brigade, a Scouts section and a Girls' Friendly Society, Mothers' Meetings, Band of Hope, and Sunday school. For music there was a Kippington Drum and Fife Band, a Choral and Orchestral Society and the Church Choir. Mutual help was provided by the Provident Coal and Clothing Club, and the 'Slate Club' was a sort

31 *William James Thompson, 1817-1904, the founder of the church on his Kippington estate.*

of insurance scheme which figures in the parish accounts, with contributions shared out as sick pay or for funeral expenses. Though charity was mainly at home, the Church Missionary Society was strongly supported, as can be seen

32 *Architectural drawing of St Mary, Kippington, by J.M. Hooker, the architect, c.1876.*

33 *'The Iron Church', Granville Road, c.1935. For many years this served as a parish centre for Kippington parish church.*

from the parish accounts and the 'Red Letter Notes from the Mission Field', which were included in every copy of the magazine. There was also a special link with a poor parish in Deptford. The Temperance Society appears to have been popular: the average attendance at meetings, where lectures or slide shows might be given, was fifty-five. An enjoyable picnic is recorded in 1906, when 30 members of the society visited the grounds of 'Frankfield', home of Horace Wilkinson in Seal Chart. During the First World War a Soldiers' Temperance canteen and reading rooms were provided.

William Thompson played a leading part in planning the church, and the architecture and fittings reflect his sincere Christian beliefs, as revealed in the little guidebook written by his son, Henry Percy Thompson, who subsequently became vicar of St Mary's from 1895-1919. 'Man cannot approach to God but in a spirit of Faith and Humility', so above the entrance is a statue of Faith. In the porch we are reminded by words from Psalm 11:4 to enter with reverence: 'The Lord is in His Holy Temple'. No expense was spared or detail overlooked. The font is of Italian marble, specially designed, and the pulpit is of alabaster with marble shafts. The nave is long, and the chancel arch is high and wide, leading up to the sanctuary with its painted ceiling representing Heaven with singing angels and sprinkled stars. The best of Victorian craftsmanship is here, from the lovingly carved wooden bench ends, each one different and carved by local craftsmen, to the curly, stiff leaf capitals and intricate stonework. The whole building expresses Victorian confidence and prosperity, and, as in so many similarly endowed churches in England, a strong sense of family. There are moving memorials to the founder's sister

34 *Children's nativity play at St Mary Kippington, 2001. Christmas is a busy time for churches. Many people who do not regularly attend church come to the various Christmas services. Sometimes it is to see their children perform in nativity plays, a standard fare for Sunday schools since the 19th century.*

Esther, who also helped to endow the church, and to two pairs of brothers killed in the First World War; several record the inevitable childhood deaths: 'it is well with the child'. There are family portraits discernible in some of the stained glass windows, notably 'The Heavenly Choir' (after Fra Angelico) in the chancel, installed by friends of the family, where all nine of the Thompson children are recognisably represented.

The church has served the area steadfastly throughout the last 120 years, without any great changes architecturally, but moving sufficiently with the times, representing a continuous tradition of middle-of-the-road Anglicanism, probably much as the founder intended. The electoral roll now numbers 239, and the congregations average about a hundred at the main services, with the church full for the major festivals. The building is also used by local schools for their carol services, and the open chancel makes it a good venue for concerts, supported by the newly-restored Brindley & Foster organ. There is a thriving Sunday school and youth group, and two choirs. Many activities take place in the adjoining parish centre, and the church is still a place of social interaction, mutual support and Christian witness in this part of Sevenoaks.

4

ST JOHN THE BAPTIST, SEVENOAKS

Jim Cheeseman

In the 1830s the St John's area of Sevenoaks parish, on sandy soils sloping north into the Vale of Holmesdale, was mainly wooded with fields. A few houses stood at the bottom of St John's Hill at the intersection of the two turnpike roads. From 1841 a new working-class village, with a public house, shops, and Baptist chapel, was built on a 13-acre greenfield site at Hartslands, close to the existing town gas works. By 1850 the population of Hartslands had grown to 350 and it was the 'poorest and most thickly populated part of the parish', but, lamented a local newspaper, it was without a 'Church', meaning an Anglican place of worship.

A public meeting in December 1858 made plans for a railway to link the town to London via the Darent valley, with a station at Bat and Ball. The expectation was that the population of the area would grow. It was, therefore, not surprising that at the same time Thomas Curteis, the rector of St Nicholas, made arrangements for a chapel of ease to be built in the St John's area. The funds were subscribed by 'noblemen and gentlemen resident', the land was given by the Marquess of Camden, while the ragstone came from quarries at Knole. St John's was dedicated in November 1858, and the original building formed the nave of the present church.[1]

The railway line was completed in 1862 and the population of the area continued to grow, but not as rapidly as had been hoped. However, in 1878 St John's was made a separate parish. By then it had its own National School, built opposite the church in 1870. The Revd E.K.B. Morgan, who had been in charge of the church since 1875, became the first vicar. The rector of Sevenoaks, Thomas Samuel Curteis (the fifth and last Curteis to be rector), became the patron of St John's in his own right rather than as rector.

It was T.S. Curteis who was responsible for enlarging the church with the addition of the north aisle and the provision of a baptistery in 1878. It is to the same cleric that St John's owes its High Church tradition, as he was a strong supporter of the Oxford Movement, or, as it is sometimes called, the Catholic Revival, in the Church of England. Despite the efforts of the Curteis family the second vicar of the parish, the Revd J.S. Bartlett (1882-1900), remarked that the building could 'boast but little architectural beauty in itself'.

In 1900 The Revd J. Palliser David became the third vicar of the parish. His incumbency saw the greatest period of building at St John's. A magnificent redbrick church was planned, with two aisles and a Lady Chapel. The first stage

35 *St John the Baptist, St John's Hill, Sevenoaks. St John's is a composite building constructed of different local materials at different times.*

of this was the east end of the present church, built between 1901 and 1905 and dedicated by the Bishop of Dover, as Sevenoaks was then in the Archdiocese of Canterbury. The next project was the building of the present adjoining parish room, completed in 1910.

In 1913 Mr David resigned the living. A year later the Great War started and the plans for the completion of St John's Church were postponed. For nearly fifty years that was the way it remained. It was very obvious that the work was not complete as the brickwork by the Lady Chapel was left so that it could be continued and the joining of the two buildings was clearly temporary. Eventually it was realised that the new St John's would never be completed and the outer fabric of the church took its present form.

Thomas Samuel Curteis died in 1913 and his executors sold the patronage of St John's to the Guild of All Souls, a society which promotes prayer for the dying and the dead, for the sum of £300.[2] This transaction ensured that St John's would always have a vicar in the Catholic tradition. It is also because of this link that the vestments which were made for a Requiem Mass for Queen Victoria are on permanent loan to St John's and are used for funeral Masses of parishioners. The first appointment made by the Guild was the Revd Edward Hawkes, or Father Hawkes as he was always known. He became vicar in 1920 and continued in office until 1957. Vestments were already in use, but he instituted the daily Mass which has been celebrated each day without interruption. Reservation of the Blessed Sacrament was introduced in 1924, and incense in 1925. Thus Father Hawkes established the spiritual life of St John's in the form which continues to this day.

There was no further building but damage was sustained during the Second World War (1939-45), including the destruction of the east window. The damage was duly made good and this prepared the way for the refurbishment of the interior of the church in the 1960s, when Father Martin Heal was vicar. These changes were inspired by the movement for liturgical revision that started in the last half of the 20th century. In this period were added the magnificent High Altar, hanging crucifix and many other ornaments.

The foundation stone bears the Latin inscription 'For the greater glory of God'. That is the reason for the existence of St John's. It is the hope that all that we have and do points to God, and our meeting with his crucified and risen Son, in the Blessed Sacrament of the altar. It is to this end that the daily Mass is celebrated both for the congregation and all who live and work in the parish. The church is, therefore, open for prayer and worship at nine o'clock every morning. There is a strong link with the Shrine of Our Lady of Walsingham, with a parish pilgrimage the weekend after Easter and participation in at least three other pilgrimages throughout the year. A feature is also made of combining social events with major festivals.

5

ST LUKE'S, SEVENOAKS

J. Jill Garner

The foundation of St Luke's church was partly a result of the railway that came to Sevenoaks in 1868. Immediately south of Tubs Hill station the railway ran through a deep cutting which divided part of the newly created parish of St Mary's, Kippington, endowed by local philanthropist William Thompson. Parishioners living in new houses found it difficult to reach St Mary's, and Thompson's proposal to build a light suspension bridge over the railway proved to be expensive and unacceptable to the railway company.[1] The temporary solution to the problem was to utilise a small iron church, which had been erected in 1878 in Granville Road, for worship whilst St Mary's was being completed.

A more permanent solution was needed; in 1902 land in Eardley Road was acquired for £380. The new church was dedicated to St Luke the physician, an appropriate title as the building stood near the local Hip Hospital. The foundation stone was laid by the Bishop of Dover on 22 July 1903.[2] John Thomas Lee FRIBA provided sketch plans for a permanent church but these had to be greatly reduced because of the cost.[3] However, the first part of the church, consecrated on 15 June 1904, comprised 'the chancel, transept, vestry and organ chamber, a north chapel designed for the future clergy, a choir vestry and a temporary nave built within the piers of the arcade of the future nave and aisles'.[4]

Parishioners of St Mary's (particularly the potential worshippers at the new church) raised funds to complete this modest building. Gifts were made, including Francesco Albani's painting 'The Last Supper'.[5]

The next portion of the church was built in 1909, and included the gift of an organ. The modern pulpit was replaced by one dating from around 1625, which had served as a cupboard in a builder's workshop. The north aisle was lengthened so that the carriages in which the children from the Hip Hospital lay could be drawn into the Children's Chapel. Following this and the outbreak of the First World War all further work ceased. After the war children were no longer brought in from the Hip Hospital; their chapel became a choir vestry, the vestry on the north of the sanctuary becoming the present Lady Chapel. Today patients from the nursing home that replaced the hospital, together with patients from the Mulberry Centre, regularly attend Sunday morning services.[6]

No major building work took place until 1942 when Archdeacon William James Gray was appointed to St Mary's. 'He at once took up the question of

36 *Memorial service for Canon Richard Mason, St Luke's, November 1997. At the service were present three Bishops of Rochester: Michael Turnbull, then bishop of Durham, David Say, who now assists in the diocese of Canterbury, and the present bishop, Michael Nazir-Ali. They are seen here with the vicar, Robert Chavner, and the churchwardens Joy Pennells and John Bullock.*

finishing St Luke's Church and had a completion fund opened which … in 1957 stood at about £4,500.'[7] The architect Frederick Pite, who had family connections with St Luke's, was appointed to complete the building. Simpler plans than those envisaged by Lee were drawn up and approved, and work was completed by Spring 1959. Archdeacon Gray instigated the arrangement whereby curates had a special responsibility for St Luke's until, in 1958, Ministers of the Conventional District were appointed, the first being Oscar Stanway, who had been the curate in charge since 1950.[8] He retired in 1965; the fund in his memory was used to provide the clergy vestry known as the Stanway Room.

During the next 30 years minor changes were made to the building and the furnishings: particularly in the Lady Chapel. Simple kneelers were designed and made for the chapel and, later, more complicated ones for the nave, by members of the congregation. A memorial window was installed in the west wall of the church in 1980 contrasting with the east window.[9] In the next decade a memorial window by Judy Hill, depicting the Agnus Dei, was positioned in the south transept in memory of Judge John Newey.

John Hargreaves succeeded Stanway as the new minister. John was a former missionary with a young family who quickly involved themselves in church activities. He and his wife instigated an annual parish walk which still takes

37 *St Luke's Lady Chapel. This shows the altar table and cross designed and made by Geoffrey Gilbert, a skilled cabinet maker and also organist at the church from 1966 to 1971.*

place, giving participants the chance to talk to worshippers they might not normally meet. Canon Richard Mason, a former journalist, followed John in 1983. He was very familiar with Sevenoaks, having served in several local churches. Appointed Archdeacon of Tonbridge in 1977, he was a very erudite man with a strong sense of humour, and much loved by the congregation. His involvement in the parishes outside St Luke's widened the congregation's perception of the area within which they worshipped and brought new visitors to the church.

With the appointment in 1996 of Robert Chavner as minister the time was considered ripe to make St Luke's a fully independent parish, which it became later that year, he becoming the first vicar.[10] As a professional counter-tenor with musical connections Robert Chavner brought many people to the church for concerts and other musical events. He wrote in *Crossway*, the parish magazine, in November 2001:

> We have a thriving Junior Church for children, we have a choir for singers, we have study groups for thinkers and prayers, we have a church that is open every day and available for baptisms, weddings and funerals; we run fairs, coffee mornings, lunches, midweek recitals; we have TOTS for parents and very young children, an 1830s group for young people,

38 *Parish outing to Germany. A party of parishioners outside St Luke's before leaving for a visit to Oberammergau in 2000.*

a team of Pastoral visitors, a Mothers' Union and a Women's fellowship, we have a library, we hold many different forms of worship. Here is a fellowship which welcomes newcomers, visitors, enquirers and those who are lost and lonely or bereaved; and we reach out to them in their homes.

Centenary plans for extending the building have improved the facilities for both the congregation and visitors to St Luke's. Like the acorns which grew into the oaks after which this town is named and known, the growth of St Luke's was slow, but a sound building and a healthy, thriving parish is the result.

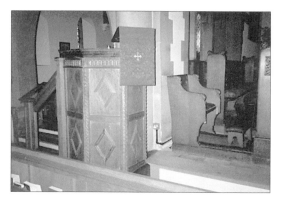

39 *Jacobean pulpit, St Luke's. Bought in 1912 from an antique dealer, the pulpit was originally in Lynsted parish church in mid-Kent.*

6

VINE BAPTIST CHURCH

Helen and Leslie Ellis

The first known reference to Baptists in Sevenoaks dates from the 1640s, a decade when there was considerable religious freedom. A church book records that 'about the years … 1646 and 1647 there was a small people of Believers Baptized that did usually assemble at Bradbourn, and Orpington … for the publique worship of God'.[1] Among the leaders was William Jeffery, a clothworker. Following the Restoration in 1660 persecution of dissenters increased, and Jeffery was imprisoned for his faith. By 1716 the General Baptists were meeting in their own building at Bessels Green.[2]

By the mid-18th century dissenters could worship more freely although the group of Particular Baptists, who began meeting at the home of Michael and Elizabeth Bligh at Bessels Green in May 1748, were threatened by local people. Bligh moved to Sevenoaks and became an ordained minister in 1753, able to preside over communion services in new-found premises rented for two guineas a year. By the 1770s the congregation had resolved 'to build a place of public worship for promoting and establishing his pure gospel amongst us', and in 1776 they bought a dwelling house and site for a chapel in the London Road for £120 from David Ball, a corn chandler. The Particular Baptist Church was opened by Michael Bligh in October of that year, and became the first dissenting church in the town.[3] Thomas Shirley became minister in 1810 and during his 42-year ministry membership steadily increased. By 1834 there were 110 members and 120 children in the Sunday school. A General Baptist church opened, also in the London Road, but it later closed and the congregation moved to a new chapel in Hartslands, built in 1842. By 1851 there were more than 200 people meeting at the

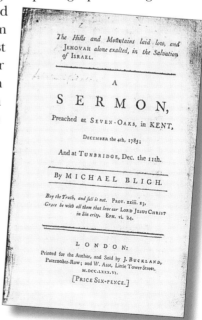

40 *Published sermon. Sermons were often published in the 18th and 19th centuries. This one was preached in December 1785 by Michael Bligh, the first minister of the Particular Baptist church.*

89

1832   It was agreed to exclude Joseph Harvey he having left us and united himself with the Wesleyans.

1833   It was agreed that several brethren should be appointed to wait upon members particularly those who are in the habit of neglecting prayer and church meetings and weekday lectures, to remind them of their duty as church members and to stir them up to greater diligence in the way of the Lord.

1840   It was decided to read the Discipline of the church at the next church meeting.

1842   Mr Filkin from the General Baptists offered to let us join them in purchasing a piece of ground for a burying ground, but friends present thought we had better have one of our own. Brother Read offered the church a piece which cost him £50 for £25 which was considered a very liberal offer ... none but members and their family should be allowed to be buried there.

1846   Mrs Keyse was excluded for having her child christened.
       The case of Brother Whiteman was considered who has failed in business and it was agreed that his conduct for several years past was calculated to bring religion into contempt for obtaining money in a dishonourable way.

41   *Baptist discipline and order. The Sevenoaks Baptist church minute book offers an insight into the standards expected of members and also how church business was conducted.*

Particular Baptist church in the London Road, and around a hundred and fifty who met each Sunday in the General Baptist chapel in Hartslands.

By the 1860s there was pressure for congregationally-minded Christians to join together in a Union chapel, something which the Particular Baptists resisted. The failing number of General Baptists at Hartslands made that church more favourable to such a scheme and most members joined with the new Congregational Church when it opened in St John's Hill in 1866. In the London Road, the new minister of the Particular Baptists was John Jackson, a product of C.H. Spurgeon's newly opened training college in London. He served the church for 10 years (1864-74); after a few years in Surrey he returned to Sevenoaks to run a school, to be prominent in the affairs of the church and also active in local politics. Under Jackson's ministry the Baptists resolved that Christians of other denominations could join them for communion, but membership remained open only to believers who had been baptised by full immersion.

By the late 1870s the Baptists in the London Road decided to move to a new building. A site was eventually bought on the edge of the Vine Court estate where the present Baptist church was opened in mid-1887. Over the next 10 years membership increased; by 1899 there were 222 members and 140 in the Sunday school. Mission has always been a strong interest of the church and from early days there was outreach in the villages around Sevenoaks. In 1916 Seal Mission was given to the church and a work continued there until 1986 when that chapel and cottage were sold. For many years members have trained for the ministry and others have served in overseas mission in India, Kenya and South Africa. By the end of the 20th century the church was supporting missionaries with the Baptist Missionary Society, Latin Link

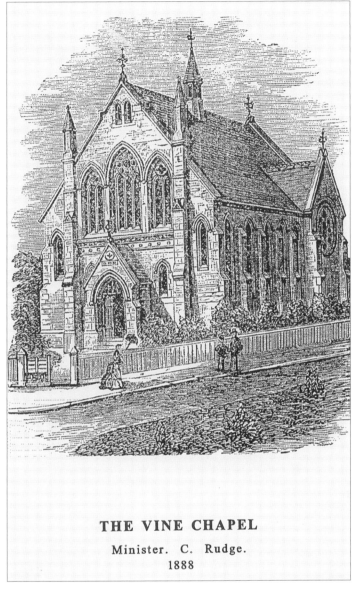

THE VINE CHAPEL

Minister. C. Rudge.
1888

42 *Cover of Sevenoaks Baptist Church Magazine, 1888. From the 19th century many churches published a weekly or monthly magazine. Although few complete runs have survived they are a valuable source of information, not only about members and church activities but also the wider community.*

and the Overseas Missionary Fellowship. In 1990 the church was twinned with Sofia Baptist Church, Bulgaria, and money continues to be contributed to its winter fund.

The original building has also been extended – to include: a chapel keeper's cottage, and the Spurgeon Memorial Hall built in 1924. Further work in 1990 refurbished the Spurgeon Hall and kitchen giving the church a lounge and

43 *The interior of the Baptist chapel in the London Road, 1863. This is an artist's impression of the candle-lit Baptist chapel in the London Road from the description given by Jane Edwards in her 'Recollections and Conversations about old Sevenoaks', written down in 1863.*

44 *John Jackson, Baptist minister, teacher and local politician. Jackson was the Baptist minister in Sevenoaks from 1864-74. He served in other Baptist churches but returned to Sevenoaks where he and his wife ran a school for many years. Jackson was active in local Liberal politics and he was elected to the new Urban District Council in 1894. He was an energetic campaigner for nonconformist rights.*

modern catering facilities. For well over 300 years Baptists have worshipped Jesus Christ in Sevenoaks. That witness continues by a fellowship committed to worship God, show God's love in their lives by serving the community, sharing the good news with others, and growing towards Christian maturity.

7

QUAKERS: THE SOCIETY OF FRIENDS

Gillian Draper

Quakerism emerged as a sect in the political, social and religious upheavals of the mid-17th century when Oliver Cromwell was 'Protector'. Quakers held a range of radical beliefs and declined to attend church or to pay tithes and other church taxes, or even secular ones. They refused to take oaths, which were necessary in many courts and legal procedures, or to undertake service in the militia. Quakers believed in their own direct inspiration from God to act and speak in their meetings. This applied to both women and men. They had no formal rites of admission such as baptism, nor lists of members, but referred to each other as Friends and their tenets as Truth.[1]

Converts to Quakerism were made in Kent by two missionaries from northern England who visited churches and chapels to proclaim the Quaker message. Their radicalism had a poor reception among most of the population of the county, but many converts were made among Baptist groups. Quaker meetings were held in Sevenoaks, and many other places including the Weald, north-west and eastern Kent, and Romney Marsh. The meetings in Sevenoaks were held at the home of Nathaniel Owen, where a Quaker related to the leading Friend, George Fox, came to preach.

After the Restoration of the monarchy in 1660, Quaker beliefs became the focus for great 'persecution', and Quakers such as Nathaniel Owen of Sevenoaks were prosecuted for holding meetings and for refusing to attend the parish church. An important reason for meeting at Owen's house during this severe persecution was its distance from the town centre and the parish church of St Nicholas. The 'persecutors' of Quakers were often churchwardens and rectors, and action was especially likely to be taken against Quakers who had the temerity to hold their meetings 'in front of the town'.[2] Prosecution could not always be avoided; in 1675 certain men informed two Justices of the Peace and local landowners that Owen had held a Quaker meeting at his home and he was heavily fined.

Under persecution the Quakers began to make written records of the beliefs and actions which had brought them into conflict with others, putting a spiritual interpretation on their practices and calling them 'Sufferings'. Some people, however, left the movement as it became more purely religious and less political. Others ignored or avoided Quaker precepts such as resistance to tithe-paying. The movement came more fully under the control of George

45 *The house of Nathaniel Owen. This house is on the junction of Quakers Hall Lane and Bayham Road, Sevenoaks, where Quaker meetings were held in the 17th century.*

Fox with a system of local and central meetings which aimed to support 'suffering' or persecuted Friends, but which also monitored and controlled their personal lives. Henry Thrum, who disagreed with Fox's direction of the movement, was disciplined 'for his Adultery with one and for being mariad by A Priest to another'.[3] Such Friends were sometimes required to produce statements of their shortcomings in writing, called 'Condemnations'.[4]

About 1690 Thomas Marche, an east Kent Quaker, edited and rewrote the records of the movement in the county, such as the 'Condemnations'. Marche's aim was to emphasise the core beliefs, such as refusing to pay tithes and take oaths, and to call his generation to observe them faithfully. He altered the records concerning early Quakers who had subsequently left the movement, suggesting, for example, that it was because of 'Persecution growing Hott', that Henry Thrum 'left Truth and went nowhere'. Marche did not concern himself with west Kent, however, where meetings such as that in Sevenoaks were becoming weaker and numbers of Quakers fewer.

Nathaniel Owen's house, a timber-framed, tiled building, gave its name to the Quakers Hall Lane area of Sevenoaks. It still stands, lying close to the junction of Quakers Hall Lane, Bayham Road and Kennedy Gardens. In the 17th century, this 'house and Warehouse' were the centre of Owen's operations as a cloth merchant, where he kept linen, woollen and other sorts of cloth. In the 18th century, when Owen's descendants lived here, the area was mainly agricultural. A map of 1760 showed two farms, an orchard, a dipping place for animals, a barn and a 'Lande Way leading to the Fields'.[5] A 'Plot for the new House' was also marked, and that new house was built in what is now Bayham Road. The name of Owen's house, Quakers Hall, was given to this 18th-century house, and his own house became known as Quakers Hall Cottage.

Eighteenth-century decline and twentieth-century revival

By the 18th century, the Quaker movement had become institutionalised and conventional. Within the meetings, for example, gender roles became much more traditional, with women having supporting, rather than leadership or preaching, responsibilities. As Quakerism here became less radical, Friends quietly found ways to pay tithes or go through legal procedures needing an oath: Nathaniel Owen's relatives had his will proved, for example. In Kent Quakerism provided alternative religious and social functions to those of the established Church, carrying out marriages and supplying poor relief to people

46 *Quaker activism. A vigil outside Sevenoaks Station in support of International Women's Day in March 1984. The Quakers have been active in supporting many social and political causes. On this occasion the vigil was to advocate freedom, democracy and disarmament.*

who were prepared to risk the penalties of being known as a Quaker. Some remained in the religious practice in which they had been born to ensure they would receive its benefits. A contemporary noted that Quakers here were 'not so industrious to make proselytes as others are', and there were few conversions. As a result numbers declined, and some Quaker meetings finally disappeared, including that in Sevenoaks.

A Quaker meeting was re-established in Sevenoaks in the 1930s, and grew to have approximately seventy members and attenders. The Friends' Meeting House in Hollybush Lane opened in 1960 (by coincidence near where the earliest meetings had been held in Sevenoaks). This meeting has been a place of quiet contemplative Christian worship, and a centre for social concern and action in the local and wider community.[6] Local Quakers have joined others to support, for example, Sevenoaks Peace Forum and International Women's Day. Modern priorities such as these can be traced back to Quakerism's earliest days.

47 *Quaker self-help. Working party in the garden of the newly opened Friends Meeting House in Hollybush Lane, Sevenoaks, in 1960.*

8

METHODISM IN SEVENOAKS

Adrienne Rogers

Methodism has flourished in Sevenoaks for around two hundred and fifty years: from the first meetings in a private house to the fine church now standing in The Drive.[1] Methodism was first brought to Sevenoaks by its founder John Wesley. He first preached in Sevenoaks in 1746 while visiting his friend the Revd Vincent Perronet, vicar of Shoreham. In the first of his 24 sermons to be preached in Sevenoaks, Wesley declared, 'There is no difference; for all have sinned, and come short of the Glory of God'.

In the 1750s Mrs Amy George, a local businesswoman, suffered the deaths of her husband and one of her four children. A neighbour told her of the preaching of the Methodists in London, so she went to hear them on her next visit in 1753. She was moved by the preaching and wanted others to share the experience, so she and her friend invited the preachers to Sevenoaks. This led to the formation of a Methodist Society in the town, meeting in Mrs George's house that same year. She not only provided the meeting room but offered hospitality to visiting preachers including John Wesley, who stayed at her house on a number of occasions.[2]

48 *Mrs Amy George's house in Hill's Yard, Redman's Place. The earliest Methodist meetings in the town were held in this house in the centre of Sevenoaks from 1753.*

The Society grew despite strong local opposition, some of which came from Mrs George's customers. The room in her house in Hill's Yard, Redmans Place, was no longer large enough and an upstairs room was rented in the 'Grainery' in Coffee House Yard. Methodism, and the George family, prospered, and William George, son of Mrs Amy George, was able to build a chapel at his own expense at Hill's Yard, which was rented by the Society. The chapel was opened by John Wesley in 1774, and he continued to visit it until 1790, only five months before his death in 1791. This period was one of growth of Methodism in the southeast. The Methodist Society in Shoreham was formed in 1763, and a chapel of very similar design to the one in Hill's Yard still stands there. The chapel in Hill's Yard was demolished in the 1960s.

The Sunday school at the Hill's Yard chapel was started in 1810 and by 1846 the average attendance was 112 with 53 teachers. The chapel was becoming rather too small for these numbers and in 1843 it was decided to work towards a new Wesleyan Chapel and Sunday school. Fund-raising started immediately and included tea meetings, collecting boxes and a bazaar held over three days during which the grand total of £134 10s. 11d. was raised. A plot of land was acquired in Bank Street and building work started in 1852; the chapel was opened in 1853. This was the first chapel to be owned by the Sevenoaks Methodists. The adjacent Sunday school was built in 1862 at a cost of £300. The chapel and Sunday school are still standing, having been converted to shops and restaurants.

49 *Hill's Yard chapel, from a drawing made in 1920. This early Methodist chapel was opened by John Wesley in 1774. It remained in use until 1853 and was only demolished in the 1960s.*

In the early days hymn singing was led by flutes and stringed instruments. At some time a harmonium was introduced, but by 1883 it was wearing out. A fund was started to raise money for a pipe organ and a bazaar was held in 1884 at the *Royal Crown Hotel* Assembly Rooms. The pipe organ was installed in 1884, moved to The Drive church in 1904 and remained in use until it was replaced by a new pipe organ in 2001. A move from Bank Street chapel was first suggested in 1899. For a church with a membership of 133 and a debt of £10 19s. 9d., this was rather an ambitious plan.

The story of The Drive church and associated buildings is essentially the story of Henry Swaffield J.P. (1834-1912). Born at St Austell, Cornwall, he moved to London in 1856 and then to Cornwall House, Granville Road, Sevenoaks, in 1876. He made his money on the stock market, and was a very generous benefactor. The site at The Drive was purchased for £500. Henry Swaffield visited the Wesleyan church at St Leonards, in Sussex, and suggested a similar building for The Drive; anyone

50 *Wesleyan chapel in Bank Street, Sevenoaks. The chapel was in use from 1853-1904. Today many people walk past it unaware that it was once a place of worship.*

51   *Opening of The Drive Methodist church, Sevenoaks, 9 March 1904; (left) Order of Service; (right) Opening ceremony.*

visiting St Leonards can see the similarity. The foundation stone was laid on 20 May 1903 and the opening ceremony took place ten months later.

Of the total cost of £7,640 9s. 9d. for building and fitting out the church, Henry Swaffield contributed £5,030. In addition he provided and endowed The Retreat, 'housing for aged people', which opened in 1904, also on The Drive site. He paid for and equipped the Cornwall Hall in 1906, named because of his Cornish origin. The manse in Pembroke Road, for which he paid, was named Carn Brae, after a hill outside Redruth, Cornwall. The name was later transferred to The Drive manse.

Swaffield's benefactions were not confined to the Methodists; he also gave the bandstand on the Vine (opened 1894), a fountain, two shelters, and the Band practice room on the Vine (1902). He renovated the Market House for use as a reading room for the YMCA (1900) and gave a site in The Drive for the Carnegie library. Henry Swaffield was elected a member of the Sevenoaks Urban District Council in 1894. He is buried in St Nicholas' churchyard.

Whereas the town centre church was Wesleyan Methodist, the church at St John's Hill was started by one of the variants of Methodism, the Bible Christian Methodists, in 1882. By 1907 it had become a United Methodist chapel. In the 1920s it was struggling to continue and in 1930 asked the Wesleyans for help. Assistance was given in the form of pastoral care but no direct financial help. However, individual members of The Drive gave generous gifts towards clearing the debt and for urgent building repairs. Even after the union of all branches of Methodism in 1932, they only became part of the same circuit in 1939. The church closed in 1961 and the building is now a Masonic Hall.

Frederick Ibbett, writing in *Sevenoaks News* in 1937, recalled that Henry Swaffield had seen a cinematograph display in London and wanted to have one for the regular Saturday evening entertainment, an aspect of the temperance movement, held in the Cornwall Hall. He bought a set of

52 *Children's group, Drive Methodist, 2001. The 'Little Drivers' toddler group for children aged up to four years, together with a parent, grandparent or other person in charge of them, is an important part of the church's contact with the wider community. The majority of people in the group are from outside the church, but some are introduced to the church in this way and start attending services. Helpers from the congregation provide refreshments and toys and also play with the children.*

equipment on condition that Ibbett worked it, so Sevenoaks was introduced to the cinematograph in its very early days. The date is not known, but Henry Swaffield died in 1912.

The Cornwall Hall played a part in both World Wars. In the first it was used for entertaining soldiers billeted in the town, and then served as a military hospital for four and a half years. In the Second World War soldiers again attended the church, some helping with the Sunday school. The Cornwall Hall was used as a British Restaurant until 1947. In 1976 the possibility of selling or leasing either the church or Cornwall Hall was discussed, due to the rising cost of maintenance. However, because of difficult access it was decided to keep them both, much to the relief of members at the end of the century when the Cornwall Hall had become a source of considerable income from lettings as well as being used for many church activities.

In the mid-1990s there was a debate with strong feelings on both sides about a proposal to replace the church pews with chairs. The 'chairs' lobby wanted the flexibility of seating, while the 'pews' group pointed out the practicality of the pews, which had lasted for nearly a century and were good for many more years, as opposed to chairs, which would need replacing after a relatively short time. On a vote at a church meeting 'pews' won by a comfortable majority. The debate seems likely to reoccur.

In the 21st century, The Drive Methodist is a thriving, busy town-centre church with weekday activities such as the toddlers' group, country walking and a worship band, in addition to Bible study house groups and Sunday worship. It also takes part in the ecumenical events in the town.

53 *The Junior Choir, 2001. They meet regularly and sing at church services and church entertainments.*

9
ST JOHN'S HILL UNITED REFORMED CHURCH

John Lurcook

Congregational ideas developed in the late 16th and early 17th centuries when small groups of dissenters rejected the rules and hierarchy of the established Church of England. Many of the early Independents, or nonconformists, suffered persecution for their faith. In 1672 conditions improved slightly although dissenters' meetings had to be licensed. The first such licence in Sevenoaks was granted in that year, possibly for a meeting held at the house of Lady Boswell.

The early history of a separate Congregational church in Sevenoaks is somewhat obscure. The line demarcating Baptists and Congregationalist was often narrow although they were divided over the questions of baptism, qualifications for church membership, and admission to communion. In 1861 a group of Christians formed themselves into a committee for the purpose of establishing a new and Independent Congregation in Sevenoaks. An appeal launched in 1863 proposed that both Baptists and Congregationalists should worship together 'on equal terms, irrespective of their differences on the subject of baptism, and to welcome to the Church, without distinction, all who love the Lord Jesus Christ'. A disused chapel, formerly built and used by General Baptists, in Cedar Terrace in the Hartslands area, was purchased, to be known as the United Congregational Chapel. The opening services were held on 9 August 1863.[1]

Within 18 months, to quote from the appeal for funds, 'a new chapel having become absolutely necessary to meet the requirements of the surrounding population – a Freehold Site, commandingly situated, has been purchased' at the top of St John's Hill. The foundation stone of the new church was laid by Samuel Morley and the Dedication Service held on 16 August 1866.[2] The original chapel was retained 'for Day and Sunday School purposes, also for Lectures and other means of mental and moral improvement for the working classes'. The costs of the building project had risen from £2,500 to over £4,400, placing a heavy burden on the minister and the small congregation, which ultimately led to the Revd Amos Attenborough, who was the first minister from 1864, resigning in 1871. The neighbourhood had not developed as quickly as had been anticipated and the hopes of a growing church in a growing suburb began to fade. For three months the church was closed and the congregation dispersed.

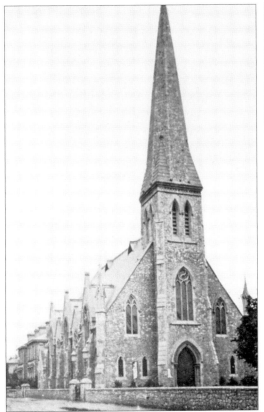

54·5 *St John's Congregational Church. Built in 1865-6, the perpendicular Gothic Congregational church, with a 130 ft spire, was constructed in Kentish ragstone from the quarries in Knole. By the late 1870s the fabric of the tower and spire was a cause for concern, and the spire was removed in 1880 and replaced by pinnacles on the four corners of the tower. These had to be removed in the 1970s as they, too, became unsafe.*

The church reopened in May 1871 with a new minister, and in the next few years the outstanding debt was cleared. About this time the Revd J.J. Feaston, a retired minister, and his wife joined the Church. He became superintendent of the Sunday school, which met morning and afternoon in the Hartslands chapel with '200 scholars in regular attendance', while his wife led a Bible Class. Mr Feaston also started 'Psalmody Exercises' in the church on winter evenings to improve congregational singing: when the only instrument available was a harmonium. This seems to have been successful as between two and three hundred people attended.

Congregational work expanded. In 1873 the church undertook the care of a small daughter chapel built in London Road, Dunton Green, which remained in use until 1937 when a new church, known as Dunton Green Free Church, was built in Station Road; this became independent of the Sevenoaks church in the 1950s. A mission hall was also built in the mid-1880s in Greatness Road to provide local services: a Sunday school, adult classes and meetings, and, for a time, the Boys' Brigade when a company was formed in 1924. The building has since been converted into a private house.

In the late 1880s the Hartslands chapel was becoming dilapidated and too small for the growing Sunday school, so a new hall was built in Holly Bush Lane. Known as St John's Hall, it opened in 1888 and was used for the 200 pupils of the Sunday school, the Band of Hope, Christian Endeavour, and

56 *Samuel Morley (1809-86). Morley, a hosiery manufacturer, leading Congregationalist and Liberal MP who lived in Leigh, was active in religious and philanthropic affairs. Between 1864-70 he gave £14,000 for the building of chapels, as well as considerable support to St John's Congregational church and the original chapel, for which he was treasurer.*

Musical Drill Classes. During the First World War the hall was taken over as a VAD hospital for British and Belgian soldiers. After the war the Sunday school returned to the hall, which was also used by the Boys' Brigade, Girl Guides, youth and adult groups, for church meetings, badminton, and jumble sales. As part of its social work the church formed a Benevolent and Maternal Dorcas Society to provide garments and clothing materials 'for deserving poor families', and bags of 'useful articles' for mothers.[3] For many years there was a 'Dorcas Room' in St John's Hall.

With the development of Junior Church, which brought children into Sunday morning worship in place of a separate Sunday school, it became increasingly inconvenient to have the hall separate from the church. In 1991-2 an ambitious scheme was undertaken to remodel and renovate the church by inserting an additional floor, thus accommodating the sanctuary above, with meeting halls and associated facilities below at ground level. The hall in Holly Bush Lane thus became redundant and was sold.

For almost a hundred and forty years many people have given, and continue to give, devoted service to the church, which started as a small local community and now draws its membership from a very wide area. Many founder members

57 *St John's URC: The remodelled worship area, 1992.*

were local business people, some of whose names are still well-known in the town: J. Salmon (printer and stationer), Palmer & Young (department store), J.H. Marchant (haberdashery), H.E. Warren (gold/silversmith, watchmaker), Edwin Pain (chemist), and J.H. Lorimer (stationer & bookseller). Other early members were Frederick Vallins, secretary of Sevenoaks Water Company, and George Whale, a local schoolteacher for 43 years. Some held posts for many years as church secretary, treasurer or Sunday school superintendent. Much could also be said of the 11 ministers since 1865 who have contributed so much to the life and work of the church and locality.

A union of the Congregational Church in England and Wales and the English Presbyterian Church had been talked about for many years and in October 1972 the union was completed with the creation of the United Reformed Church. In some

58 *Christian concern for 'Third World' needs. A Traidcraft stall at St John's URC, Sevenoaks.*

areas this entailed the formation of a joint congregation, but in Sevenoaks the numbers of worshippers at both Christ Church and St John's Hill enabled the two churches to continue individually. However, in January 2002 simultaneous church meetings voted unanimously in favour of the formation of a a single elders' meeting to serve both fellowships with a shared vision for the future, and which is preparing for the time when one minister will have oversight of both congregations. One Lord, one Church, two congregations.

IO

CHRIST CHURCH UNITED
REFORMED CHURCH, SEVENOAKS

Pat Davies

Early in 1941, despite the preoccupations of war, a small group of Sevenoaks residents began to explore the possibility of founding a Presbyterian church in the town. This was in the knowledge that since the beginning of the war many Presbyterians, Scottish or otherwise, had been evacuated to the area and had not joined any local church. The initial work was pioneered by Charles and Agnes Slater who had some experience of helping to establish a Presbyterian church in Malaya. A list of likely supporters was drawn up and contacts made, and a series of monthly services was advertised in the *Sevenoaks Chronicle*, the first to take place in mid-July.

The project had received encouragement and support from a central committee and from ministers of Presbyterian churches in surrounding areas; one report made special mention of the minister of St Paul's Church, Croydon, who '… did all the splendid spade work, visiting on foot people whose names had been given as interested, even on icy days after his bus ride from Croydon setting off on a round of visits'.

TO ALL PRESBYTERIANS.

PRESBYTERIAN SERVICES

will be held on

Sunday, July 13th,

at

OAK SCHOOL, GRANVILLE ROAD

(near Tubs Hill Station)

at 11 a.m. and 6.30 p.m.,

conducted by

REV. P. B. HAWKRIDGE, M.A.

(of St. Paul's Presbyterian Church, Reigate), under the auspices of the CHURCH EXTENSION COMMITTEE OF THE PRESBYTERY OF SOUTH LONDON.

All Presbyterians and any others interested are cordially invited.

59 *Advertisement for the first Presbyterian services in Sevenoaks, July 1941.*

In less than a year the monthly morning services had become weekly, held at various locations in the town: initially a wooden hut in Granville Road but later, for several years, at the Cheyne Hospital (now the Emily Jackson). But with a permanent minister and a growing congregation it was becoming essential to start looking for a plot on which to build a church, and in 1949 the present site was acquired at the corner of Kippington Road and London Road. This was an ideal position as there was no other nonconformist church in that part of the town and it was well placed for people then settling in to the nearby, and rapidly expanding, Montreal Park estate. A dual purpose church/church hall was completed in 1953 and the church itself 11 years later.

The funding of the church buildings was greatly helped by the allocation by the Presbyterian Church authorities of part of a war damage claim for a church at Wandsworth, South London, which had not been rebuilt after its destruction in 1940. This church had been erected in 1872 to commemorate the tercentenary of the founding of a presbytery at Wandsworth. The undamaged memorial stone from the Wandsworth church, showing the two dates 1572 and 1872, was given a place of honour in a wall in the vestibule of the new Christ Church, Sevenoaks.

60 *Laying the foundation stone of Christ Church, 1 June 1963.*

The first ministers, Hastings Eastwood and Geoffrey Sirkett, covered the period from 1943 to 1961, each contributing much to the consolidation and growth of the congregation. Michael Whitehorn, the next appointed minister, served the church for 21 years. His and his wife Margaret's early years of ministry were marked by big strides towards increasing church membership and the numbers attending Sunday school. Guides, Brownies, Scouts and Cubs were further important additions to the church family.

There was an increasing awareness of the need to develop church unity and Michael Whitehorn was closely associated with setting up the North-West Fellowship of Churches and the creation of opportunities for congregations to share in worship or social events. This inter-relationship extended to groups from overseas, in particular from the Lutheran Church of Bavaria and the Waldensian Church of Italy, whose members have been hospitably received by the Sevenoaks congregation.

In October 1972 the much discussed amalgamation of the Congregational Church of England and Wales and the English Presbyterian Church occurred to form the United Reformed Church (URC). In many centres this union resulted in the formation of joint congregations but in Sevenoaks the numbers of worshippers enabled the two churches (Christ Church and the Congregational church on St John's Hill) to carry on individually.

61 *The completed Christ Church, June 1964.*

62 *Party of Bavarian Lutherans visiting Christ Church in June 1966. The photograph was taken outside the old railway station at Tubs Hill.*

In 1983 the appointment as minister of Bruce Stuart, an American, brought in new approaches, although patterns of worship and activities remained substantially unchanged. There was much emphasis on pastoral care. During his ministry, work was carried out at the church to give full wheelchair access, and the Littlecourt Lunch Club was set up (a joint venture with St Mary's, Riverhead and Age Concern, with recent involvement by St John's Hill URC) using the church hall to provide lunch and weekly fellowship to about fifty elderly people.

Andrew Francis was inducted as minister in 1994, but on a less than full-time basis in view of his commitment to work with a number of other URC churches in the furtherance of lay ministry. Under his direction there have been several additions to the church calendar, including the 'quiet communion', the Iona-style service and a prayer service, which are held monthly and precede the normal Sunday morning worship. Alpha courses have been introduced, and the holding of lay-led home groups, concentrating on Bible study, has considerably increased in scale. Very recently a mother and toddler group, Christ Church Chums, has been formed and is receiving good support. In 1995 a room known as The Bridge, which had been added to the church buildings many years previously, was made available to the Sevenoaks Christian Counselling Service.

A feature in recent times has been the increasing role of the elders in leading worship, principally to prepare for the time when the minister will have oversight of more than one church, a result of reduced deployment quotas. Sharing a minister will, in fact, happen quite soon between the two URC congregations and the two fellowships are working in very close collaboration, aiming to establish (in the words of a recently issued statement) 'two congregations and two sets of premises but with a single eldership and a shared vision for the future'.

VINE EVANGELICAL CHURCH

Arthur Duke

The Vine Evangelical Church originated in a group of people who were part of a movement known as the Brethren, the founders of which had in 1825-30 determined to meet together with other Christians of any denomination in a simple way, following the example of the early church. Their purpose was to enjoy fellowship, study the scriptures and observe the Lord's Supper weekly. A distinguishing feature of this movement was that they saw no need for an ordained ministry or central authority. Each local church was independent, with its affairs administered by elders, or overseers.

In 1892 Vine Hall was recognised by the Registration District of Tunbridge Wells for the solemnisation of marriages, and the Official Guide to Sevenoaks, published in 1901, declares that the church was known as 'Vine Hall, the Meeting House of the Open Brethren, and seats 150 persons'.

The doctrines and practices of the Brethren were similar throughout the world, and wholeheartedly evangelical. Jesus Christ was recognised as the sole and all-sufficient Saviour of those who put their trust in Him. They practised baptism by immersion and extended it only to those who made a personal and public profession of faith in Christ. Prominent

63 *A holiday Sunday school certificate from the second decade of the 20th century. Throughout the 19th and for much of the 20th centuries most nonconformist and Anglican churches had Sunday schools. They often met on a Sunday afternoon. Various means were used to encourage children to attend. Regular attendance resulted in prizes (usually a Bible or a book of 'an improving nature'), and joining the annual outing and the Christmas party. This form of card was commonly used by many churches so that children on holiday could have a certificate of attendance at Sunday school.*

Vine Hall Sunday School, Sevenoaks.

————————————191

DEAR FRIEND AND FELLOW WORKER,

———————————— who is one of our Scholars, proposes spending a holiday in your neighbourhood, and during that time will probably attend your School.

I shall be very much obliged if you will kindly certify such attendance on the form below and return this paper to me by the above-named Scholar.

If the School is only open once on Sunday please make a note to that effect.

Yours very truly,

————————————

Secretary.

Certificate.

I hereby certify that————————————

has attended the————————————
Sunday School as follows :—

Date.........................					
Morning					
Afternoon					

(Signed)

Superintendent (or Secretary).

64 *Farewell gathering in the 1960s. The Christian Brethren were noted for their warmth and hospitality to each other. Here some of the members of Vine Hall, as it was then known, gather to send off the Sharman family who were emigrating to New Zealand. Many nonconformist chapels had a biblical text displayed prominently on a wall; the verse shown here is part of Romans 6:23. All mainstream churches were run and led by men. Although this gradually changed in the late 20th century, the Christian Brethren maintained male dominance. Until recently women were expected to wear hats and the wearing of trousers by women was frowned upon.*

in their teachings were biblical prophecy, typological teaching from the Old Testament and readiness for the return of the Lord. There developed a great interest in missionary work, undertaken by people who set out in faith that God would meet their needs.[1] Many followed the pioneers with the help of 'Echoes of Service', a missionary agency now located in Bath. In the earlier years George Müller (1805-98), of Bristol Orphanage fame, was a great supporter of these missionaries.

From the beginning the Vine Hall congregation had a great interest in Sunday school work locally. It was so popular that the numbers attending became very large. As a result advance application forms were made available to register the very young for later admission when numbers permitted. Forms were also devised for the children to take on holiday with them, certifying attendance at other Sunday Schools, so that those Sundays might be taken into account for attendance prizes at the year end.

Vine Hall was (and is) located on a road junction. Its entrance was in Hitchen Hatch Lane, but the adjoining premises were entered from Dartford Road. The latter was known as Vinehurst, the residence in the 1900s of William Henry Jenkins, who owned both premises. Earlier the whole property had been intended for use as a hotel, but a licence for this purpose was not granted. Accordingly, the church (or assembly, as it was known) continued to enjoy the use of Vine Hall. In 1906 William Jenkins sold both properties for £2,000 to Echoes of Service. The money for this purchase had been donated by two individuals, with the stipulation that the rental proceeds should be used to support missionary work.

By 1963 Vinehurst had become more of a liability than an asset for Echoes of Service. It had been divided into rooms mainly occupied by elderly ladies at a very small rent. This income was insufficient to cover the cost of appropriate upkeep, and the facilities were not of an acceptable standard. Things came to a head when the Sevenoaks Urban District Council served notice requiring extensive modernisation of the property. In 1964 proposals were drawn up to demolish Vinehurst and construct a new building on the whole site for use by the church, but planning permission could not be obtained. Eventually in June 1971 the whole property was purchased by the church for £2,000 and

65 *The music group at a baptism service, Vine Evangelical church. The Christian Brethren and the Baptists practise believers' baptism by immersion. Most of their places of worship have a baptismal pool, usually placed near to the pulpit or platform. Nearly all other denominations baptise infants. In the 19th century many Brethren services had hymns sung without musical accompaniment. Organs and pianos were only slowly accepted, but by the end of the 20th century many churches, including Vine Evangelical, were using a variety of musical instruments to accompany singing.*

vested in a group of seven trustees with a view to ensuring that the church continues to adhere to the doctrines and practices set out in the trust deed, and that the buildings are maintained in good order.

Since that time the buildings have been modernised, but a local church primarily consists of the people who compose it. The main downstairs room, in which Sunday services are held, is furnished simply to permit flexibility of use. During the week the property is used for various purposes such as 'Mothers & Others', a popular opportunity for small children from the local community to enjoy a time of play watched over by their mothers and carers. There are also off-site activities such as weekly home groups for worship, study, prayer and fellowship; there is also a fortnightly football evening for local men.

While VEC (as the church is often referred to) has seen many changes over the years, the fundamental principles guiding its founders remain in place. The scriptures are regarded as the final authority in matters of personal faith and practice, and also in patterns of corporate worship and church life. While VEC is a member of the Evangelical Alliance it remains independent and autonomous, and the overall leadership is in the hands of elders and a leadership team. Every member is encouraged to play a vital role in contributing to the health and growth of the church, with a mission to reach out in friendship to those who do not yet know Christ, in order that He might make them His friends and disciples. This is encapsulated in a recently adopted evangelism vision statement: 'Making friends for Kingdom ends'. VEC's traditional interest in young people and the spread of the Gospel continue to be reflected in active youth groups and in its support of several people who have been sent out from the church to devote themselves to full-time Christian work in other parts of the UK and overseas.

12

THE CATHOLIC CHURCH OF
ST THOMAS OF CANTERBURY, SEVENOAKS

Christopher Bell

The Catholic Church in this country is unique in that it existed for nearly a thousand years, was suppressed at the Protestant Reformation and virtually disappeared for the next three hundred years, and then reappeared in the middle of the 19th century.

During the long years while the Catholic Mass was prohibited, those recusants who continued to practise their faith had to do so in the strictest secrecy in private houses or chapels. Inevitably there were many martyrs to the faith, particularly priests. There were others who outwardly conformed to the newly established national church, in order to retain their positions in their professions or society, or to protect their families, while privately remaining loyal to their Catholic beliefs. They were categorised as Church Papists.

Much historical research has been done (and, indeed, continues to be done) into Catholic recusancy, and there is some indication of the survival of Catholicism in the Sevenoaks area at least during the early years of what were known as the Penal Times.[1] A number of the Sackvilles of Knole, for example, retained their allegiance to

66 *The interior today of St Thomas's church. The decoration of the apse, added in 1930, shows Christ enthroned and flanked by Saints John Fisher, Thomas Becket, Thomas More, and Edith of Kemsing. Roman Catholics and Anglo-Catholics place considerable significance on certain people whose lives were a particular example of godliness. The Roman Catholic Church continues to beatify people: Mother Teresa of Calcutta, for example. Nonconformist and Low Churches acknowledge the sainthood of all Christian believers and do not single out any one for particular veneration. In practice, however, all churches have their founding fathers and favourite sons and daughters.*

110

67 *Opening Ceremony of St Thomas's, 15 July 1896. The principal celebrant at the Mass was Francis Bourne, Coadjutor Bishop of Southwark. He was later to succeed Herbert Vaughan (seen preaching here) as Cardinal Archbishop of Westminster.*

Catholicism. Foremost among them was Thomas Sackville, Lord Buckhurst and the Ist Earl of Dorset (1536-1608). This family's adherence to their faith is particularly notable, given that they continued to play a leading part in the politics of the realm.

Another well-known local family with many recusant members were the Bosvilles of Bradbourne. In 1592 Sir Henry Bosville was disarmed, along with other recusants, his arms being given to John Pett of Sevenoaks. One of Sir Henry's sons, John, was sent to Douai in France to be educated in the Catholic faith, and was subsequently ordained a priest at the Valladolid seminary in Spain in 1589. He was arrested in England in 1603, charged with the treason of being a seminary priest, and imprisoned in Newgate Gaol in London. He reappeared in Rome in 1607, and later still, in 1623, was back in England as Archdeacon of Warwickshire and Worcestershire. Finally, he is recorded as having been Vicar General of the West Midlands in 1625. He was one of those lucky few who did not lose their life for their priesthood. One of John's nephews, Edward Maddison, took the same route to Douai, was ordained a priest at Arras, and was sent to England in 1617. He too appears to have escaped the ultimate penalty, having eventually become a monk in Spain.

Another strongly recusant family were the Loanes (also spelt Lone and Lowe) of St Julian's and Sevenoaks Park. In 1592, Samuel Loane's arms were

68 *St Thomas's church in its peaceful setting as it was between 1896 and 1926.*

confiscated, the recipient again being Thomas Pett of Sevenoaks. The family continued to suffer fines and sequestration of land over the years for their refusal to conform to the Church of England. Finally, in 1654, George Loane, no longer able to pay his debts, was forced to sell both Rumshed Manor and Sevenoaks Park to Thomas Lambarde of Westerham. Thus constancy to their Catholic faith resulted in the loss of the family's lands in Sevenoaks, and the Protestant Lambardes took their place as the largest estate owners in the town.

The Theobolds were a further prominent Catholic family, and were originally of Stidulf's Place. Oliver Theobold and his wife were indicted for recusancy in the 1660s, and Oliver, this time described as a doctor of medicine, was indicted again at the Assizes in 1674. A later list of recusants, covering the period 1678 to 1688, also includes Oliver's son, John. Oliver had another son, Richard, who took the Oath of Allegiance to the King in 1680, but not the Oath of Supremacy. This halfway house resulted in his being bound over to appear at the King's Bench, but unfortunately there is no record of the outcome.

Notwithstanding the existence of these and other examples, there are no firm grounds to infer the continuity of Catholic practice for the full 300 years of proscription, and so, in the current absence of evidence to the contrary, it must be presumed that the practice of Catholicism in the Sevenoaks area

69 *Nave extension to St Thomas's under construction, 1926.*

probably did eventually die out. However, three centuries of oppression came to an end with the passing of the Catholic Emancipation Bill in 1829. The Catholic hierarchy was finally restored in England and Wales in 1850, and the first Cardinal Archbishop of Westminster was Nicholas Wiseman. He and his bishops immediately set about the establishment of Catholic churches and schools.

We are now on much firmer ground with regard to Sevenoaks, and know that a Mass took place in the home of a Mr and Mrs Buchanan in Granville Road in February 1880. The congregation that day numbered seven, but it very soon increased sufficiently for a temporary iron church to be erected in October of that year. The first rector was Father Ignatius Lazzari, who had been acting as tutor to the Buchanans' son.

There is little information available concerning parish activities in the very early days, but there is a report of a meeting of the Sevenoaks Branch of the Catholic Total Abstinence League of The Cross that took place in March 1881. Father Lazzari, who chaired the meeting, spoke on the evils of alcohol and encouraged his congregation to sign the abstinence pledge.[2] Contemporaneous parish records indicate that regular meetings continued for a number of years, but the League appears to have failed owing to lack of support by 1893.

By 1884 the rector had raised adequate funds to build a permanent, albeit small, brick church to replace the existing iron one. It comprised what is now the sacristy of the modern St Thomas's Church, and a Latin inscription over the sacristy door still clearly records the fact. The new church was initially dedicated to The Most Holy Trinity because the altar had been acquired from a church of that name and bore (as it does to this day) a diagrammatic

70 *St Thomas's today, with the Father Tom Quinn Memorial Porch. Tom Quinn, a Holy Ghost Father, was a much loved assistant priest at St Thomas's from 1978 until his untimely death in 1991.*

representation of the Holy Trinity on its front. Among the early benefactors who made the project possible were the Duke of Norfolk, the 3rd Marquess of Bute and the Empress Eugenie, widow of the Emperor Napoleon III of France, who was then living in exile in Chislehurst.

Father Lazzari left Sevenoaks in 1892 and was succeeded as rector by Father William Cunningham. The latter's great contribution was to raise funds for, and oversee the building of, a further extension, which now constitutes the sanctuary, spire and top end of the nave of the present St Thomas' Church. The work was completed in 1896, at which point the previous building became the sacristy. The new church had been referred to during the planning and fund-raising stage as the Manning Memorial Church (although it never actually bore that name) in memory of the late and popular Cardinal Manning, Wiseman's successor as Archbishop of Westminster, who had lived at nearby Combe Bank as a boy. Henry Manning had been the Anglican Archdeacon of Chichester before converting to Catholicism, and is perhaps best remembered for his concern for London's poor and the part he played in solving the London Dockers' Strike of 1889. The opening ceremony, with Pontifical High Mass, was conducted by Manning's successor at Westminster, Cardinal Herbert Vaughan.

The congregation continued to grow, and was temporarily increased further during the Great War by the influx of Catholic troops from Lancashire who were billeted in the town. Within a very short time of their departure for the Western Front, the Sunday notices began to include requests for prayers for those soldiers who had been, in the stark words of the then rector, slain.

One parishioner very active in fund-raising, from her arrival in 1890 until the 1920s, was Victoria, later to be Lady Sackville, the youngest daughter of Lionel Sackville-West, the 2nd Lord Sackville, and his Spanish mistress Pepita. Since 1916 the rector had been Father Joseph Phillips, and it had fallen to him to extend the nave to its present length. The building was completed in 1926 and eventually consecrated in 1935 when the large parish debt had finally been paid off. For some years the church had retained its original dedication to the Most Holy Trinity together, since 1896, with that to St Thomas of Canterbury, but by 1935 it had become simply the Church of St Thomas of Canterbury.

As the parish grew, so activities and organisations blossomed. In September 1918, Father Phillips introduced an annual pilgrimage across the fields to St Edith's Well at Kemsing, a devotional practice that had been very popular in earlier centuries. In 1931, the Sevenoaks section of the Catholic Women's League (CWL) was established with its motto of Charity, Work and Loyalty, and it was active in the parish for the next 60 years. A parish school was built and staffed, and a Youth Club and Scout and Guide groups were formed. The Sevenoaks Catholic Association, which was formed in 1947, organised welfare work, fund-raising events and social functions, while waging campaigns on a variety of fronts on behalf of the Catholic community.

In later years the Society of St Vincent de Paul (SVP) has done much charitable work with the poor, housebound and lonely in the district. Similar activity has been undertaken by the Co-Workers of Mother Teresa, and much valued assistance to the priests, particularly of a catechetical nature, was, until recently, provided by the Franciscan Missionary Sisters for Africa from their convent in South Park.

Prior to the building of their own churches, the Catholics of Westerham and Biggin Hill were served from Sevenoaks. In the days before nearly universal motor car ownership, the Sevenoaks priests offered Mass for the Catholics of Ide Hill in private houses in their village. Although the geographical boundaries of the Sevenoaks parish are now reduced, there are still affiliated churches, served by the priests of St Thomas's, in Otford, Weald, Borough Green and West Kingsdown. All these locations, except Weald, support thriving communities, with a total of more than a thousand people regularly attending Mass. There is an ongoing busy preparation of children for their first Holy Communion and confirmation, as well as courses for adults who wish to join the church, or who would merely like to learn more about the Catholic faith.

13
First Church of Christ, Scientist, Sevenoaks

Kate Bettley

Mary Baker Eddy, an American, discovered 'the Science of divine metaphysical healing which I afterwards named Christian Science' in February 1866.[1] She published her foundational work *Science and Health with Key to the Scriptures* in 1875. The First Church of Christ, Scientist, known as the Mother Church, was founded in Boston in 1879 'to commemorate the word and works of our Master, which should reinstate primitive Christianity and its lost element of healing'.[2] The followers of Christian Science first met for services in London in 1896.

The first Christian Science gathering in Sevenoaks met in 1904 at the house of a Mr James whose healing through Christian Science had attracted the enquiry of a small number of people. Two years later meetings were being held in the Oddfellows Hall in London Road. In 1908, the ground floor at the back of a shop in the High Street was rented to provide space for a reading room where people could find out more about the movement; this was later temporarily moved to a hut near the railway station.

In August 1910 the Sevenoaks Christian Science Society was organised and advertised in the *Christian Science Journal*. Two services were held on Sundays and there was a testimony meeting once a month where members could tell of healings; a lecture by a member of the Board of Lectureship of the Mother Church was also hosted annually. Literature distribution throughout the local area had also begun by 1910, and new rooms for the services were found in the Market Place, High Street, which were large enough to accommodate a reading room-cum-Sunday school as well. In 1912, a plot of land near the old main post office in South Park was given to the Society by a member of the church, and in 1915 a temporary church was erected together with accommodation for a reading room and, for people up to the age of 20, a Sunday school.

By 1925 the Society had grown to become the First Church of Christ, Scientist, Sevenoaks, a branch of the Mother Church in Boston, Massachusetts, and thereafter weekly testimony meetings were held. By this time the reading room and Sunday school were situated in an upstairs suite of offices in the London Road. In 1930, literature distribution broadened with the establishment of a Monitor Circulation Committee.[3]

Later a building fund was started for a permanent church, the erection of which was made possible following a substantial donation by a Christian Scientist in 1934. Building work began in late 1935 on the site of the boating pool of the old *Lime Tree Hotel* (almost next door to the old church), to a

71 *First Church of Christ, Scientist, Sevenoaks, in South Park. This shows the building with the modern Reading Room to the right.*

design by wartime comedienne Joyce Grenfell's father, Paul Phipps. Space for a congregation of just over 200 and a temporary Sunday school in the rear lobby was provided and the first services were held in November 1936. An extension for a permanent Sunday school was built onto the back of the church in 1954, but was later demolished when the rear land was sold in the 1970s; the present Sunday school lies within the church.

Mary Baker Eddy defined church as: 'The structure of Truth and Love; whatever rests upon and proceeds from divine Principle'. This is reflected in the Christian Science Church's impersonal pastor: the Bible, *Science and Health with Key to the Scriptures*, and a weekly Lesson Sermon, given centrally from Boston, which is studied and read in all branch churches across the world. The major contribution offered to the community by Christian Science churches is healing. That is summed up in the following statement:

> A Church of Christ, Scientist, promotes the recognition and acceptance
> of the healing Christ in the community ... It provides individuals with
> an open door to recognising their true identity by guiding them to
> an understanding of identity as God-with-us, Love-with-us, health-and-
> holiness-with-us consciousness.[4]

In Sevenoaks the practice of Christian Science is manifested through, for example, church members' prayers for the community and the work of local Christian Science practitioners, while members of the congregation continue to share news of healings at weekly testimony meetings. One typical account, a member recalls, was related by Norman Duncan, who was healed of a serious

DIVINE LOVE ALWAYS HAS MET
AND ALWAYS WILL MEET
EVERY HUMAN NEED

72 *Inside First Church of Christ, Scientist, Sevenoaks, 2000. This photograph shows past and present Readers Chris Miller (left), Jonathan Webb and the late Minnie Holbrook.*

head wound he had received during the First World War from which he was not expected to recover. He went on to become the church organist for many years, and his son, Sir Val Duncan, then chairman of the mining company Rio Tinto, became a Christian Scientist and taught in the Sunday school.

In addition, the movement has three care homes in Britain, including one in Farningham, that 'support the practice of Christian Science and the mission of the Church of Christ, Scientist, in an atmosphere which promotes spiritual growth and healing'. For those seeking healing solely through prayer and radical reliance on the teaching of the Bible, together with the Christian Science textbook and other writings by Mary Baker Eddy, 24-hour nursing care by specially trained nurses who support the patient's reliance on God for healing is also provided.

The present, purpose-built reading room serves as both a bookshop for Christian Science publications and as a public reference and study centre. Annual lectures continue to be hosted in local venues such as the Stag Theatre, while the work is further promoted by exhibits at, for example, the annual Kent County Show.

14

SEVENOAKS TOWN CHURCH

Andrew Wilkinson

In 1871 William Wallis and his wife began a Sunday school on their farm in the parish of Cudham. Adult interest grew and the congregation built a chapel on the farm, which was named Cudham Baptist Chapel. The church flourished and mission works were started at Leaves Green and Biggin Hill Valley. In the 1920s Biggin Hill grew into a village and a new Baptist church was built at the heart of the community. After 1945 the congregation gradually declined in strength and also in spiritual purpose so that even baptism was considered optional.

The 1970s were a time of spiritual renewal in all the mainstream churches in Britain. At Biggin Hill Baptist the prayerful search of some members was rewarded as joy and faith returned, with teaching and experience of the gifts of the Holy Spirit. Renewed focus on the Bible brought about a restructuring of church government and life, with deeper mutual accountability. In the late 1970s the Baptist church became part of a movement called 'Coastlands', now New Frontiers International, one of several groups of churches having a similar experience of the Holy Spirit.[1]

Among the now vibrant congregation was a small group of close friends from Sevenoaks. In time these people felt a call to start a similar church in their home town. In September 1983 they began to meet there in a private home for Bible study, fellowship and prayer, and to proffer the Gospel on the street. In this they were supported both by the Biggin Hill Baptist Church and by Kemsing Free Church, which had been established in the 1930s. After a year, numbers had increased from 10 to 30, as friends were invited in. The group then began meeting publicly in the hall behind *Bligh's Hotel* in Sevenoaks, becoming an independent congregation in June 1985. One elder recalls that the fellowship grew as 'we saw people responding to Gospel calls [who were] healed from sickness [or] emotional problems [and given] hope and happiness'.

In January 1986 a new church was formed by merging with Kemsing Free Church, and was called the Sevenoaks Town Church. In the late 1970s many members of Kemsing Free Church believed that God wanted them to experience greater freedom in worship and prayer. New leaders were appointed in 1981 and the church became part of New Frontiers International. From 1981 to 1986 membership nearly tripled, rising from 24 to 70. To quote

73 *The Town Church have a celebration of praise at a Sunday meeting. The members of the Town Church acknowledge that God's Holy Spirit is at work in their lives, and many members raise their arms in praise to God as they sing or pray.*

one leader: 'We worked to discover more of church life as we find it in the New Testament'.

From early on people met mid-weekly in private homes for Bible study, prayer and praise, and there was a strong emphasis on the need to evangelise. These themes continue and, since 1996, groups are taught to see themselves as churches in microcosm. In 1992 the Town Church moved from the rather unsuitable hall behind *Bligh's Hotel* to meet on Sundays in Wildernesse School at the north end of the town. This continued for the next 10 years.

Right from the beginning there was the desire to share the good news of Jesus Christ with people in Sevenoaks and the surrounding villages: hence the name 'Town Church'. The vision grew to include working with other churches in the area and, where possible, to support them with help and resources. The Town Church thus prays and works with several local churches, and there are also preaching and pastoring ministries to groups of Christians in the Lake District and overseas in Mexico and France.

The Town Church is itself still youthful, and has many young members. There is a Children's Fellowship for those aged 3-11 years. 'The aims for all groups', a teacher says, 'are for them to have fun, friendship and fellowship whilst learning truths about God ... each morning includes games, stories, teaching ... and prayer ... As the children get older there is more emphasis on their walk with God.' Teenagers are encouraged to support one another and the younger children. A young helper writes: 'When they even do simple things like showing you a picture they're proud of, you feel like you're doing something really worthwhile.' A recent development is for children to have their own worship with a live youth band monthly. Teenagers encourage one another in their own groups or cells so that, in the words

74 *The new building of the Town Church. For several years the Town Church met for Sunday worship in rented halls. Other meetings were held in members' houses. Eventually a site was acquired on the north side of Seal Road, and a church was built in 2001-2.*

of one, the 'cell provides an environment where we can worship and share our friendship'.

Many of the younger members of the Town Church are passionate about working with teenagers and those in their twenties. From 1996-2000 a well-attended monthly nightclub for 13-17 year olds was run from Raley's Gym in Plymouth Drive, Sevenoaks. It provided safe, good quality entertainment with good music.

For several years a search continued for fixed premises. Eventually a disused car repair centre was bought in the Greatness area of Sevenoaks. The hangar-like structure was stripped down to its concrete frames and a new building formed around these. Various facilities have been included – offices, kitchens, toilets and meeting areas. The aim is to increase the current adult membership of about one hundred and forty people. It is also seen as a home base for reaching out with God's love into the Sevenoaks area. Named 'The Mill Lane Centre', it came into use in March 2002.

15

VINEYARD CHURCH

Tony Cornfield

The founding pastors, Tony and Pam Cornfield, encountered the Vineyard style of church through visits to St Peter's Anglican church in Hextable, near Swanley, in 1989. The combination of modern, and yet intimate, worship, with biblical teaching and practices that had an expectation of God's active involvement with His people, transformed their image of church.

Ten years later, following study at Spurgeon's College, in London, and on-the-job training as members of Redhill Vineyard Church in Surrey, Tony and Pam were commissioned, and sent out to 'plant' a Vineyard Church in Sevenoaks, on 28 March 1999. The following Sunday, they held their first public worship service at The Bradbourne School. It was Easter Sunday, and about fifty adults attended: friends, well-wishers, and 'seekers' who had responded to local advertising. At its birth, Sevenoaks Vineyard became the 55th Vineyard Church in Britain. The Vineyard denomination, with its origins in the mid-1970s under the leadership of the late John Wimber, comprises more than a thousand churches worldwide, which share common values, purposes and priorities. Broadly speaking, they aim to combine the best of evangelicalism with the best of the charismatic movement.

75 *Members giving away chocolate cream eggs to passers-by simply to say 'God loves you'. The Servant Evangelism card is given to people with the free gift of a lemon, or flowers, or a chocolate cream egg.*

The leaders felt called by God to establish a church in Sevenoaks that was both contemporary in style and based on the Bible, which would equip people to worship God and continue the ministry of Jesus empowered by the Holy Spirit. They aim to gather both people who recognised that there must be more to life than their current experience and Christians who had not yet found a church home, and draw them into a vibrant relationship with their heavenly Father, and to advance the Kingdom of God and see people develop a closer intimacy with him, thereby creating an environment where emotional and physical healing were possible. Lives can

76 *Vineyard Church meeting for worship and fellowship. The Vineyard Church is a relatively newly-formed fellowship of believers meeting in Sevenoaks. As with many similar groups of Christians, meetings are held in private homes, while members meet for Sunday worship in a local school hall.*

be changed as people practise their faith with compassion, acceptance and love. The expectation is that ordinary believers can be released to minister to God in worship, and equipped to minister to their neighbours in the church and in the community, both locally and further afield, as God directs. The church adopted a mission statement: 'Our primary purpose is to know Jesus and make Him known'.

After two years the church moved to Sevenoaks Primary School for its Sunday morning service. Here a warm, friendly and relaxed environment gives one the freedom to worship and learn practical truths whilst being changed by the presence and power of God. Starting with contemporary worship-music that is not 'happy clappy', the service moves, after a coffee and doughnut break, to a positive message culminating in prayer ministry that has the potential to change lives.

The Vineyard Church recognises that there is more to church than a Sunday service; at the heart of the church are the midweek fellowship groups. These groups meet in people's homes and typically have between eight and 12 participants of all ages and backgrounds. They provide an informal setting where people can get to know each other better. Worship, teaching and prayer ministry, where members pray for one another, are typical elements of these meetings. The main focus is on developing relationships with God and with one another. The groups are safe places in which members can learn how to minister in the gifts of the Holy Spirit as they mature in faith. There is the security to take our masks off and be real, as we seek to share our lives together.

We just want to say "God Loves You", in a practical way, with no strings attached.

sevenoaks
Vineyard Church

The Vineyard is a Christian church that has a contemporary style. Our highest priorities are to worship God and be "family" in our community.

We hope

this simple

gift made

you smile

and

brightened

your day!

We meet together for a worship service at 10.30am each Sunday at Sevenoaks Primary School in Bradbourne Park Road

If we can be of help, or you would like more details, phone:

01732 452062

Sevenoaks Vineyard Church

On midweek evenings we meet at 8.00pm in local housegroups for Worship, Teaching & Fellowship i.e, Food, Friendship and Fun

77 *The Servant Evangelism card. This is handed to people in the streets as an invitation to come to the church.*

From time to time people gather in groups, both large and small, to pray specifically for the work of the church, to examine specific topics through bible study, and to pray for the local community. Some of these evenings of prayer and worship have been with other local churches, thus demonstrating the unity that we have in Christ Jesus our Lord.

Throughout the year the Vineyard Church looks for opportunities to be a blessing to the local community through simple acts of kindness: typically by giving things away in order to encourage people to smile and to be able to tell them that God loves them. Examples of this include giving away fresh lemons before pancake day, single carnations close to Valentine's Day, small bunches of flowers near Mothering Sunday, cream eggs before Easter and paying for people's car park tickets at the 'Pay and Display' machine.

A major purpose of the worldwide church, and a constant element in the Vineyard ministry, is to share the Gospel, the good news of the redeeming grace of Jesus Christ. One way of reaching out to people is through Alpha courses: these are part of a national programme which involves informal gatherings over a meal, after which the Gospel is explained and Jesus' claims are discussed. As a result of these courses, several people have come to faith and joined the church. Christian faith also leads to a concern for our neighbours and the local community. Through liaison with local organisations, both voluntary and statutory, opportunities have presented themselves for people to give their time to visit the elderly and disadvantaged, to talk or provide practical help. One example, of practical help to parents, is a Breakfast Club offered in a local primary school that provides breakfast before school starts for any child that needs, or would like to have, this service.

Essentially 'church' is all about relationships. Primarily this relationship is with God, to whom we aim to draw close in worship through his word and in prayer; the Westminster Confession reminds us that 'the chief end of man is to glorify God and enjoy Him forever'. Secondly, the New Testament writers remind us again and again to 'love one another', so at the Vineyard Church there are regular opportunities to meet together simply for food, fellowship and fun.

16

BESSELS GREEN BAPTIST CHURCH

Richard Bevan

The 17th and 18th centuries were times of change for the nonconformist groups and worshippers who had begun to flourish following the Reformation and the English Civil War. For Baptists this time saw two groupings develop: the General and the Particular Baptists. The General Baptists held Arminian views while the Particular Baptists had Calvinist views on salvation. In the Sevenoaks area a group of General Baptists first met in the Bradbourne area, mainly in private homes, but by 1716 they had built a Meeting House on the Westerham Road at Bessels Green. Theological differences between worshippers led, in 1747, to a group breaking away and establishing their own meeting in Sevenoaks. In 1769 a further division occurred within the Bessels Green Baptist church, principally over the doctrine of the Trinity.

Under the leadership of John Stanger (1743-1823), the assistant pastor, a company of men and women separated from the General Baptist congregation meeting in Westerham Road (now the Unitarian church) and met together to establish a new church, which now looks back on a history spanning over 230 years.[1] Initially the new group met in homes, and then, due to the gift of a portion of Great Barn Field from Charles Polhill of Chipstead Place, a new Meeting House and residence for the Minister was constructed; it opened for worship on Sunday 23 December 1770. The same building in Bessels Green Road remains in use to the present day, although over the years various congregations have modified and added to the accommodation.

The 34 founding members appointed John Stanger as the first pastor: a position in which he was to serve for 54 years. During this time he was present at and shared in many key events in Baptist history, including the ordination of William Carey in 1787 and the 1812 gathering at which the formation of the Baptist Union was decided upon.[2] Stanger was active among young people in the district by continuing a school that he had previously founded when first moving to the area. A Sunday school was established in 1807 and this has continued uninterrupted to this day.

Worship in the early years was very different from today. It was not until 1844 that the fellowship agreed to allow music and stated 'that two instruments be permitted subject to an understanding that this was to be used with moderation and in a devout and serious manner'. Sunday services were held at 10.30 a.m., 3.00 p.m. and 6.30 p.m. (the afternoon service was discontinued in 1857). The fellowship were particular about whom they chose

78 *Bessels Green Baptist Church, 2002. The Meeting House dates from the late 1770s. For some time the minister's house was the area to the right, which is now incorporated within the church building. An extension was constructed behind the church in the late 1980s.*

as pastor. In 1845 a candidate was invited to preach for two Sundays, then a further four, and finally a further six before any decision was made. In the final third of the 19th century the church benefited from the support of Sir Samuel Morton Peto, an MP and major railway contractor, and his wife, who lived at Chipstead Place. They supported the fellowship and funded improvements to the church building and the minister's house. In 1891 an outreach mission was established at Goathurst Common, Ide Hill, which continued to be supported by Bessels Green until the 1960s, when it was closed and the building sold to become a private house.

The 1980s saw significant growth in attendance figures and an expansion of activities. The membership increased from 74 in 1980 to 133 in 1990 with increased numbers attending Sunday worship. This growth put pressure on accommodation as the original 1770 Meeting House was able to seat only 135, and the adjacent Victorian hall was in need of significant renovation. Numbers attending on Sunday mornings meant that it was necessary to hold two morning services: one at 9 a.m. and the second at 10.30 a.m.

In 1986 a separate house for the minster was purchased, allowing the original minister's accommodation adjoining the church premises to be adapted and used for offices, Sunday school and small group activities. In 1989 the fellowship was able to build a new hall capable of seating two hundred. This allowed the Sunday morning services to be combined and held in the hall. This hall was the first step and, with continued growth in numbers, 1997 saw the old Victorian hall demolished, enabling the original Meeting House to be refurbished and extended as a modern worship area seating 275.

79 *Sunday Morning worship at Bessels Green Baptist Church. Many Baptist churches have ministers who live in a nearby manse. The minister, usually a graduate with a degree in theology, is called by the congregation to serve the church. His stipend, or salary, is provided by church members. New or struggling churches often receive financial aid from denominational bodies; in the case of many Baptists it would be the Baptist Union. Lay preachers are a common feature in many nonconformist churches. The baptismal pool is beneath the platform on which the minister is standing. Many churches in the late 20th century have made increasing use of a range of musical instruments and various means to aid services and illustrate sermons.*

Since John Stanger and the original members began the work at Bessels Green, 26 other pastors have led the fellowship through what have been some of the most challenging and changing years imaginable. At the start of 2002 the formal membership numbered 157 although on Sunday mornings between 200 and 225 adults and children worship God together. During the week a variety of clubs are held to cater for children and young people of every age group. A fortnightly luncheon club is held for older members of the community, and the fellowship meets midweek in small groups for prayer and Bible study in home groups spread throughout the district.

Today, looking back to 1770, from the opening years of the 21st century, it is difficult to imagine the district as it was and the lifestyle of our predecessors. We must dismiss the urban sprawl of commuter housing, motorways and emails and imagine a district devoted to agriculture, where travel was on foot, horseback, cart or coach on a dirt track and there were great houses at Chevening, Chipstead Park, Bradborne, Montreal and Cole (Cold) Harbour. Water came from the well, and lighting was by candle and oil lamps.

With an active congregation the history of Bessels Green Baptist Church is still being written. Many things have changed but the fellowship at Bessels Green Baptist Church continues to proclaim the message of God's love in sending Jesus Christ into our world. This remains central to all worship and activities, and the challenge is to present the Gospel in culturally understandable ways for a new millennium.

17

Bessels Green Unitarian Church

Sheila Crosskey

The distinctive claim of Unitarians was (and is) for freedom of conscience without credal statements, recognising a diversity of spiritual pathways within the broad band of a liberal Christian heritage. Each congregation is an independent self-governing entity and neither their histories nor their present standpoints are uniform. The roots of the congregation in the Bessels Green Old Meeting House are to be found among the Old General Baptists, who professed General Redemption and the six principles derived from Hebrews 6:1-2. They merged with other strands of radical dissent to become Unitarians in the late 18th century, but at Bessels Green they did not relinquish the rite of baptism by adult immersion until midway through the 19th century, and still recognised their General Baptist traditions beyond that date. It is the ethos, rather than the theological views, of these forbears which has remained formative for succeeding generations of this congregation. We take care that every member 'has a voice in church affairs', as explicitly laid down in the old minute book, and we recognise (in the words of a celebrated epitaph) 'that the differences of the earnest make the world freer and wider'.[1] From its foundation, this church covenanted to live according to the teachings of Jesus, but it discouraged defining the margins of permissible belief, which was seen as both presumptuous (for 'mere humans') and divisive.

Led by William Jeffery, the church first assembled around 1650, but their earliest records have not survived. We know that by 1697 they were meeting at Brittains in Sevenoaks. When the second Church Book (1697-1813)[2] opens they were engaged in an ambitious plan to 'gather churches for Jesus Christ in Virginia'. Tragedy overtook this attempt which had collapsed by 1725. It was during the preparation of this venture that the Sevenoaks General Baptists resolved to build themselves a Meeting House. Their deacon and benefactor, William Cox of Lullingstone, purchased the Meadow at Bessels Green and paid to erect the building and its attached dwelling house. It opened for worship in December 1716. William Cox directed that rent from the cottage and meadow should provide for needy members of the church. A natural spring in the meadow became an outdoor baptistery. The burial ground was added in 1738. William Cox (d.1719), and perhaps other church members, are interred at the Crockenhill Old Burying Ground laid out on land belonging to the Cox family.[3] In 1747 a newcomer from Bedfordshire, Michael Bligh, drew away seven

80 *The east front of the Old Meeting House, Bessels Green. The dormer windows are not original but date from 1905. Several older nonconformist churches have burial grounds. This one at Bessels Green is the oldest in the area. Others are to be found at the Bessels Green Baptist church, behind the old chapel in Hartslands, Sevenoaks, and by the chapels at Goathurst Common and Ide Hill. Many nonconformists, especially Methodists, were buried in Anglican churchyards for much of the 19th century. These tombstones, like those in most Anglican churchyards, face towards the east, in the belief that the dead will be resurrected to meet Christ when he returns.*

members of the church to found his own Baptist congregation in Sevenoaks. They threw a charitable veil over their differences which (deliberately) remain unspecified, and in 1760 an amicable arrangement was agreed for his church to share the burial ground at Bessels Green.

A second split occurred in 1768 when John Stanger, a young stocking weaver from the Northamptonshire General Baptist Association, was recruited as assistant minister to Samuel Benge. He turned out to hold irreconcilably different views from the trustees and officers of the church. This complex conflict had many layers. John Stanger was an evangelical who apparently preached Calvinism to a congregation which professed General Redemption. But there were grave personal affronts and difficulties on both sides, culminating in a credible threat to eject the incumbent congregation from their property, based on a legal omission of 30 years before. John Stanger took away part of the membership to found his own New Connection General Baptist church in Bessels Green, where he was honoured with a memorial for his long and devoted life as pastor and itinerant preacher.

What had become the Old General Baptist Society at the Meeting House joined with the Unitarians to campaign for civil and religious liberty.

81 *New extension to the Old Meeting House and the manse cottage, 2001. Most church buildings have been altered in one way or another over the years to meet the needs of a different age and a new congregation. Few, if any, of the churches in the area remain as they were originally built.*

Traditionally looking across the Atlantic for freedom from persecution they went on to applaud the American Revolution, and some then clamoured for radical political change at home. In 1795 Robert Colgate and John Austen, with a large party of their family members, fled to America to escape a charge of treason, under which they were suspected of supporting republicanism on the example of the French Revolution. In America Robert Colgate founded the Colgate soap firm, later developed in New York by his eldest son William.[4]

The silence of our surviving records on this crisis in the life of the church speaks eloquently of the threat it constituted to the remaining membership. Samuel Love, who came of a long General Baptist lineage, appears to have moved immediately into Filstone Hall, Robert Colgate's farm near Shoreham. He was elected an elder in 1802 and a trustee of the Meeting House in 1803, along with Ambrose Austen, who also emigrated to America, probably around 1811, without any note being recorded of his departure. Few further minutes were entered in the surviving Church Book and from 1813 on there is a long hiatus. A Unitarian minister, the Revd John Briggs, was called to the pulpit in 1822, succeeded by his son the Revd John Atkinson Briggs in 1851. In 1828 John Boys, a notable benefactor, paid to build Park Point Manse for John Briggs Sr, on a site already incorporated into the Meeting House land on the north-east boundary of the burial ground. His benefaction formed the core of the Ministers Residence Charity which has been of such importance to the church.

Samuel Love's son, another Samuel Love of Filstone Hall, became the next managing trustee in 1836. However, it was his sister Elizabeth Love, also of Filstone Hall, who undertook most of the administration until her death in 1873, when the church was in woeful decline. The only records of this period are a handful of letters and some bills relating to property maintenance. It seems that both finance and membership had collapsed. Two years later it fell to Samuel Love Green, nephew of the above, to try to set things in order. From 1898 he leased most of the Meadow for building, and a decade later, after long negotiations, he obtained a charitable scheme which revised the original Trust in line with developments during the first 200 years of its existence. The Meadow passed out of the possession of the church in 1973.

At the start of the 20th century the small congregation was beset with financial problems. For more than sixty years services were maintained by visiting preachers and devoted lay members, under the oversight of the London (Unitarian) District Minister. In 1974 a shared pastorate was arranged with Maidstone Unitarian Church. The trustees sold Park Point Manse in 1986, and a recent period of growth has culminated with building extensions to the Meeting House and manse cottage, where a settled minister will soon be in residence. The resurgence in numbers and activities (there are between thirty and forty members and attenders), has been self-sustaining and, in addition to, Sunday services, includes social events, adult religious education, concerts, contacts with Sevenoaks charities and societies and, importantly, participation in Unitarian affairs at local, regional and international levels.

18

CHEVENING

Katharine Draper and Beryl Duncan

The ancient parish church, aptly dedicated to St Botolph, patron saint of travellers, lies just south of the intersection of the prehistoric track, now known as the Pilgrims' Way, and the Rye Road. The oldest section of its stone walls only dates back to the end of the 12th century, though the parish was established in Saxon times. Built as a place of Christian worship, gradually enlarged and continuously cared for, it has also played a focal part in the civil governance of the parish. The history of the church and its community can be read in the different architectural styles of the present building, its internal ornaments and the documents of both the parish chest and the Stanhope archives.

Chevening was a daughter church of Shoreham Minster, from where missionaries would have crossed the Darent Valley to convert the inhabitants of *Civilinga* (Chevening), a small Jutish settlement on the Downs at the western border of Otford Manor. The first known documentary evidence is the payment of 9d. by the parish of *Civilinga* recorded in the *Textus Roffensis* of around 1120.

The oldest portion of the church building is the south wall of the south aisle, built largely of local flint, ragstone, rubble and Roman tiles, the remains of a small two-celled church. Built on demesne land, it is contemporary with the first record of a resident lord of the manor, Adam of Chevening, in 1199. Chevening was sub-infeudated from the manor of Otford, which had been ceded by the Mercian Kings to the Archbishop of Canterbury between 785 and 822. It remained in his possession until it was given to Henry VIII in 1537, but the advowson of the parish remains with the archbishop to this day. The first rector, Reginald, held office in 1262. With tithes and glebe land for support, he and his successors were expected to assist the poor of the parish. Social organisation was exercised through the manorial courts.

The increasing number of pilgrims making their way to Canterbury, after the murder of Thomas Becket in 1170 and growth of traffic from London to the coast, especially the fish trade, would have brought increased prosperity. A fish market was established in the hamlet of Chipstead a mile south of the church so that by 1291 Chevening was assessed for a payment of £16 13s. 4d. under the taxation of Pope Nicholas.[1] There was a further boost to the economy

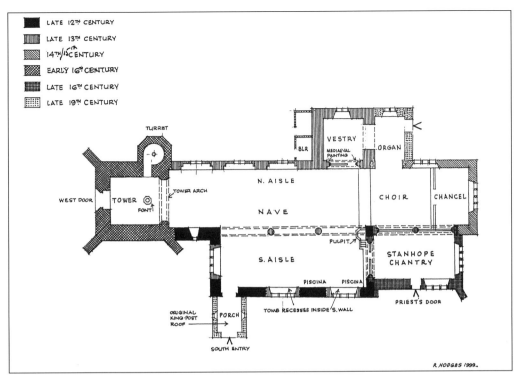

82 *St Botolph's Church, Chevening. The gradual expansion of the building over the centuries can be seen in this plan. The tower was added in 1518. The Stanhope Chantry was the last significant addition.*

when Edward III created a staging post at Chipstead towards the end of the 14th century.

After the Act of Supremacy in 1534 legislation was used to impose Protestant practices on the Church of England, and all links with Rome were severed (except for the brief interlude of Queen Mary's reign). The social upheavals of this period led to a significant increase in the number of dispossessed and vagrant people, who became the responsibility of the parish. While the manorial courts continued to meet in Chevening into the 19th century, their concern was now property.

The vestry meeting, usually chaired by the rector, was responsible from the 1530s for the civil administration of the parish and also for the care of the poor. It was empowered to raise church rates but sometimes found difficulty in keeping a correct account of these multifarious activities. The minutes of the Vestry of Chevening held on 10 January 1819 contains the transcript of a long and irate letter from the 4th Earl of Stanhope. He wrote that: 'the accounts have been kept in a manner extremely irregular, confused and unsatisfactory ... though no imputation of dishonest or dishonourable conduct exists'. He also strongly criticised the 'charges [varying from four guineas to five pounds each] towards defraying the expenses of a public dinner on the day of Visitation' and 'charges of four guineas each for "Feasts to the Singers"'.[2]

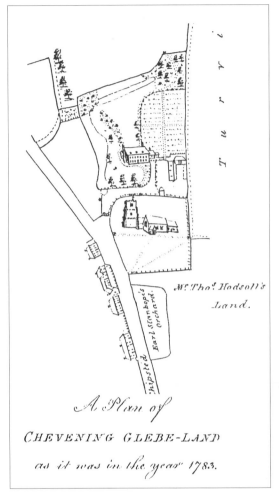

83 *Plan of the Rectory and glebe land, Chevening 1783. After Chevening House was enlarged the Rectory became an elegant Georgian house with large gardens. Until the early 20th century many rectors and vicars, often the sons of gentry, had private incomes from landed property and lived in elegant houses paid for by the parish. In the 18th and 19th centuries there were poor curates in the Church of England who struggled on low incomes and did much of the parish work, but the image of the absentee and indifferent incumbent has been somewhat exaggerated. (Abraham Barham)*

The parish records, originally kept in the parish chest, contained the registers of baptisms, marriages and burials, and the various documents generated by the vestry. An analysis of them provides a substantial body of evidence of contemporary life.[3] A few are surprising: such as the baptism on 12 February 1687 'of John, an Ethiopian or black-moor, Servant to the Lady Katherine Strode of Chepsted, being eighteen years of age or thereabouts as is supposed'. There are also church briefs, or royal mandates, which authorised collections for disasters as far afield as Edinburgh and Copenhagen.

Only a few years after the upheaval of the Reformation, John Lennard bought the Chevening estate. This prosperous legal family lived at Chevening for six generations and rebuilt the house between 1616 and 1630. The chantry in the south-east corner of the church was built about 1585 to house their splendid monuments. It is now renamed the Stanhope Chantry, after the family who bought and enlarged Chevening House in 1717. Ennobled by George I, the family lived at Chevening until the childless 7th earl died in 1967. A board on the wall at the back of the nave records the foundation, in 1722, of the Lucy, Countess Stanhope Charity for apprentices. This charity is still active, partly thanks to this record.

In 1851, when the population numbered just below a thousand, an average congregation in the parish church was 190 in both the morning and afternoon.[4] A pew plan of a few years earlier indicates where people sat in church and thus the social hierarchy of the parish.[5] By the middle of the century the tithe, glebe, and fees for Chevening added up to £612 5s., but tithe reforms meant that this was not a source of income upon which the parish could continue to rely. Letters and subscription lists in the Stanhope archive show the effort to raise the funds needed to maintain the fabric of the church. At one point in the 19th century even the bells were sold to pay for repairs after an outbreak of dry rot, although they were restored in time for the millennium.

Chevening was a long, narrow, straggling parish. Most people lived in the hamlet of Chipstead, a mile to the south of the church. In 1894 it was decided to build a mission hall in Chipstead that was used for Sunday schools, classes, and even as a hospital during the First World War. In 1926 the Bishop of Rochester agreed to the creation of the Chapel of the Good Shepherd in the east end. A few years later the Rectory was built beside the mission hall, so the church had moved nearer to the majority of its congregation.

84 *Public notice advertising the opening of the Methodist chapel, Chipstead 1859. Many churches in the 19th century had services in the afternoon and the evening. It was not uncommon for women to preach in Methodist churches.*

Gatherings of nonconformists were illegal during the Restoration period and so their discovered activities can be seen in the records of the West Kent Quarter Sessions. James Calverley of Chevening, a farmer, was fined five shillings for attending a gathering on Easter Day 1675 at the house of the widow Peller, under a hill called Toys Hill: 'A person unknown was standing upon a stool, and a great multitude to the number of a hundred persons standing about him ... he was preaching and exhorting and citing many texts from the scriptures'. Calverley was also fined £8 as part share of the £20 fine for the unknown preacher. Unrepentant, he was fined £20 in 1687 for attending a further gathering.[6]

The Old Meeting House at Bessels Green was built as soon as the law permitted, in 1716, becoming the first nonconformist chapel in the district. In the mid-18th century the congregation split: the Meeting House became Unitarian, and in 1769 the Baptists built a new chapel further along the road. The Religious Census of 1851 reported that, together, the two churches had an average attendance at services of 149 in the morning, 139 in the afternoon and 100 in the evening. And, as with many churches and chapels in the area, 'Bessels Green being a mere hamlet in a rural district the number of hearers is dependent on the weather'.[7] A small chapel in Chipstead High Street was opened in 1859 as a New Free Methodist Chapel, later to be designated as

85 *A Rogation Sunday at St Botolph's, Chevening. The children are holding sunflower seeds given to them by the Revd Christopher Johnson during the Rogation service. The children will plant them and then at harvest time prizes will be given for the tallest and biggest flowers. Before the Reformation, Rogationtide was the three days before Ascension Day, a time for fasting and prayer for the coming harvest. It was also a time when parishioners perambulated the boundaries of the parish. Before the tithe award surveys of the 1830s, and the Ordnance Survey, many parish boundaries were not mapped. It was important for the parish authorities to know the boundaries because this helped decide who had local rights to poor relief.*

Bible Christian, a branch of Methodism. By 1895 the chapel was in secular use; it has since become a private dwelling.

It was only a vigorous protest led by the Parish Council that prevented Chevening church from being cut off from its congregation by the construction of the M25 orbital road. The parish still has its own rector, and the present incumbent, Christopher Johnson, writes:

> Jesus said 'God is not the God of the dead but of the living' (Mark 12: 27), and though St Botolphs has a long and distinguished history it is still a living church, serving the Parish of some 3,500 people. There are 246 people on the church's electoral roll and as well as regular worship there are prayer groups, a bible study group, and several children's and young people's groups. There are strong links with Chevening School, which is a church school and with the Chipstead Lake Cheshire Home. The Parish Hall is administered by the church but it is a facility available to the whole parish. The church has always existed to glorify God and to make His love known to the world and this is still the aim of St Botolphs Chevening.

19

HALSTEAD

Geoffrey Kitchener

St Margaret's Church at Halstead, an unpretentious building with bell turret, low sweeping roof and knapped flint walls, is Victorian. Inside, however, its memorials name members of the community back to the 14th century, and these were taken from the old church, when it was demolished in 1880-1. The remains of that building lie some two hundred metres away, in the former grounds of Halstead Place, and most of its remaining memorials have been vandalised, largely in recent years.

There are some sources available which help to infer the early origins of the church and community. First, a church at Haltesteda is recorded in the *Textus Roffensis* (*c*.1120), as part of a list of churches believed to be based on a Saxon original. Secondly the site adjoined, and lay well within the private grounds of, Halstead Place. This was an 18th-century mansion that replaced an earlier manor house, which suggests a continuity of relationship between church and principal landowner. In conjunction with the evidence of *Textus Roffensis*, this could point to an origin as a private chapel erected by a Saxon thane next to his residence. Place-name evidence suggests that, in common with many other settlements ending in '-stead' high up on the downland, Halstead was an outlying secondary settlement, perhaps used for stock grazing, from middle or later Saxon times.

The church was rebuilt in the 13th century. Halstead does not enjoy the richness of medieval ecclesiastical records that the neighbouring parishes of Otford and Shoreham possess. There are records of church bequests, proceedings for debt against the rector, and even the excommunication of William Bebyngton, the incumbent, in 1419. But the general paucity of information reflects the fact that this was a very small and impoverished parish. In 1377 only 38 people over 14 years of age paid their groats for the poll tax. In 1535 the living was assessed as worth £5 17s. 10d. per annum, plus an additional 3s. 4d. allocated solely to the priest. By way of comparison, Shoreham was, with Otford, worth £56 gross, Chevening, £21 6s. 8d. and Brasted, £32 6s. 8d.

The parish was sometimes fortunate in possessing a rector who was able to devote care and attention. Examples include John Hoadly (rector from 1678 to 1725), who kept school 'when I was young and Able',[1] and John Cottingham, for whose appointment during the Civil War the parishioners petitioned the House

137

86 *Halstead old church next to Halstead Place, c.1872. The preservation of old buildings as part of the national heritage was largely a 20th-century idea. The Arts and Crafts Movement and the Society for the Protection of Ancient Buildings (1877) were small and weak pressure groups. Early legislation was voluntary and largely focused on ancient sites. Late Victorian clergy and church patrons 'restored' churches with little let or hindrance. At Halstead the old church building was demolished and a new one built nearby.*

of Lords. Although in 1653 the Commonwealth took the conduct of marriage ceremonies away from clergymen, the marriage register shows that Cottingham was still prepared to marry in the old way. These rectors may be contrasted with the non-resident Carswell Winder (rector from 1742-70), who was 'better known as a Foxhunter than as a Divine', according to the historian Streatfeild.[2]

Halstead's community began expanding in the 19th century with the growth of the London fruit market. Woods were grubbed, and the ground laid to soft fruit. Halstead became famous for strawberries: the fields and the fruit pickers' huts are depicted in one of the south windows of the present church. Several rectors commented on the tensions created by fruit growing, especially the drunkenness that resulted from money being earned, and anti-clerical feeling amongst farmers. By 1885 there were some fifty dissenters in the parish, with a focal point provided by Albert Bath of Colgates farm, described by the *Bromley Journal* in that year as 'a well-known local politician holding advanced radical views'.[3] He campaigned through the Farmers Alliance against the extraordinary tithe rent charge payable on hops, obliging the Halstead rector to seize his produce to secure payment.

With Halstead's expansion came a proposal to demolish the old church and build anew.[4] Four factors may have been involved. First, it has been claimed that the old church was pulled down because it was in a dangerous condition; the evidence for this is not convincing. Second, the population was increasing; yet average congregations were in the order of two-thirds of the church capacity. Thirdly, the Victorian period was one in which substantial private benefactions for religion were not uncommon. Fourthly, T.F. Burnaby-Atkins had inherited Halstead Place in 1872. He contributed most of the building costs and would have been conscious of the advantages of removing both the access to the church through his grounds, and the bells from outside his windows.

The old church was pulled down in 1880-1, and the new one built in the separate cemetery grounds, converting a burial chapel of 1855 into the chancel. An unfortunate omission marred the transfer of the church. The rights of the old church as a place for the solemnisation of marriage were

87 *St Margaret's Church, Halstead, 1977.*

not transferred, with the result that the 112 marriages celebrated at the new building until 1919 were, strictly speaking, invalid. A sizeable proportion of the village population was accordingly illegitimate, until the marriages were validated by an Order, confirmed by a special Act of Parliament in 1920.

Halstead's population was increased by migratory fruit-pickers, leading Harry Cumberlege (rector from 1891-1900) to institute open-air services for them on summer Sundays, as well as providing a class on Saturdays for the children. He continued Sunday schools, which had been run by his predecessors from at least the 1870s (attendance was about thirty in 1876, 50 in 1880 and 87 in 1885). Fruit-pickers' children were also encouraged to attend Sunday school by Francis Deane (rector from 1903-15), by the added attractions of lemonade, ABC biscuits and 'hundreds and thousands'. His wife ran temperance socials for young men and women, where tea was provided in huge urns. A frequent injunction to her daughter was 'Take this strong one to so-and-so, who is here drunk again'![5]

Civil and ecclesiastical parishes were then smaller than at present. Most of Otford Lane lay in Shoreham parish, and the fruit growers there faced a walk of two or three miles to their proper parish church. The Otford Lane Mission Church, a small wooden building, was opened for their benefit in 1891. Other straggling communities in the large Shoreham parish were similarly served by mission churches at Twitton (1890) and Well Hill (1893).

88 *Mission to fruit-pickers at Halstead, c.1910. Itinerant seasonal workers, such as hop and fruit pickers, temporarily increased the population of certain parishes. Halstead's clergy responded by providing a special mission for workers and their children. In this photograph Miss Shrimpton is sitting at the portable harmonium.*

89 *Otford Lane Mission Church, 1892. A congregation of fruit grower families with the Shoreham rector, the Revd R.A. Bullen. The boys' uniform caps probably denote membership of the Band of Hope, one of the national temperance organisations formed in the 19th century.*

Both Otford Lane and Badgers Mount, which had no separate church, were brought into the Halstead ecclesiastical parish in 1938.

Nowell Wood (rector from 1967-73) had experienced many years of commercial life before entering into the ministry, and brought with him a variety of skills and enthusiasms that benefited both church and village. During his incumbency several organisations were started, including St Margaret's Players and the Ladies' Fellowship. His successors have all held the position of chaplain at Fort Halstead, and during the early 1970s the Director of the Fort, Fred East, was also lay reader.

The communities of Knockholt and Halstead were brought closer together with the appointment of Malcolm Bury as rector in 1983. The opportunity was taken to combine both livings, although separate parochial church councils were continued. His vision and commitment led to the building of the North Room onto the church in 1992, which accommodates crèche facilities during services and informal gatherings after them. However, the closure of the Otford Lane Mission Church in 1985, with a residual congregation of about eight people, marked the disappearance from Halstead of the fruit growing that had originally given rise to the Mission Church's foundation.

There are many groups within St Margaret's: the Ladies' and Men's Fellowship, the Saturday club for children, a Flower Team, the Prayer Team, the Churchyard Team and others; all contribute to a lively and enthusiastic church, whose members have also led the community in organising Millennium and Golden Jubilee celebrations. The combination with Knockholt has facilitated the provision (as at 2002) of a broad range of services that cater for many different tastes and traditions: early morning said Holy Communion, choral matins and choral evensong, all based on the Book of Common Prayer; family services, family communion and evening sung Holy Communion, all based on Common Worship; and a reflective candle service.

20

KEMSING

V.E. Bowden

The dedication of a church to St Mary the Virgin at Kemsing indicates a foundation date in the 10th or 11th century. The architecture also points to an original building date of about 1060. However, nothing is known about the founder, or of any officiating priest, until 1265. Edith, daughter of King Edgar, was born in a convent in Kemsing in 961, which shows that Christianity was well established by then. The manor of Kemsing held the two parishes of Seal and Kemsing, and a continuous line of incumbents served both churches up to 1874. Some of these priests also held other livings and neglected Kemsing. For example, when in 1399 the advowson was acquired from the rector by the abbey of Bermondsey, a vicar was not inducted until 1402.

During the 14th and 15th centuries the church sought to educate an illiterate population by means of coloured windows, murals and images of saints, together with the celebration of holy days, and pilgrimages to venerated shrines. A shrine was set up in the churchyard with a statue of St Edith, possibly containing a relic of the saint, and as it was situated on the pilgrim road to Canterbury this attracted many visitors: probably to the spiritual and secular advantage of local people.

It is possible that the major changes in religious observance in the early 16th century only affected Kemsing slowly. For instance, the instruction in 1538 that all churches must keep registers of baptisms and marriages seems not to have been observed in Kemsing until 1561. The many Protestant reforms to worship in the reigns of Edward VI, Mary, and Elizabeth I may have bewildered many in the village congregation. By the end of that century the interior of the church had been deprived of all the colourful decorations and many of the glass windows had been destroyed. Outside, the shrine to St Edith was demolished.

Until the end of the 19th century the vicars of Kemsing lived in or near Seal, leaving Kemsing to the care of curates. How the population reacted to this treatment is not known, but it can be conjectured that the changes made in the mid-17th century to religious practice and worship possibly encouraged a growth of interest in Puritanism. Certainly in 1650 one of Cromwell's 'pastors' replaced the vicar. Following the Restoration many of the restrictions of the Commonwealth years were removed. A new vicar in 1674 took more interest in Kemsing and had the church building repaired, re-decorated and fitted with new oak pews, a pulpit and a western gallery.

90 *St Mary the Virgin, Kemsing. A pencil drawing of the northern elevation by A.M. Parkin, 1967.*

The churchwardens' accounts for the period after 1660 indicate that the village was largely self-supporting. Within the church building the village hierarchy was clearly defined by seating in the box pews. The high walls of the front pews were for the gentry; the lower walls behind them were for the successful farmers and tradesmen; and at the back were the benches for servants and labourers.

In 1721 a new vicar, albeit an absentee one, arranged for repairs and redecoration to be carried out to 'beautify' the church. There followed a succession of vicars who appeared to do little for Kemsing, preferring the larger village of Seal. It was the last of these, the Revd Thomas O. Blackall, who realised that the parish was too large to be cared for by one vicar. He hived off areas which each had a church and a separate incumbent, forming the new parishes of Underriver (1866), Seal St Lawrence (1868), and Seal (1874).

In the mid-19th century the majority of the 420 people in Kemsing were poor. Attendance at the parish church had been 'indifferent' for many years. However, the coming of the railway in 1874 improved communications and local economic opportunities, and also brought new, more prosperous, families to some of the larger houses. The new incumbent in 1875, the Revd George Bridges Lewis, set about improving matters. He deemed that many of the inhabitants of the village ignored religion and behaved in a rough and disorderly manner. To amend this he reproved publicans for encouraging heavy drinking, and persuaded farmers to cooperate in the training of children by allowing them time to attend the National School that had been opened in 1850. This school was replaced by a larger one in 1885, and was mainly

91 *The Kemsing Music Book, c.1750. This book contains 76 pages of hymns in rhyming verse based on various psalms, as well as anthems and pages on musical theory. The tunes include 'Otford' and 'Kemsing'. The choir performed in the West Gallery of the parish church (removed in 1870) accompanied by instrumentalists. The Music Book is in the Centre for Kentish Studies, Maidstone (cat. No. P205/1/8), and is reproduced by permission.*

governed by the Anglican church. Sunday schools were held throughout this period. The erection by Lewis of a mission hall at Noah's Ark in 1887 was an attempt to encourage the residents of that hamlet to take more interest in church life.

Nevertheless, an archdeacon's report of 1880 noted that there were no Roman Catholics in Kemsing and only a few nonconformists. These were mainly Methodists or Bible Christians who had built a chapel in the village in 1846. By the middle of the 20th century this fellowship had become an evangelical Free Church meeting in a building at the west end of the village. In the 1980s it merged with the Town Church in Sevenoaks and the old building was later demolished. Attempts by the parish church to take it over failed, leaving no place for worship in this quite heavily populated area.

An organ was installed in the parish church in 1878. Music played by an organist and a choir led the singing. During the ministry of the Revd Thomas Carleton Skarratt (1889-1908) a new organ was installed and notable musicians were invited to give recitals. A growing congregation required an enlarged building, and a north aisle and new vestries were erected. At the same time the architect John Ninian Comper was asked to redecorate the chancel and to design four windows. Skarratt introduced Anglo-Catholic church practices that were only gradually dropped after his death in 1908; it was not until the mid-20th century that vestments were reintroduced.

Although the population of Kemsing increased rapidly after the Second World War, to more than 4,000, church attendance declined. Since the formation of the Parochial Church Council in 1920 the number of names on the church electoral role has remained in the region of three to four hundred.

21

OTFORD

David Fowdrey and Cliff Ward

In 821 the King of Kent gave lands at Otford to the Archbishopric of Canterbury. Over the next 700 years the manor of Otford became one of the most important of the archiepiscopal properties, controlling estates from the Thames to the Sussex border. When the archbishop (or if the see were vacant, the king) stayed in Otford with his retinue, he lived in the manor house, otherwise known as the Palace, which had its own chapel. Thus, despite its proximity to the Palace, the parish church remained separate and at the heart of the village.

It is known that there was an Anglo-Saxon church in Otford. The core of the present building dates from the mid-11th century, when the structure was of stone with a thatched roof, which almost certainly replaced an earlier timber building. The west tower was constructed in Norman times and additions which probably included a spire were made in the later medieval period. A stone chancel was built between about 1315 and 1325 and was subsequently enlarged. The south aisle and lady chapel date from around 1520-30. A disastrous fire in 1630 led to much reconstruction and refurbishment. A document for 1637 gives details of a collection in Brasted for Otford church, following a serious fire; this suggests a second fire at that time. The tiled, wooden west porch bears the date 1637.

In 1863 the celebrated architect, G.E. Street, made substantial modifications including an arcade and chancel arch, box pews, and a new pulpit to replace the earlier 'three decker'. However the nave, aisle, and chancel retain much of the timber of the mid-17th century. Following war damage in 1940 and later, substantial repairs were made to the tower and some of the stained glass windows. The damaged east window was repaired incorporating glass salvaged from the window installed in 1845 by the Polhill family. The glass had been purchased in Rome by David Polhill during his 'grand tour' in 1696. The tower's two original bells, of 1622 and 1674 respectively, were joined in 2000 by four new bells, in memory of a local resident; and since then a team of bell ringers has been trained and established.

There are several features of the interior of the building that merit notice. The Easter Sepulchre dates from 1510-27 with decorations that incorporate the Tudor Rose and the pomegranate badge of Catherine of Aragon. There are funerary hatchments and a number of imposing monuments,

92 *The four churches of Otford. The best known view of St Bartholomew, Otford parish church, is from the pond looking across the village green (a). The clock was placed in the massive Norman tower in 1883, replacing an earlier one. The three other churches in the village were built of brick in the 20th century. The oldest is the Methodist church (b) opened in 1935. Originally it had a rural setting until adjacent industrial development was allowed in the 1960s. The local public library was constructed on part of the site in 1980. Otford Evangelical Free Church (c) stands on the western edge of the village on the Pilgrims' Way. The original wooden hut serving the fellowship was replaced by the present brick structure in 1987. The most recent building is the Roman Catholic church of the Most Holy Trinity (d) built near the River Darent in 1980.*

some commemorating the Polhill family, one of which, to Charles (*d.*1755), dominates the chancel. A font cover in carved wood dates from the 17th century. And still to be seen is the firm anti-Jacobin political point made by David Polhill in 1697 when he hung the royal coat of arms of William and Mary in St Bartholomew's.[1]

The original brick-built parish room, erected in 1737, stood on the Green until 1910. That year a new parish hall was built in the High Street, designed by the distinguished architect Edwin Lutyens, brother of the then vicar, the Revd William Lutyens. Today it has been enhanced by the addition of the Otford Millennium Mosaic that depicts 4,000 years of the village's history. The small Anglican Mission of the Good Shepherd was built at Twitton in 1890; it closed in 1982.

John Wesley, the founder of Methodism, visited Shoreham and Otford frequently between 1746 and 1790. The first Methodist meeting place was built in 1800 thanks to the generosity of a local farmer, James Martyr, who gave land in The Street (now the High Street). Like many early Methodists,

93   *Otford Crusaders, as it became, was a thriving Bible class. It met in a private home, at first on Sunday afternoons and then on Saturday afternoons and evenings. At its peak well over a hundred and fifty children attended each week (c-d). The first camp was held in the garden (a) but thereafter it was hosted at various other sites, including Carroty Wood, near Tonbridge (b, e), and Hall's Green, south of Weald village. Various events were held at Hildenborough Hall, now Oak Hall, and there was an annual prize giving service in the parish hall. The Crusaders national organisation began in 1907. There were, and still are, other Crusader Bible classes in the area: most notably in Sevenoaks and Underriver, and also Covenanter Bible classes.*

Martyr was a member of the established Church. Originally a private chapel, the meeting place was officially conveyed to the Wesleyan Methodists in 1813. The society had a small membership until the early 1930s. In that decade, when a large increase in the population of the village was predicted owing to the planned new London airport for Swanley, a field was purchased opposite the chapel and a new church built, which opened in 1935. The population of Otford did increase but the Darent valley was preserved when the airport went to Heathrow. All the halls in the village are used extensively for both Christian and secular activities. The old chapel was sold and later used by the small Roman Catholic community. It is now a private house but still carries the builder's tablet: 'J.M.E.1800' for '*James Martyr Erexit*'.

Other evangelical Christians began a ministry in Otford and founded a church during the 1920s. In 1931 profits from a good apple harvest funded the erection of a wooden hut, then called the Pilgrims' Way Gospel Hall. The Church Trust of that time stipulated that the sole purpose of the land and its buildings must be for 'the public worship of Almighty God and preaching of the Gospel and a Sunday school'. The trust has been kept faithfully ever since. In 1987 the church changed its name to the Otford Evangelical Free Church, reflecting its affiliation to the Fellowship of Independent Evangelical Churches. The same year saw the completion of the present church building, to which a hall was added in 1991. In 1994 the church appointed its first full-time pastor. Evangelicals in the village also found encouragement from the work of the Hildenborough Hall Evangelical Trust, founded by Tom Rees, a former lay worker at St Nicholas, Sevenoaks, that ran a variety of activities from Shorehill, above Kemsing, and also from the trust's successor Oak Hall, a Christian organisation which sends aid to the Balkans and runs overseas expeditions, primarily for young people.

In the early 20th century the small number of Roman Catholics in Otford was served by St Thomas's church in Sevenoaks, opened in 1896. In the late 1920s the Southwark Catholic Travelling Mission set up a chapel at Little Timberden in Shoreham, through the generosity of the Berkeley family. An unusual feature of this mission was the hospitality given to tramps. The chapel suffered bomb damage in 1944, but Maud Berkeley had already purchased the old Methodist chapel in Otford High Street and this became a chapel of ease to St Thomas's from 1944-81. By the 1970s it became clear that a new and larger Catholic church was needed. Not only had the congregation grown but the chapel was said to be 'held up by not much more than prayer and plaster'. A site was bought near the river and a large brick building was completed in December 1980. The dedication of the church, and the consecration of the altar, were carried out in May 1981 by the Archbishop of Southwark.

Both the parish church and the Methodists have long had Sunday schools. Although these had been large in the 1920s by the 1960s fewer children were attracted to traditional classes in a church building. In the early 1970s a number of Christians in the village were concerned for children and began a Sunday afternoon Bible class in a private home. At first this attracted the children of neighbours, but it gradually grew to have nearly two hundred young people, including many teenagers. The group affiliated with Crusaders, a national young people's organisation. For over twenty years many young people went through the class with its programme of Bible teaching, camps, holidays, and leisure activities. In addition there were Bible study groups for women that developed from contact with their children. Today both churches run several groups on Sundays for children and young people, as well as supporting weekday activities and a joint group for parents and infants.

In an age of increasing secularism it is encouraging to note that the Otford churches are flourishing and providing for the spiritual needs of young people, older people and the community as a whole, including an industrial chaplaincy. Regular joint ecumenical services and activities in the village are well supported.

22

SEAL

Peter Mountfield

There is no mention of a church at Seal in Domesday Book (1086). There is a reference in the margins of the *Textus Roffensis*, in around 1120, but this may have been a later insertion.[1] The earliest physical evidence is a carved stone dug up on the site, now preserved in the church, identified as an abacus from an arch, dating from about 1180.[2] This Norman church disappeared, possibly destroyed by fire, and the oldest parts of the present building are the nave and south aisle, both of late 13th-century style. There was almost certainly a church on the site by 1283, when a fair was established in the village on the festival of St Peter and St Paul, the patron saints.

By then Seal shared a vicar with Kemsing, appointed by the Cluniac abbey of Bermondsey. Some authorities maintain that Seal was a daughter church of Kemsing.[3] There is a full list of vicars from 1317, and two earlier references.[4] Two priests were replaced during the Black Death (1348 and 1354) so may have died then, but there is no record of the impact this had on the rest of the parish. The oldest tomb in the church is a fine memorial brass to Sir William de Bryene, who died here in 1395.[5] Little else is known of the fabric of the church until the 15th century, when the present chancel was added, in addition to a chapel at the end of the south aisle of roughly the same date. Very few records exist about the parishioners at this time.

The present south porch and the great west tower were added in the perpendicular style before 1529 (prior to the break with Rome) making Seal much bigger than the older church at Kemsing.[6] In 1524 a local man, Thomas Theobald, became vicar, but left his duties to a curate, who eventually succeeded him. Theobald travelled extensively abroad, and studied at the universities of Louvain and of Tubingen (the latter a centre of Protestant learning). He also acted as an intelligence agent on behalf of Thomas Boleyn of Hever (one of the leaders of the Protestant party) and of Archbishop Cranmer, although Theobald himself died a Catholic.[7] His curate, Thomas Lightstone, meanwhile accepted the new regime and, like most of the local clergy, renounced the Pope's supremacy in 1534.[8] But the church was not, apparently, stripped of traditional symbols, and the rood screen survived until the Civil War. In the 1550s the Protestant incumbent, Thomas Hicklyng, was deprived of his benefice under the Catholic Queen Mary.

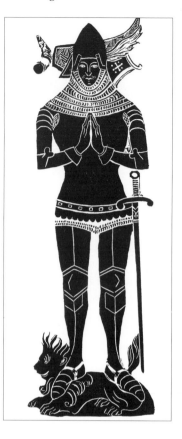

94 *Memorial brass to Sir William de Bryene, Lord of the Manor of Seal (d.1395). Brasses were memorials formed from engraved metal plates, usually fixed to the floor or wall. Sir William de Bryene is shown as a knight with a lion at his feet. At his head is his hunting horn crest.*

From the mid-16th century parishes became responsible for the administration of the poor law and of highways, but no records for Seal survive from this time. The parish registers start in 1561, and for the first time provide some hard evidence about the people of the parish. So do the wills, many of them written for a semi-literate population by the vicar.[9] Their wording suggests a largely Protestant parish. Bequests for masses and candles were of course barred by now. A hundred years later, during the Civil War and Commonwealth, similar evidence from wills suggests that Seal had few Puritans; and the church's small library (recorded in the register) contained basic Anglican, rather than Presbyterian or independent, titles. The registers also record something odd, as yet unexplained: there was a steep increase in the number of baptisms and marriages at Seal at the end of the Civil War (1647-49), as there was at nearby Shipbourne; this was matched by a corresponding fall at Sevenoaks, headquarters of the Parliamentary party in Kent. This may mark some preference for a more traditional ministry at Seal.[10] The next vicar (or minister), John Stevens, served Seal from 1654 (under the Commonwealth) until 1668 (well after Charles II's restoration). Maximilian Buck, vicar from 1674 until 1720, was also chaplain to the Duke of Dorset at Knole; a surviving sermon of his on the 'martyrdom' of Charles I indicates a high Anglican position.[11] As part of a survey undertaken for the government in 1675 he reported that there were no dissenters or recusants in the parish.[12]

A similar pattern continued throughout the 18th century. Seal seems to have been a fairly typical rural Anglican parish, apparently untouched by the early days of the Wesleyan revival. The first Wesleyan congregation was founded in 1805[13] (in a house at the corner of the present Zion Lane, where a chapel briefly stood later in the century). The local population continued to grow, and a gallery was added to the parish church in about 1825, indicating that church attendance remained high (which the church records largely confirm). Derek Lucas's reconstruction, based on contemporary documents, shows the nave and east end at about this time. In the 1851 religious census, about one third of the total population attended various Sunday services (it was a cold wet day), including that held in the recently opened 'Licensed Schoolroom' at Underriver. The census also recorded two, apparently rival, Wesleyan Methodist congregations in the village and another meeting at Stone Street, all of which were quite small. The parish church was extended

95 *Church of St Peter and St Paul, Seal. Built of local ragstone with a battlemented tower dating from around 1520-9.*

in 1855 by the great Victorian architect George Gilbert Scott, who built the north aisle in an unobtrusive copy of the south (but didn't actually increase the seating because the gallery was removed at the same time). Very unusually for the time, the drawings preserved in the church are signed by a woman draftsman.[14] The church, along with the inns, clearly provided the focus of the local community, whose more prosperous members (gentry, farmers and traders) provided the churchwardens and other officers. Another Methodist group, the Bible Christians, arrived in 1881, and built a chapel (now a private house) in Church Street in 1886. It was sold to the Baptists in 1916 and closed only in 1980.

In 1874, Seal was formally separated from Kemsing parish and each received its own vicar. At about the same time Seal St Lawrence and Underriver became separate parishes too. The local landowners (Bickerstaffes in the early 18th century, Pratts (Marquess Camden) from 1760 to 1865, and the Mills family (Lord Hillingdon) until 1920), dominated Seal village. They endowed many of the local charities, built the two National (i.e. Church) schools, employed a large part of the local population, and their monuments are prominent in the church.[15] Although the remaining civic duties of the vestry and churchwardens passed to local government at the end of the 19th century, there was a considerable overlap of offices. One vicar, Charles Few, was the first chairman of the new civil Parish Council in 1894.

At the beginning of the 20th century Seal was still a rural parish. The pattern only changed after the 1914-18 war as the Sevenoaks area gradually became part of the commuter belt round London. The parish church continued to provide the main focus of village life, surrounded by Sunday schools, choir, youth clubs, the Mothers Union and its successors, and similar organisations. By the end of the millennium, the population of the old parish

96 *Interior of Seal parish church, c.1825. A modest interior with box pews and the 17th-century pulpit on the north wall. The building was candle-lit by an 18th-century brass chandelier. Most parish churches of this period had minimal heating in winter although coal-fired stoves were installed in some.*

had increased to over 2,500. The estate once occupied by the Hillingdons had been carved up into sizeable plots for designer housing and Oak Bank School had given way to five substantial houses marketed at over £1 million each. North of the A25, along Childsbridge Lane, cul-de-sac after cul-de-sac of houses was added between the village and the railway line. The early developments were of 'affordable housing'; later developments were more 'up-market'. A small number remembered the time when it was still 'a proper lane and all fields'.

The church continues to baptise, to marry and to bury (now ashes more often than bodies), and to provide opportunities for regular worship for all who want it, moving from the Book of Common Prayer, through the Alternative Service Book to Common Worship. The worship was significantly enhanced in the 1990s by rebuilding the organ at a cost of £40,000. The church continues to maintain strong links with the village Church of England school, and to reach out beyond the parish to support local and national projects and its linked missionaries in Brazil.

97 *Seal parish church: late Victorian interior. A view of the interior of St Peter and St Paul after the extension designed by George Gilbert Scott in 1855.*

23

SEAL ST LAWRENCE

Gretel Wakeham and Elspeth Cooke

In the mid-19th century Seal Chart, Stone Street and Bitchet were somewhat remote parts of the eastern end of the scattered 'chapelry' of Seal in the parish of Kemsing. A small group of Wesleyan Methodist Reformers met for worship in a building at Stone Street, and the vicar of Kemsing conducted occasional services in a barn belonging to Stone Street Farm. It was a long walk to the parish church in Seal for regular Anglican services, and bad weather deterred many from attending. In 1867-8 Horace and Anne Wilkinson, who were then having Frankfield House built (he was a stockbroker and landowner), paid for the building of St Lawrence Church in memory of their eldest child Mary Rachel, who had died aged six at St Lawrence, Isle of Wight.

The new church was constructed of Kentish ragstone, cut from the local Foxbury quarry, and modelled on the old church of St Lawrence, Isle of Wight. The foundation stone was laid by Mary's little sister, Esther Mabel, on 8 October, and with it a bottle containing a small parchment record of why the church was built, some coins of the year, and a photograph of Mary Rachel aged 14 months. One month later, St Lawrence Seal, consisting of Seal Chart, Stone Street and Bitchet Green, was confirmed as a separate parish. An extract from notes compiled by Teresa Wilkinson, granddaughter of the founder, in 1935-6 recalls the consecration of St Lawrence church:

> On 20th June 1868, the anniversary of Mary Rachel's birthday, the church was consecrated by Dr Longley, Archbishop of Canterbury. The Archbishop robed at Frankfield and drove to the church where he was met by about thirty robed clergy. Old inhabitants still recall details of the consecration Service – such as the text of the Archbishop's address (Luke XVI.31) and the fact that the carriages conveying him and members of the congregation from Frankfield to the church, drove straight across the meadow not then fenced in; the Archbishop remarking that it was more like driving to a cricket match than to a consecration.

On the afternoon of the same day the foundation stone was laid for St Lawrence School, which was adjacent to the church, and also funded by Horace Wilkinson.

98 *The newly built church at Seal St Lawrence in the 1870s. A tower with a peal of bells was added in 1888. Church bells were an important part of the auditory landscape of England. They were rung to call people to worship, for weddings, on special occasions, and as a warning in times of trouble. Bells were also tolled for funerals. Bell ringing was often an important activity which generated enthusiasts, networks, and organisations.*

In 1876 the church was enlarged in memory of the third daughter of Horace and Annie Wilkinson, Annie Clare, who died in that year aged 14. The enlargement took the form of the two transepts. The Wilkinson's dead daughters are represented as angels in the stained glass windows. In 1888 the tower with its peal of six bells was added, and the nave lengthened, in memory of Sarah Wilkinson, the founder's sister. At this time the original porch was moved to form a lych gate.

St Lawrence has had an unbroken tradition of bell ringing since 1888. At midday on 1 January 2000, the team of six ringers joined with parishes around the country to ring in the new millennium. In the early days of the church, the church choir was also an important village activity involving the young people from the parish. Today there is an enthusiastic choir of mixed ages who sing at parish events such as the harvest supper, which brings together many people from the local community.

In March 2000, St Lawrence's was privileged to be the first church in Kent to sign a formal Declaration of Ecumenical Welcome and Commitment. As the only church building in the parish, the congregation undertook to give pastoral care to all who desire it, to incorporate the riches of other Christian traditions as appropriate, and generally to lead the way forward in focusing on what brings Christians together. This initiative was encouraged by the Methodist and United Reformed churches in the Sevenoaks area, whose representatives signed in support of this intention.

99 *Mary Rachel Wilkinson aged 14 months. Mary's grieving parents paid for the building of the church at Seal St Lawrence in her memory in 1867-8. Other parish churches in the area (at Kippington, Underriver, and Halstead) were built by wealthy landowners during the mid- and late 19th century.*

100 *The choir, Seal St Lawrence parish church, 1924. Choir stalls were introduced by Victorian clergy in the chancels of their churches. Cathedral choirs consisted of boys and men. Many choirmasters in parish churches would have liked to copy the great choirs but had to be more realistic and use women and girls.*

At the start of the 21st century the population of the ecclesiastical parish numbered about 350; in 2001 there were 93 people on the electoral roll. The congregation of all ages meets every Sunday and there is a monthly Sunday school. The variety of services includes both the modern and traditional. A regular service of healing and wholeness was introduced in 2000; a Taizé-style service is held during the Week of Prayer for Christian Unity and attracts

101   Celebrating Pentecost 2000 St Lawrence style!

Christians from all traditions in the Sevenoaks area. The beautiful setting of the church makes it an ideal venue for summer evening concerts in which the local community participates. Close links are maintained with St Lawrence School and other local organisations. St Lawrence is a small church with a happy family atmosphere that helps to bring together people from all parts of this scattered semi-rural community and beyond.

102   Children from the Church school of Seal St Lawrence planting a garden in the churchyard, 1997.

24

SHOREHAM

Ken Wilson

A parish church has stood on the present site of St Peter and St Paul since the 11th century.[1] The original building only consisted of a chancel, probably built of timber and roofed with thatch. A nave was added later and major extensions were undertaken in the 17th century, including the construction of a tower on the west wall. The tower collapsed, and was replaced, in 1775, by a square brick-laced structure with flint panels. Five of the eight bells in the belfry are from the 17th century; three others were added in the 19th century. A carillon did not last long; its three tune barrels played 14 songs including 'Drink to me only with thine eyes'! The entrance to the 15th-century porch is formed from the base of a single oak tree, split down the centre and upended, the natural shape creating a pointed gothic arch which was then squared and decoratively carved.

Dividing the nave from the chancel is a rood screen which, very unusually for Kent, survived destruction in the 16th century. The octagonal stone font is lined with lead and of sufficient size to immerse the whole baby, which was the early custom. The only windows to survive a Second World War bomb were one small roundel of medieval stained glass, and the Burne-Jones memorial window to geologist Sir Joseph Prestwich, made in the William Morris workshop. In 1999 a new stained glass window, financed from village donations, was installed to celebrate the millennium. The organ and the pulpit came from Westminster Abbey in the 19th century.

Until major renovations by the Mildmay family in the 1860s the pews faced north towards a three-tier pulpit. On the lower level sat the vestry clerk who, in the 17th century, kept a check on absentees from compulsory services; on the middle level sat the vicar, or curate, conducting the service; the sermon was preached from the highest tier. The separate chapel was used as a family pew by the lord of the manor, a practice continued by the Mildmays as part of their alterations. The middle classes sat in rented box pews in the body of the nave. Free seats for the poor were identified by the word 'Free' painted in large letters. Music was provided by a choir in the balcony on the west wall, a barrel organ and, on occasions, by a small string ensemble.

In 1758 the vicar, Vincent Perronet, reported that the parish had a single dissenter, a Baptist. As an ardent supporter of John Wesley he did not include the Methodists who were then a group within the Anglican

103   *The rood screen, Shoreham parish church. The rood (from Old English rod meaning 'cross'), was a carved image of the crucifix. In pre-Reformation churches the rood screen, a decorated stone or wooden screen, separated the chancel from the nave (the chancel being the place where the priest conducted mass). As the nave was often used as a gathering place for the community, and dogs also wandered in and out, the screen protected the dignity of the solemn eucharistic service. During the Reformation most rood screens were removed. Many were replaced, often in an elaborate way, in the 19th century. The wooden rood screen survived at Shoreham and is unique in Kent, stretching across the church and retaining the rood loft. It has fan vaulting and the carved pomegranate emblem of Catherine of Aragon. She is reported to have visited the church with Henry VIII en route from Otford Palace to the Field of the Cloth of Gold, in France, in 1520.*

church. When in 1744, Charles Wesley first preached in the parish church, the congregation protested strongly and 'rioters followed us to Mr Perronet's house'. As separate groups Wesleyan Methodists first met in private houses. A chapel was eventually built in Chapel Alley in 1836; this was in 1878 replaced by a larger building in the High Street, which closed in 1962. Wesleyan Reformers met separately in the mid-19th century, while at Romney Street there was another chapel built from flints that had been hand-picked from the fields. The religious census of 1851 indicates that a large number of people in the parish attended Sunday services at one or other of the various churches. A Baptist church was built in Crown Road in 1896, and services were held there until 1982.

Maud Berkeley, a Roman Catholic who had come to the village as a land girl during the First World War, settled at Little Timberden. She converted one of the barns into a church in connection with her work for the Southwark Catholic Travelling Mission with sequestered villages in the south east. In 1938 this was taken over by American Franciscans, but in 1940 worship was transferred to Otford.

104 *A traveller's return. Commander Verney Lovett Cameron RN went to Africa in search of David Livingstone, but he then continued crossing the continent from the east to the west coast. In this painting, by Charles West Cope RA, Cameron, and his African servant Jacko, are being greeted by his father, the vicar of Shoreham, on his return in April 1876. Jacko, a Yao from what is now Tanzania, was baptised and worked in the rectory as a servant.*

In his Annual Report for 2001 the Revd Richard Freeman, priest in charge since January 2001, shows an Electoral Roll of 147, with an average Sunday attendance of 70 adults and ten under 16s. There is a Sunday school which, due to shortage of space, meets in a room in a local public house. There was also a special group for 10 to 14-year-olds, with drama, but this had to close because of the need to have at least two supervisors. A midweek Home Group is held in members' homes. A church school has existed in the village since 1841, and now has some 70 pupils.

An innovation in 2002 was to hold the annual Harvest Supper in the church instead of the village hall. An amazing transformation greeted the 120 guests as the church had become a very exclusive restaurant with cold food prepared by the Home Group. Entertainment was provided by Juggling John who displayed his skills not only at the tables, but on stilts. He concluded his act with an intriguing religious homily. A range of music from song to Jazz (by Pastiche, a new trio), added a novel atmosphere to a traditional event.

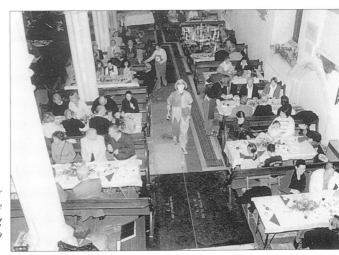

105 *The Harvest Supper was, for the first time in 2002, held in the church. The photo shows Juggling John moving between tables to entertain the guests.*

25

SUNDRIDGE

Bruce Walker

There is evidence for Christian worship in Sundridge for at least a thousand years, but the history of the early years of St Mary's at Sundridge is confusing and contradictory. A church certainly stood here before the Norman Conquest, probably around 900. Sundridge gets its first recorded mention in 862 in a charter of King Ethelbert, brother of Alfred the Great, giving land to Dryhtwald. Some time between 966 and the Norman Conquest Sundridge began an association with the see of Canterbury. The archbishop is still the patron of the Sundridge living. It has been suggested that Sundridge was a missionary church founded by the great Theodore of Tarsus, archbishop from around 668-690.

Mention in Domesday that Sundridge had a church indicates the existence of a church in Saxon times. Many Saxon churches are not mentioned in Domesday and the fact that Sundridge is mentioned suggests it was of some importance to the Normans. The church is also mentioned in the early 12th-century *Textus Roffensis*. One can presume a wooden structure, similar to that at Greensted in Essex, with painted walls and an interior lit by small windows (with no glass but closed with shutters). The choir, if there was one, would have stood on a platform in the centre of the nave.

Around 1100 the Saxon church was dismantled, and a tower and nave were built in stone. The original Norman plan is plainly visible in the existing building. It is possible to imagine a nave with solid walls whose height is indicated by offsets running along the nave walls above the arches. At the end of the 13th century, or early in the 14th century, there were major alterations to the building. One of the chantry chapels was probably for John Delarue because two stone slabs date from this period: one, formerly inlaid with a brass cross and lettering in Lombardic script, commemorates John Delarue (*d.*1351) and offers 120 days' pardon to those who pray for his soul. The other chapel could have been for the Isley family, of Brook Place, who were benefactors until the 16th century.

In about 1450 there were further alterations, and the decorated tracery in the windows was replaced by perpendicular tracery to show off the splendid blaze of colour from the recently improved stained glass. From this period also dates the perpendicular altar tomb, now in the north chantry chapel, which at one time had brasses for John Isley and his wife (1484), and a

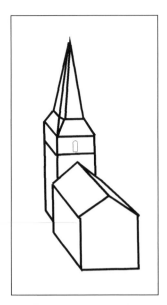

106 *Development of St Mary the Virgin, Sundridge.*
(a) The original Norman building c.1150.
(b) 1200-1300: the roof was raised and two side aisles and chapels were added.
(c) The walls of the north and south aisles were raised in height c.1450.

memorial to Roger Isley, Lord of Sundridge and Farningham (1429). This major rebuilding took place in the midst of the turmoil of the Cade rebellion and the Wars of the Roses (1450-87).

Early in the following century there is a memorial to Thomas Isley and his wife, who had ten sons and three daughters (1515); one of them was Sir Henry Isley, a sheriff of Kent, who was executed in February 1554 at Sevenoaks for his complicity in the Wyatt rebellion against the marriage of Queen Mary to Phillip of Spain. There is still a Sanctus bell, which originally dated from this period but was recast in 1937.

In the 17th century four bells were hung, one before the Commonwealth period and three afterwards, doubtless in celebration. The Revd Samuel Sharpe was inducted in 1645 and he succeeded in holding the living, through the Commonwealth and the Restoration, until 1680. In 1650 there was a Commonwealth commission that reported the living as being worth £100 per annum and that 'the church is not conveniently situated for the parishioners … it is not convenient to unite their church to any other … and … there is no place to build a new church': indeed much the same as now.

In March 1882 a fire, started in a stove chimney, destroyed the chancel roof, the remains of the rood screen, ancient stained glass (including three coats of arms of members of the Isley family) and a medieval confessional chair. The Combe Bank Fire Brigade was called out from its garage on the Main Road. The jet was not powerful enough to reach the burning timbers in the chancel so the firemen climbed onto the roof and successfully extinguished the fire. During the rebuilding, the west gallery was taken down.

107 *St Mary the Virgin, Sundridge. The parish church stands on the south side of the Vale of Holmesdale well above the old flood plain of the river Darent.*

A faculty issued in 1923 included lowering the floor of the north chantry 'to the ancient level'. This was paid for by William Plender (1861-1946), an accountant and public servant who, together with his two wives, is buried in Sundridge Churchyard, and is now known as the Plender Chapel. W.D. Caröe, the architect for the modifications to the Plender Chapel, wrote that he considered the existing window of 1862, commemorating a past rector (Dr D'Oyle), to be, 'a real Victorian hideosity of the worst type and is not a memorial window'. He continued, 'I should be sorry were the advisory committee to stand in the way of the removal, when occasion offers itself, of some of the disfigurements and disgraces of which this is one of the worst the Revival Era has left us in the matter of stained glass windows'. Caröe refers earlier in this letter to designs that 'did not fit in with the smug Victorian minds ... and so they [the Victorians] changed them'. Caröe was architect to the Ecclesiastical Commissioners and did work in Canterbury Cathedral (including the tomb of Archbishop Frederick Temple) as well as designing new churches in Kent, so he had a stance to make. The D'Oyle window was repositioned a few years later in the west window of the tower.

In the 1840s the workhouse for the new Sevenoaks Union was built one mile south of St Mary's. It regularly had over 250 inmates (mainly the elderly and sick, and orphaned children), with a resident chaplain, and also a burial ground. The main industry in the village was the 'paper manufactory' astride the Darent. Several nonconformists lived in Sundridge. By the middle of the century a Wesleyan Methodist chapel held morning and evening services

108 *Morning service, St Mary the Virgin, Sundridge, c.1950. The photograph was taken looking east to the chancel and shows the congregation, bowed in prayer, and the minister, who appears to be giving the benediction at the end of the morning service, or matins. The service would have been based on the Prayer Book and probably included two scripture readings (one from the Old Testament and one from the New Testament), and a sermon preached from the pulpit to the right of the nave. In all probability the parson would have conducted the whole service. As can be seen from the hymn boards displayed on the columns, Psalm 15 was sung or chanted and four hymns, numbers 541, 573, 776 and 337, were sung, all probably from* Hymns Ancient & Modern. *The two poles at the end of the pews are the staffs of office of the two churchwardens, one a vicar's warden, the other the people's warden. Until the 1960s it was customary for most women to wear a hat to church; men and boys wore their 'Sunday best' suit of clothes and polished shoes.*

with an average attendance of between thirty-five and sixty. At the same time there was another Independent Calvinistic chapel on the high chart lands to the south of the parish at Ide Hill. Later in the century a further dissenting chapel, an off-shoot of Bessels Green Baptist, was built on Goathurst Common. A wooden building, known as The Ark, it was demolished in 1941.

In the first part of the 20th century St Mary the Virgin was High Anglican. The rector, the Revd Herbert E. Edwards, wrote on 21 January 1938 that the Sanctus bell was rung during Holy Communion, at the words of the Institution, in the Prayer of Consecration and also at the end of the prayer. In 1936 a new altar (which includes consecration crosses on its top), was given by Lord Plender in memory of his late wife, Marian Elizabeth. The faculty papers were for a 'new altar in Australian oak to replace a small and inadequate one. The old altar might be offered to some mission church in the Diocese at the Bishop's discretion'.

Since then Sundridge has weathered storm and the Second World War and is still much cherished by those who worship within the building, which has stood on that site for most of the last millennium. In 1973 the parish was joined with that of Ide Hill, and it required the hard work and sympathetic

109 *A forgotten Wesleyan Methodist chapel, Sundridge. The Wesleyan Methodist chapel at Sundridge is now barely recognisable. It stands on the A25, south-east of the crossroad and traffic lights at the centre of the village. It opened after 1800 and closed in the early 20th century; it is now a furniture shop.*

touch of the next three rectors to meld the two parishes into one congregation and community. The merger resulted in an influx of people and energy which has allowed the combined church to expand into youth work, and also pram services for mothers with very young children. Although part of a rural community, the congregations are slowly increasing, and the average age of the congregations is significantly falling. Whilst Sundridge church is still, as stated in the Commonwealth Commission of 1650, 'not conveniently situated for its parishioners', it is alive and much loved by its congregation. It is a large church seating about 200 comfortably and there have been congregations of over 400 for special funerals and events.

26

UNDERRIVER

Jennifer Fair

'Thus by their fruit you will recognise them.' Matthew 7:20.

Underriver, a small village south-east of Sevenoaks, consists of about 130 scattered homes. It was formerly part of Seal parish. Before the church was built, the vicar held occasional services in a one-room building known as Francis Woodgate's 'chapel of ease'. Thomas Offspring Blackall pioneered the separation of the parishes in 1866 and he also gave £400 for the building of the church. The ragstone church of St Margaret was paid for by John Davison in 1867 in memory of his mother, Margaret Pearson Davison. It was designed by George Gilbert Scott, famed for his gothic churches, and cost £1939 14s. 2½d. It is an extremely pretty building, light but quite plain. In 1869 Davison's wife died and his children were brought up by their aunt, Maria Foster Wood, to whom there is a loving memorial in the church. Davison became Judge Advocate General in 1870 but died the following year. His son Arthur, also of Underriver House, was vicar's warden in 1893.

In 1878 Horace Beaumont became people's warden, a position that he held for more than forty years. The Parochial Church Council (PCC) minutes frequently record grateful thanks for all he did, including making good the year's deficit, trouble taken over a 'warming apparatus', and for his 'energy and efficiency'. The rural dean, reporting in 1886, said that though he found the church 'in a fair state of repair', it lacked a decent surplice, there was no inventory or book of services, and the churchyard was unconsecrated. As result people dying in Underriver had to be buried in Seal: 'a distance of about 3½ miles, up a very long & very steep hill, so that the expense of funerals to poor persons is excessive, and the fatigue to relations excessive'. Finally, he commented, 'a parsonage house is much required'.

In 1900 Sydney Stapleton Adkins became vicar and remained for 36 years living in the new vicarage. Under his ministry the church progressed and he helped to furnish the building, including the gift of the handsome eagle lectern in memory of his mother. D. Henry T. Peploe, elected as vicar's warden, was 'congratulated on the marked improvement in the singing under his tuition'. He too lived at Underriver House, leasing it from Arthur Davison. He left the parish in 1918 but later returned to Fawke House. In 1917 the vicar appointed Robert Herries, of St Julians, as vicar's warden. The PCC minutes record thanks 'for the energy and sympathy he displayed in furthering the

110   *St Margaret's, Underriver. This is the earliest known photograph of the church, probably taken in the 1870s or 1880s. The adjoining vicarage was built in 1891.*

spiritual work of the parish', with specific reference to his work in conducting services when the vicar was assisting at Shipbourne, whose vicar was engaged in war work in France.

For many years the church school played a central part in village life. Built in 1850, and extended in 1897, it remained under the church's control. The pupils attended services in the church on saints' days. The vicars called at the school regularly and gave instruction. Nativity plays regularly took place in the village hall, watched by 'an enthusiastic audience'. In 1937 an official inspection reported: 'It is difficult to picture a school with a happier spirit that that which prevails here'. In 1939 the Diocesan Inspector reported: 'It only needs the co-operation of the parents to make this a live centre of the Christian faith.' Sadly the school was closed in 1974 due to falling rolls.

As in many small communities there was much goodwill between people and the church. Many gave their services free: Miss Clara King played the organ for many years; Miss Herries gave curtains; Mr W. Powell, in the 1930s, gave

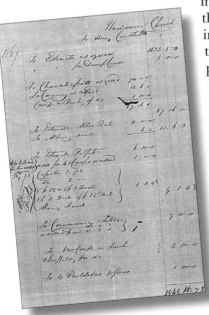

111   *Estimates for building St Margaret's, Underriver.*

many gifts including altar hangings and stoles, and, after the vestry had been built, a magnificent organ with a case designed by W.D. Caröe. The money for the vestry was raised by innumerable concerts, jumble sales, and gift fairs. Much of the construction work within the church was done by Mr Jenner, the skilful village carpenter.

In the years 1936-50 the church had an active Mothers' Union. When the vicar retired in 1950 the PCC, in recommending a new incumbent, stated that he was 'to conduct a normal, not high church service; he should own a car or at least a bicycle; he should take a strong interest in the school and try to win the confidence of the children and the adults; he should put the interests of Underriver before outside activities.' The Revd W.R.O. Taylor became vicar and in 1951 there were 107 names on the electoral roll.

Many women played an active part in maintaining the church furnishings. For example in 1962 the PCC minutes record that: 'Mrs Taylor, Mrs MacPherson and Mrs Hume renovated and repaired embroidery and have enjoyed the active support of Mrs Bentley whose brilliant

112 *John R. Davison QC, MP. It was not uncommon in the 19th century for wealthy people to pay to have a church built either on their own estate or in 'their' village. Davison did this at Underriver. In 1880 in the neighbouring parish of Shipbourne Edward Cazalett, of Fairlawne, paid for the demolition of St Giles (designed by Gibbs in 1720) and for a new church building.*

needlework on the vicar's white stole is a wonderful contribution to the beauty of our little church.' In 1980 Donald Lynch, at the age of 69, became priest in charge. He was a Queen's Chaplain, a prebendary of St Paul's Cathedral, and had been head of the Church Army training school. He was an inspirational priest. He wrote: 'Growth in the Christian way of life involves participation in the life of the church where people find the support of Christian fellowship ... Most of us are not called to be professional evangelists but we are called to witness for Christ by word and action.' During his incumbency, in 1983, Jill Scott produced the People's Passion Play. There was a cast of 150 and it was performed in Rochester Cathedral. Rachel Carr, one of St Margaret's organists, wrote the music and she and Jill underpinned the whole with prayer.

Other Christian work also took place within the village community. Max and Sue Sinclair ran a Crusader class in their home, teaching young people what it meant to be a Christian. This involved not only Bible study groups, but also camps and other activities. They were also involved in couples' evenings, Easter sunrise services, parents' evenings, and marriage counselling. For the millennium celebration Ann Taylor designed new and beautiful kneelers. A service, 'In the Footsteps of the Saints', was held with readings and music celebrating Christianity throughout the centuries.

113 *National School at Underriver, early 20th century. This typical village school, usually with a single teacher plus an apprentice, catered for children aged 5-12 years. Miss Eleanor Long, seen here with the children, was headmistress of the school from 1900-23.*

St Margaret's continues to serve the community with services to cater for various tastes. In 2001 there were 77 people on the electoral roll. On a typical Sunday there will be 22 adults at matins and more at the children's service. There is a steadfast band of women who come each week to clean, polish, and 'do the flowers'. Over the past 130 years many people have contributed to the spiritual life of the parish. Some held positions, were wealthy and gave gifts. Others gave their labour and their love.

114 *Church of England Temperance Society, Underriver, late 19th century. Fighting 'demon drink' was a great concern of the Victorians. Most churches organised temperance societies. The largest was the Church of England Temperance Society, founded in the 1860s, with many local branches such as this one in Underriver. As a result of the Beer Act of 1830 two beer shops opened in Underriver, much to the consternation of Robert Herries of St Julians. Although not particularly religious, he was concerned at the effects that excessive drinking might have on family life and the workers on his estate. Sevenoaks had a temperance hotel in Lime Tree Walk, opened in the early 1880s.*

27

WEALD

Beryl Higgs and Ian Mitchell-Lambert

The village of Weald formed the southern part of the parish of Sevenoaks.[1] The hamlet, as Hasted describes it in the late 18th century, lay on 'stiff clay' and was referred to as Sevenoaks Weald.[2] It was then without a church building of any form. In 1821 William Pitt, Lord Amherst of Montreal Park and Multon Lambarde of Beechmont, initiated the building of chapels-of-ease in Riverhead and Weald to enable the villagers to worship more regularly. The chapel in Weald was built on land owned by Lambarde and was completed in 1822. It consisted of a nave, rows of pews to seat 200 people, a west gallery and an organ. Dr Manners Sutton, Archbishop of Canterbury, consecrated it in May 1821 as 'a chapel built for the accommodation of the POOR in the WEALD in the parish of Sevenoaks'.[3]

A consecrated burial ground surrounded the chapel, but burials were still registered in Sevenoaks. Baptisms took place in Sevenoaks until 1830 and weddings until 1861. Services at the chapel were at first taken by the chaplain from Sevenoaks, who was expected to journey on horseback from Riverhead to Weald, a distance of about six miles over rough roads, to preside over either a morning or evening service at each chapel every Sunday. Eventually, in 1824, at a cost of £500, a vicarage was built next to the chapel, on land previously owned by Lambarde. The chapel was enlarged in 1839, at a cost of over £1,300, and a chancel was added in 1870, designed by T.G. Jackson, the son-in-law of William Lambarde. In 1861 St George's Church ceased to be a chapel-of-ease and became a parish church with a vicar, its own parish registers and parochial administration. By the 1890s the stonework of the tower was in such a decayed state that the tower had to be lowered by twenty feet.

Almshouses were built opposite the chapel for the out-pensioners of the town and parish of Sevenoaks, again at the instigation of Multon Lambarde (d.1836), and completed by his son, William. A small church school was built between the two blocks of almshouses between 1836 and 1842, with a playground to the north of the church.

Parish churches are not renowned for their physical comfort. Comfort and audibility were gradually improved. Electricity was installed in St George's in the 1930s, welcome electric heating followed in 1956. This was upgraded in 1990 with efficient radiant heating, and a loop system for the hard of hearing, and the building was fully carpeted. Church activities increased and

115   *Church Army evangelistic caravan in Weald, 1930s. The Church Army was founded in 1883 by Wilson Carlile, an evangelical businessman who had been ordained. It was an organisation of uniformed lay evangelists and the Church of England's response to the Salvation Army. By 1900 some fifty horse-drawn vans, or caravans, toured towns and villages throughout England. As can be seen in the photograph, caravans were usually inscribed with Biblical texts.*

more people drove to church. Funds were raised to build a new hall and car park. However, in 1985, in common with many other parishes, Weald was considered too small to warrant a full-time incumbent. Patronage passed from the Rector of St Nicholas, Sevenoaks, to the Bishop of Rochester.

Among the many memorials inside the church is one to Maude Royden (1876-1956), the outstanding Christian speaker, who supported women's suffrage and regularly preached at the City Temple, as the Anglican church that she favoured would not allow women to preach until 1992. Besides the usual services, St George's offers a wide range of weekly events for all ages that include Scouts, Guides, Brownies, Cubs, a Teens and a Thursday club for youngsters. For adults there are prayer groups, Homemakers, Men's and Women's Fellowships and a Noah's Ark group for mothers and toddlers.

The residents of Weald in the 19th century were described in the Church of England visitation reports as being mainly 'the labouring poor'. Some local farmers and smallholders were likely to have been disaffected towards the Anglican Church by its legalised dominance and the system of tithes. Wesleyan preachers in the pastoral care of Henry B. Britton had been holding meetings in Weald in members' houses. The Sevenoaks circuit sent preachers to the Weald fellowship at least as early as 1841 according to the Circuit Plan. A chapel was built in 1842-3 under the supervision of the Revd John Chettle, Superintendent of the Sevenoaks circuit. The building is reputed to be the smallest and oldest surviving Methodist chapel in the area. It was built straight

116 *Weald parish church Easter procession, 1998. Children processing to St George's parish church on Palm Sunday with Ed the donkey.*

onto bare earth, a cause of numerous damp problems. In 1888 the chapel was extended by 12 feet to its present size.

The Sevenoaks Methodist circuit, with 720 members, sent preachers on foot to outlying villages, as far away as Frant. In 1885 Henry Swaffield of Sevenoaks paid for the hire of a horse and buggy to transport preachers to their appointments. A weekly evening service was held at Weald at 6 p.m. on Sundays, but by 1849 an additional 7 p.m. service had been introduced on Fridays. One of the first fully accredited preachers from Weald in 1867 was Reuben Osbourne. Some of the early Methodists in Weald were devout and sturdy people. For example, Emma Twiner's obituary in 1907 illustrates those strong convictions:

> She was a scholar in the old chapel at Sevenoaks built by John Wesley. Her mother, Mrs Sarah Shoebridge, was a woman of sturdy convictions, and when the clergyman, a man of the old school, threatened to remove her children from the day school if she did not take them from the Methodist School, she resisted his demands and fought and won a battle for religious liberty in days when it meant more than now. Mrs Twiner was a girl when the Weald Chapel was built, she dearly loved it, and brought up her children to love it too, with the result that her son has been Society Steward for many years and a great help to the village cause; her daughter is the organist. She has often told her children of the fervour and fire of the early days of the chapel.

Today (2002) the Weald Methodist Church has a small but loyal congregation. Until recently it included Miss Win Ellis, a retired teacher aged 104, the great-grand-daughter of Mrs Sarah Shoebridge and her husband Jesse.

Samuel Morley (1809-86), wealthy manufacturer, nonconformist Liberal MP, and philanthropist, lived at Leigh. In 1871 his daughter Mary began Gospel work that was financed by her father. Morley also supported temperance causes and funded the building of Congregational chapels, including the Gospel

117 *Family weekend from St George's, Weald. By the late 20th century most people who regularly attended church went from conviction. Many churches held annual holidays or away-days for further Christian teaching, and also to provide a more informal opportunity for church members to get to know one another. This weekend in 1993 from St George's was at St Leonards-on-Sea.*

Hall in Weald. The 19 perches of land that he bought for the mission hall in Weald in 1876, from butchers Thomas Lawrence and Andrew Paris, cost £155. The chapel was nondenominational, influenced by the Plymouth Brethren, and served by lay preachers. Besides regular services and an active Sunday school the chapel operated a blanket loan service to help the poor in winter. Standing near the village centre, the mission hall was in an advantageous position and was a serious rival to St George's.

From 1912 the mission hall had several owners before passing to an evangelical trust in 1949.

During the First World War, the Gospel Hall continued to function and was used on weekdays as a rest room for soldiers who were billeted in the village. A thriving Sunday school flourished in the 1920s and 1930s: the most popular in the village, perhaps because of the Christmas 'Treat' with its tea, entertainment and presents. Most workers in Weald earned a poor wage for farm labour. Not surprising then, that some children of not notably devout parents were sent to Sunday school; some went to more than one. However, dwindling membership led to the hall's closure and it was sold and converted to a private dwelling in 1984.

The most recent church building in Weald, the ultra modern St Edward the Confessor, was built for the Roman Catholics in 1965 by the Castelli family who lived in Long Barn for several years. The architect, John J. Ayleward, was a friend of the Castellis. Officially opened in 1966, the church seats one hundred. Initially services were held on Sundays and feast days and were well attended. However, due to a reduction in the number of priests based at St Thomas's Church in Sevenoaks, services every Sunday could not be maintained. Mass is still said on the first Friday morning of each month and there are occasional weddings.

Glossary

Advowson The right to present a priest or minister to a benefice, a nomination subject to the approval of a diocesan bishop and sometimes of the Crown. The advowson was treated as a piece of property.

Altar The raised table at the east end of many Anglican and Roman Catholic churches where communion or the Mass is conducted by the clergy. Most nonconformists and evangelicals would not use the term but prefer to speak of the communion table.

Anabaptist This was the original name given to those who practised adult (or believers') baptism.

Anglican Belonging to the Church of England. The term came into use from the mid-19th century.

Anglo-Catholic That part of the Church of England that stresses historical continuity with Catholic Christianity and thus has a 'High' concept of episcopacy and of sacraments. The term came to be used in the early 19th century of those Anglicans who supported the laws against dissenters.

Apostle's Creed The statement of Trinitarian faith, dating from the fourth century. It is contained in the Book of Common Prayer.

Archbishop A senior cleric in the Church of England, or the Roman Catholic church, responsible for a province. The Archbishop of Canterbury presides over the Anglican province of Canterbury that covers the dioceses south of the river Trent, but he is also senior archbishop in the worldwide Anglican communion.

Archdeacon A senior clergy person with administrative authority delegated by a bishop. The parishes of the Sevenoaks area are within the Archdeaconry of Tonbridge. An Archdeaconry

is usually subdivided into rural deaneries. The rural dean is co-chair of a deanery synod.

Arminian A person who believes that Christ had died for all and not only, as Calvin thought, for the 'elect'. The doctrine comes from the Dutch theologian Jacobus Arminius (1564-1609).

Baptism The sacrament in which a person is made a member of the church. Most denominations practise infant baptism (paedo-baptism), sometimes referred to in the Church of England as 'Christening'; Baptists, Christian Brethren, and Free Evangelicals practise believers' baptism, often using a baptismal pool in the church for total immersion.

Baptists Originally Anabaptist In the Sevenoaks area there were two kinds of Baptists: General Baptists, who were Arminian and had usually (as at Bessels Green) adopted Unitarian theology by the late 18th century, and Particular Baptists, who were Calvinist and Trinitarian in theology.

Benefice An ecclesiastical office or the income derived from it. It usually applied to the incumbent of a parish, but it could also apply to other offices in the Anglican church.

Bishop A senior clergyman who has jurisdiction over a diocese. In the diocese of Rochester, as elsewhere, the Bishop is aided by suffragan bishops, the Bishop of Maidstone, and the Bishop of Tonbridge, who has responsibility for west Kent including the Sevenoaks area.

Calvinist A follower of the ideas of Jean Calvin (1509-64), the French theologian, who stated that only the 'elect' were predestined to salvation.

Canon A member of the clergy serving on the staff of a cathedral. Parish clergy can be appointed as non-resident canons, an unsalaried post that carries certain privileges and responsibilities.

Catholic Literally 'general' or 'universal'. Since the Reformation Roman Catholics have used the term exclusively of themselves arguing that they possess the only true source of ecclesiastical authority. Anglo-Catholics lay claim to the term arguing that they also possess an historical and continuous tradition of faith. The historic creeds accepted by all the main denominations state that there is 'one holy Catholic Church'.

Chancel Usually applied to the area of the church building at the east end which is the responsibility of the vicar or minister.

Chantry A chapel or altar within a church or on its own site, funded by a wealthy person, to support the building, and also a priest to say Mass in perpetuity for the souls of named persons or for Christians in general.

Charismatic A term used by and of people, and some churches, who claim to have experienced the power of the Holy Spirit in special ways.

Congregationalism The idea that each church or congregation is independent with authority to appoint their own leaders and to call a minister.

Curate Since the 17th century this has come to mean a minister assisting an incumbent in a parish.

Dean An official who presides over a cathedral chapter or, in earlier times, administered a Peculiar.

Diocese An area containing parishes under the jurisdiction of a bishop. In medieval England there were 14 dioceses, the oldest being Canterbury (597), London (604) and Rochester (604). Since 1836, 20 new dioceses have been created.

Dissenter A person who refused to acknowledge the authority of the Church of England (a nonconformist). The Old Dissenters were Baptists, Congregationalists, Presbyterians, and Quakers who refused to conform to the 1662 Act of Uniformity. New Dissenters, from the 18th century onwards, included Methodists although at first they were reluctant to think of themselves as such.

Erastianism A follower of the Swiss theologian Thomas Erastus (1524-83) who argued that the state had ascendancy over the church in ecclesiastical affairs.

Established Church The Church of England, 'established' by law as the official church of England.

Evangelicals Christians, who emphasise personal salvation by faith in Christ's atoning work on the Cross, hold that the Bible is the word of God, and that faith should be worked out in an active Christian life.

Gavelkind A form of land tenure peculiar to Kent where property of the intestate was divided equally among sons.

Glebe Land usually held by a parish priest from which he took income and often farmed himself.

High Church q.v. Anglo-Catholic.

Holy Communion Also the Eucharist, the Mass, Communion, or the Lord's Supper. A sacramental act in which Christians take bread and wine representing the body and blood of Jesus Christ.

Hundred An ancient administrative subdivision of a county or a shire. Sevenoaks was within the old hundred of Codsheath.

Jacobin/Jacobite A movement in the late 17th and early 18th centuries of those who wished to restore the House of Stuart. This also had a religious element in that James II, his son and his grandson, were Roman Catholics.

Knight's service Introduced by the Conqueror in 1070 as an obligation on tenants-in-chief to supply the Crown with a specified number of fully equipped knights ready for military service.

Liturgy Now commonly used to describe all kinds of services authorised by a church.

Lollards Christian group in the 14th and 15th centuries who believed that the Bible was the sole authority in religion and that people had the right to read it in their own language and interpret it for themselves.

Low Church That wing of the Church of England opposite to the 'High Church', often associated with the evangelicals within Anglicanism.

Mass (also see Holy Communion) Roman and Anglo-Catholics believe the Mass to be a re-enactment of Christ's sacrifice. The bread and wine are not mere symbols but, when consecrated by the priest, become the body and blood of Christ, a process known as transubstantiation.

Methodists A Protestant denomination that grew out of the evangelical movement in the 18th century inspired by John Wesley. Methodism flourished within the Church of England and it was not Wesley's intention that it should be other than a part of that church. However, in 1791 it formally separated. Various secessions followed and it was not until 1932 that the different groups united with the original Wesleyan Methodists to form the present Methodist Church.

Minister   Any one who administers or leads a service, although within the Church of England not necessarily a priest. Protestant churches are led by ministers (or pastors) and this is the term most commonly used in Low Churches for the vicar or rector.

Minster   Anglo-Saxon religious communities led by a priest, often sited on a royal estate, which afforded protection and was a base from where missioners could evangelise an area. Many minsters and their adjoining territory became the sites of churches or chapels with a parish.

Mortmain   Literally the 'dead hand'; it describes the conveyance of property, usually land, to the Church. The Statute of Mortmain, in 1279, was an attempt by the Crown to stop the practice and curtail the influence of the church.

Nave   The main central area of the church building.

Nonconformist   A person who refused to conform to the discipline and doctrines of the Church of England from the late 17th century. Another term for a Dissenter.

Oxford Movement   A 19th-century movement within the Church of England to restore the Church to its pre-Reformation traditions.

Parish   The smallest unit of ecclesiastical administration. Each parish contained its own church and priest supported by the dues and tithes paid by parishioners.

Parochial Church Council   Since 1919 each parish of the Church of England has had an elected lay council to administer parish affairs.

Peculiar   A parish or church exempt from the jurisdiction of the archdeacon or bishop in whose diocese it lay. Usually derived from the possession of land by a church dignitary lying within the diocese of another bishop.

Peter's Pence   A tax imposed by the Papacy in the 10th century of one penny per hearth or house per annum. The tax was not always enforced and was abolished at the Reformation.

Pluralism   The simultaneous holding by a priest of two of more benefices.

Predestination   The action of God in determining that some people were fore-ordained to salvation. It was a central doctrine of Calvinism.

Presbyterian   Someone who adhered to a system whereby the church was governed by presbyters or elders rather than bishops. Until the mid-18th century Presbyterians formed the largest group of Dissenters in England.

Priest   A member of the ordained clergy. Within Catholic traditions, both Anglican and Roman, a priest has special sacramental functions essentially related to the celebration of the Eucharist or Mass. The term would not be used by most Protestants, many of whom would accept the 'priesthood of all believers'.

Puritan   That group of Christians who in the 16th century sought a further purifying of the Church of England. They attacked acts of worship they deemed to be unscriptural and, from the 1570s onwards, the episcopal system. Puritans enjoyed a dominant position following the Civil War but declined into factions after the 1660s.

Quakers   or Society of Friends, originating in the religious turbulence of the 1650s. They had no formal ministry, and professed to follow the 'inner light' of Christ's work in individual lives. They refused to pay tithes or to engage in military action.

Rector   Originally the incumbent who received the Great Tithes. Since 1936 the term has become mainly traditional, the functions being little different from those of a vicar.

Recusant   A person who refused to submit to the authority of the Church of England. The term came to be applied to Roman Catholics.

Ritualism   A movement within the High Church that sought to promote sacramental worship.

Rogation   Traditionally a medieval festival held three days before Ascension Day, the sixth Thursday after Easter. It was also an occasion when the boundaries of the parish would be walked ('beating the bounds') and thus reasserted.

Sacrament   According to the Book of Common Prayer, 'An outward and visible sign of an inward and spiritual grace given unto us, ordained by Christ himself, as a means whereby we receive the same, and a pledge to assure us thereof'. The Church of England and the nonconformist churches emphasise two sacraments, those of baptism and Holy Communion. The Catholic tradition acknowledges five others: confirmation, penance, extreme unction, orders, and matrimony.

Saints   The veneration or invoking the aid of saints (dead Christians whom the Church recognised as having lived exemplary lives), has long been a practice within Catholic worship and prayer. In the creeds 'the Communion of Saints' means the fellowship of all Christians alive and dead.

Thirty-nine Articles   The articles drawn up in 1563, and adopted in 1571, in an attempt to define the doctrinal position of the Church of England and distinguish it from the Church of Rome. For example Article 28 denied transubstantiation.

Tithe   Tax paid to the parish incumbent by parishioners from their annual income from produce, stock, or labour, usually assessed at one tenth. Tithes were commuted to rent charges in 1836, but the system continued for another hundred years.

Tractarian   At first part of the Oxford Movement in the 1830s when academic clergy in Oxford issued a number of tracts criticising measures, including the Reform Act, that they felt reduced the position of the established Church in favour of liberals and dissenters.

Transubstantiation   see under Mass.

Trinity   A fundamental Christian doctrine of the union of three persons – Father, Son, and Holy Spirit – in one Godhead.

Unitarian   Those who deny the doctrine of the Trinity and who believe that the divinity of Christ is limited.

Vestry   A room within the church where clergy vestments are kept. From the 16th century the vestry was also the place where parish administration was conducted.

Vicar   The incumbent of a parish.

Whig   A political faction dating from the late 17th century and embracing those who wanted to curb monarchical rule and generally to promote measures of political, social, and religious reform.

Notes

Abbreviations used: *Arch. Cant.*   *Archaeologia Cantiana*
                 CKS   Centre for Kentish Studies at Maidstone, Canterbury, and Sevenoaks.

Introduction, pp.xi-xiv

1. cf. the richness of the material for Lewes in Sussex that is so splendidly handled by Jeremy Goring in *Burn Holy Fire: Religion in Lewes since the Reformation* (London, 2003).

Part One: Locality and Nation

Kentish Faith and Belief in the First Millennium, pp.1-10

1. Alan Everitt, *Continuity and Colonization: the evolution of Kentish settlement* (Leicester, 1986), p.269.
2. J.K. Wallenberg, *The Place Names of Kent* (Uppsala, 1934), p.52.
3. Charlotte Behr, 'Origins of kingship in early medieval Kent', *Journal of Early Medieval Europe*, 9,1 (2000), p.25.
4. Tacitus, *Historical Works, Vol 1, The Annals* (Dent edn, London, 1932), p.431.
5. G.W. Meates, *The Lullingstone Roman Villa, Vol. 1: The site* (Maidstone, 1979), p.35.
6. Bede, *A History of the English Church and People* (Harmondsworth, Penguin edn, 1968), p.44.
7. G.W. Meates, 'Christianity in the Darent Valley', *Arch. Cant.*, C (1984), p.59.
8. Meates, 'Christianity in the Darent Valley', p.61.
9. See S. Bassett, ed., *The Origins of the Anglo-Saxon Kingdoms* (Leicester, 1989), chapters by Brooks on Horsa and by Yorke on the Jutes.
10. Everitt, *Continuity and Colonization*, p.78.
11. Bede, *History*, p.59.
12. Walsh, R.M., 'Recent investigations at the Anglo-Saxon cemetery, Darenth Park Hospital, Dartford', *Arch. Cant.*, XCVI (1980), pp.310 and 312.
13. M. White and J. Saynor, *Shoreham, a Village in Kent* (Shoreham, 1989), p.11.
14. Bede, *History*, p.110.
15. Bede, *History*, p.130.
16. B. Philp, *Excavations in West Kent* (Kent Archaeological Rescue Unit, 1973), p.201.
17. Meates, *Lullingstone Roman Villa* (Maidstone, 1979), p.123.
18. John Newman, *West Kent and the Weald* (Harmondsworth, Buildings of England series, 1969), p.334.
19. D. Clarke and A. Stoyel, *Otford in Kent: a history* (Otford, 1975), p.69.
20. Clarke and Stoyel, *Otford in Kent*, p.69. On the mother-daughter churches see J. Blair, ed., *Minster and Parish Churches: The local church transition* (Oxford, 1989), ch. by T. Tatton-Brown on Kent.
21. Everitt, *Continuity and Colonization*, p.241.
22. Clarke and Stoyel, *Otford in Kent*, p.69.
23. J. Saynor, ed., *Bexley Mosaic, Aelfric's Collocquy*, trans. A. Watkins (Bexley W.E.A., 1977), p.83.
24. A.C. Garmonsway, ed., *Anglo-Saxon Chronicle* (London, 1975), p.40.
25. Garmonsway, *Anglo-Saxon Chronicle*, p.50.
26. Garmonsway, *Anglo-Saxon Chronicle*, p.54.
27. Clarke and Stoyel, *Otford in Kent*, p.32.
28. William of Malmesbury, 'On the Deeds of the English Kings', quoted by M. Wood, *In Search of the Dark Ages* (London, 1981), p.150.
29. Garmonsway, *Anglo-Saxon Chronicle*, p.129.

THE DEVELOPMENT OF CHURCHES AND PARISHES IN THE MIDDLE AGES, pp.11-24

1. K.P. Witney, *The Jutish Forest: a study of the Weald of Kent from 450 to 1380 AD* (London, 1976), Witney, pp.5-13; P. Brandon and B. Short, *The South East from AD 1000* (London, 1990), pp.4-12.

2. Alan Everitt, *Continuing Colonization: the evolution of Kentish settlement* (Leicester, 1986), Parts 1-3.

3. *Domesday Book: a complete translation* (Penguin Classics, Harmondsworth, 2003).

4. H. Hanley and C. Chalklin, 'The Kent Lay Subsidy Roll of 1334/5', in F.R.H. Du Boulay, ed., *Documents Illustrative of Medieval Kentish Society, Kent Records XVIII* (Ashford, 1964), especially pp.63, 66-7.

5. Everitt, *Continuing Colonization*, pp.184-5.

6. H.C. Darby and E.M.J. Campbell, *The Domesday Geography of South-East England* (Cambridge, 1962), p. 513.

7. H.E. Hallam, ed., *The Agrarian History of England and Wales: II, 1042-1350* (Cambridge, 1988), p.188; M. Mate, 'The rise and fall of markets in southeast England', *Canadian Journal of History XXXI* (1996). B.A. McLain, 'Factors in market establishment in medieval England: the evidence from Kent, 1086-1350', *Arch. Cant.*, CXVII (1997). H.W. Knocker, 'Sevenoaks: the Manor, Church and Market', *Arch. Cant.*, XXXVIII (1926).

8. McLain, 'Factors in market establishment in medieval England', map 2.

9. It is marked by a Sevenoaks Society plaque giving further details on the side of the building, now the Loch Fyne restaurant.

10. The largest group of non-Christians in England was the Jews, but there is no evidence of their presence in Sevenoaks; they were expelled from the country in 1290.

11. W.G. Birch, ed., *Cartularium Saxonicum*, 3 vols (London, 1885-91), I, No.91, but see also Nos. 367 and 370.

12. G. Ward, 'The list of Saxon churches in the Textus Roffensis', *Arch. Cant.*, XLV (1933); C. Platt, *The Parish Churches of Medieval England* (London, 1995), pp.4-5.

13. D. Clarke and A. Stoyel, *Otford in Kent: a history* (Otford, 1975), p.35.

14. F.R.J. Pateman, and others, 'St Thomas a Becket's Well, Otford', *Arch. Cant.* LXX, (1956).

15. B.J. Philp, *Excavation in the Darent Valley, Kent* (Dover, 1984), p.138.

16. F.R.H. Du Boulay, 'A note on the rebuilding of Knole by Archbishop Bourchier', *Arch. Cant.* LXIII, (1950); V. Sackville-West, *Knole* (London, 1922; 1988 edn), pp.51ff.

17. This information comes from the as yet unpublished report of the Oxford Archaeological Unit on the excavation work undertaken at St Nicholas during the building of the undercroft in 1993-5.

18. L.L. Duncan, ed., *Testamenta Cantiana: West Kent* (London, 1906), p.67.

19. Duncan, *Testamenta Cantiana*, pp.11, 57, 67, 68.

20. For St John's Hospital, see A. Hussey, 'Chapels in Kent', *Arch. Cant.* XXIX (1911), p.265, and R.D. Clarke, 'The Medieval Hospital of St John the Baptist, Sevenoaks' (typescript, 1971); A. Hussey, *Kent Chantries* (Ashford, 1936). A complete list of the Sevenoaks chantry priests is given in C.H. Fielding, *The Records of Rochester* (Dartford, 1910).

21. Graham, R., ed., *Registrum Roberti Winchelsey, Cantuariensis Archipiscopi, 1294-1313*, 2 Vols (Canterbury and York, 1952-6), I, pp.272-7; K.C. Wood-Legh, K.C., ed., *Kentish Visitations of Archbishop Warham and His Deputies, 1511-12* (Ashford, 1984), p.xi.

22. F. Du Boulay, ed., *Registrum Thome Bougchier, Cantuariensis Archiepiscopi, 1454-86* (Canterbury and York, 1957), p.345; C. Harper-Bill, *The Register of John Morton, Archbishop of Canterbury, 1486-1500*, 2 vols (Canterbury and York, 1987-91), I, pp.120-21.

23. W.H. Bliss, ed., *Calendar of Papal Registers, vol.II* (London, 1895), p. 89; Bliss and J.A. Tremlow, eds, vol. IV, ed. (London, 1902), p. 500; Bliss & Tremlow, eds, vol.V, (London, 1904), pp. 596-7; Tremlow, ed., vol. VII (London, 1906), pp.584-5.

24. J. Ward, *Women of the English Nobility and Gentry, 1066-1500* (Manchester, 1995).

25. F. Du Boulay, 'The Pipe Roll Account of the See of Canterbury', in Du Boulay, ed., *Documents Illustrative of Medieval Kentish Society*, pp.46-7; Du Boulay, *The Lordship of Canterbury* (London, 1966), p.284. C. Harper-Bill, ed., *The Register of John Morton, Archbishop of Canterbury, 1486-1500*, vol. I (Canterbury & York, 1987), pp.120-21.

26. Witney, *The Jutish Forest*, pp.201-2, 224-7; Everitt, *Continuity and Colonization*, pp.25-30; J.L. Bolton, *The Medieval English Economy, 1150-1500* (London, 1980), p.10.

27. C. Haigh, 'Anti-Clericalism and the English Reformation', *History*, LXVIII, (1983); and R.A. Cosgrave, 'English anti-Clericalism: a programmatic assessment', in P.A. Dyken and H.A. Oberman, eds., *Anticlericalism in Late Medieval and Early Modern Europe* (Leiden, 1993).

28. N. Tanner, 'Penances imposed on Kentish Lollards by Archbishop Warham, 1511-12', in M.

Aston and C. Richmond, eds., *Lollardy and the Gentry in the Later Middle Ages* (Stroud, 1997), pp.233-5; N. Tanner, ed., *Kent Heresy Proceedings, 1511-12* (Maidstone, 1997).

29. F. Du Boulay, 'Late continued demesne farming at Otford', *Arch. Cant.* LXXIII, (1959).
30. See P. Lindley and M. Ormrod, eds., *The Black Death in England* (London, 1995).
31. See J.A.F. Thomson, *The Later Lollards, 1414-1520* (Oxford, 1965); M. Aston, *Lollards and Reformers* (London, 1984); A. Kenny, ed., *Wyclif in His Times* (Oxford, 1986); A. Hudson, *The Premature Reformation* (Oxford, 1988).
32. C. Harper-Bill, *The Pre-Reformation Church in England* (London, rev. edn, 1996), p. 135. E. Duffy, *The Stripping of the Altars: traditional religion in England, c.1400-1580* (New Haven, CN, 1992).
33. L.L. Duncan, 'The renunciation of Papal authority by the clergy of West Kent, 1534', *Arch. Cant.*, XXII (1897).

Reformation, pp.25-40

1. Alan Everitt, *The Community of Kent and the Great Rebellion 1640-60* (Leicester University Press, 1973), p.36.
2. A.G. Dickens, *The English Reformation* (London, 1964), p.108.
3. Dickens, *English Reformation*, p.29.
4. Michael Zell, ed., *Early Modern Kent 1540-1640* (Woodbridge, 2000), p.184.
5. Dennis Clarke and Anthony Stoyel, *Otford in Kent, a History* (Otford, 1975), p.106.
6. William Lambarde, *A Perambulation of Kent* (1570; Bath, 1970), p.461.
7. Patrick Collinson, *The Religion of Protestants* (Oxford, 1982), p.201.
8. Eamon Duffy, *The Stripping of the Altars. Traditional religion in England c.1400-c.1580* (New Haven, 1992).
9. Lambarde, *Perambulation*, p.462.
10. Zell, *Early Modern Kent*, p.196.
11. Zell, *Early Modern Kent*, p.223.
12. Peter Clark, *English Provincial Society from the Reformation to the Revolution: religion, politics and society in Kent 1500-1640* (Harvester Press, 1977), pp.101-2.
13. Non-attendance at the parish church on Sundays.
14. For example, the commending of the soul to Jesus Christ's care, in accordance with the doctrine of justification by faith alone, as opposed to a Catholic formula which would invoke the Virgin Mary and all the saints.
15. Peter Clark, 'The prophesying movement in Kentish towns during the 1570s', *Arch. Cant.* XCIII (1977) pp.81-90.
16. John Dunlop, *The Pleasant Town of Sevenoaks. A history* (Sevenoaks, 1964), p.111.
17. Kevin Sharpe, *The Personal Rule of Charles I* (New Haven, 1992).
18. The practice, common in this and subsequent periods, whereby a single clergyman acquired a number of church 'livings', drawing the income and paying a badly-trained curate just a small portion of it to take services.
19. Everitt, *Community of Kent*, p.85.
20. Jacqueline Eales, *Community and Disunity: Kent and the English civil wars, 1640-1649* (Faversham, 2001). More generally see Nigel Yates, 'Papists and Puritans', in Yates, ed., *Religion and Society in Kent, 1640-1914* (Woodbridge, 1994), pp. 3ff.
21. F.D. Johns, 'The Royalist Rising and Parliamentary mutinies of 1645 in West Kent', *Arch. Cant.*, CX (1992).
22. Everitt, *Community of Kent*, p.165.
23. John Walker, *The Sufferings of the Clergy* (London, 1714), part ii, pp.251-2.
24. Jean Fox, 'Sevenoaks, Seal and Ightham 1560-1650', *Arch. Cant.*, CXVI (1996), p.230.
25. Christopher Hill, *The World Turned Upside Down: Radical Ideas during the English Revolution* (Harmondsworth, 1974).
26. Gillian Draper, 'The First Hundred Years of Quakerism in Kent: Part I', *Arch. Cant.*, CXII (1993), p.322.
27. Draper, 'Quakerism in Kent', p.333.
28. Robert Beddard, 'The Privileges of Christchurch, Canterbury: Archbishop Sheldon's enquiries of 1671', *Arch. Cant.*, LXXXVII (1972), pp.81-100.
29. H.C.F. Lansberry, *Sevenoaks Wills and Inventories in the Reign of Charles II* (Maidstone, 1988), p.xxiv.

Churches in the Modern Age, pp.41-65

1. A very clear recent account of changes at the grass roots level of English churches over the past five centuries is Doreen Rosman, *The Evolution of the English Churches 1500-2000* (Cambridge, 2003).

2. Peter Nouaille, of Huguenot descent, employed 80 people, mainly women and children, in his Greatness silk mill; see Parliamentary Papers. 'Minutes of Evidence Before Select Committee on State of Children Employed in Manufactories of the United Kingdom' [397] (1816). Evidence by Mr Peter Noaille(*sic*) pp.80-3.

3. John Dunlop, *The Pleasant Town of Sevenoaks* (Sevenoaks, 1963), is a useful but limited history.

4. Linda Colley, *Britons: Forging the nation 1707-1837* (New Haven, 1992), argues that Protestantism helped to create a sense of British national identity through the 18th century.

5. The Test Acts 1674, Act of Toleration 1689 and an Act of 1695 barred Roman Catholics from the professions and imposed a double land tax on them; the Act of Settlement in 1701 determined that all future monarchs should be Protestants.

6. Mary J. Dobson, 'Original Compton Census returns – the Shoreham Deanery', *Arch. Cant.*, vol.CIV (1978); Christopher Buckingham, 'Where have all the Papists gone? Or the Catholics of the Shoreham deanery in the Rochester diocese', *Kent Recusant History*, vol.2, 3-4 (1995); Michael Watts, *The Dissenters: From the Reformation to the French Revolution* (Oxford, 1978), p.509, table XII.

7. John Wesley, *The Journal of the Reverend John Wesley*, 4 vols (Longman edn, London, 1906), vol. I, p.571. For Wesley's other visits see II, pp.76, 81, IV, pp.38, 196, 492 and 513.

8. F.L. Clark, *The Peronnets of Shoreham* (London, 1984).

9. William Gibson, *The Church of England 1688-1832: Unity and accord* (London, 2003), p.1. On the 18th-century Anglican church see John Walsh, Colin Haydon, and Stephen Taylor, eds., *The Church of England c.1689-c.1833: From toleration to Tractarianism* (Cambridge, 1993).

10. Nigel Yates, 'A Kentish clerical dynasty: Curteis of Sevenoaks', *Arch. Cant.* vol.CVIII (1990) and vol.CXVII (1997).

11. See Jeffrey S. Chamberlain, 'The limits of moderation in a Latitudinarian parson: or, a High-Church zeal in a Low Churchman discover'd', in Roger D. Lund, ed., *The Margins of Orthodoxy: Heterodox writings and cultural response, 1660-1750* (Cambridge, 1995), pp.195-215.

12. John Rooker, *Parish Church of St Nicholas Sevenoaks* (Sevenoaks, 1910).

13. See Keith Thomas, *Religion and the Decline of Magic* (London, 1971); for a local study, J. Obelkevich, *Religion and Rural Society: South Lindsey 1825-1875* (Oxford, 1976).

14. Christopher Bell, 'The Speech from the Throne, 1901', *English Catholic History Association Newsletter*, 2, 18 (March 2003).

15. Churches and chapels built in the Victorian period are listed in Homan, Roger, *The Victorian Churches of Kent* (Chichester, 1984); details of alterations to mainly Anglican churches, are to be found in John Newman, *West Kent and the Weald* (Harmondsworth, Penguin Buildings of England series, 2nd edn, 1976).

16. Margaret Roake, ed., *Religious Worship in Kent: The census of 1851* (Maidstone, 1999), pp.122-33.

17. Herries papers (in private hands). Robert Herries to Charles John Herries, dd Lynmouth, 9 October 1837.

18. Susan Thorne, 'Protestant ethics and the spirit of imperialism: British Congregationalists and the London Missionary Society 1795-1925', unpub. PhD thesis, University of Michigan, 1990, pp.353-4.

19. See David Bebbington, *Evangelicalism in Modern Britain: A history from the 1730s to the 1980s* (London, 1989), especially ch.1.

20. Benjamin Field, *Sincere Devotion Exemplified in the Life of Mrs C. E. Martin of Sevenoaks* (London, 1862; 2nd edn, 1869). Catherine Martin died following the birth of her seventh child in March 1861.

21. See Rev. T. Curteis, *A Letter to the Right Honourable Sir Robert Peel, Bart., on the Principle and operation of the New Poor Law* (London, 1842).

22. John Hilton, 'A Sevenoaks church rate riot', *Bygone Kent*, vol.18, 3 (1997).

23. The National Society for Promoting the Education of the Poor in the Principles of the Established Church was formed in 1811 by the Anglican bishops as a rival body to the British and Foreign School Society which promoted non-sectarian education.

24. *Sevenoaks Chronicle*, 17 November 1911. Albert Bath, a Liberal and veteran of many radical causes, had a long history of opposing church rates and tithe payments.

25. H.W. Standen, *Kippington in Kent: Its history and its churches* (Sevenoaks, 1958).

26. The Salvation Army opened in the old Baptist church in the London Road in September 1887. The Salvationists were abused and stoned by 'the rough element' of the town; *Sevenoaks Chronicle*, 16 September 1887.

27. Birmingham University Library. YMCA Papers, A 10, Sevenoaks. The faded painted sign of the YWCA can still be seen on a building in the London Road immediately south of Bligh's car park.

28. Sevenoaks municipal cemetery, opened in 1909 on Seal Road, contains a chapel. Increasingly cremation has taken the place of burial, the nearest crematoria being at Tunbridge Wells and also having a chapel. Cremation was opposed by many religious leaders in the late 19th century and was only accepted after a lengthy campaign begun in the mid-1880s.

29. Grace Davie, *Europe: the exceptional case. Parameters of faith in the modern world* (London, 2003), p.19; see also her *Religion in Britain since 1945* (Oxford, 1994). Also Callum G. Brown, *The Death of Christian Britain* (London, 2001).

30. The Sevenoaks War Memorial, a statue of a soldier looking towards Flanders, was erected in 1920. The site, on the Vine, was hotly disputed and led to an official enquiry; see *Sevenoaks Chronicle*, 26 March 1920.

31. Yates, 'A Kentish clerical dynasty: Part II', *Arch. Cant.*, vol.CXVII (1997), although Yates is incorrect in suggesting that the introduction of ritualism to St Nicholas' was uncontested. See Sevenoaks Public Library, Local studies collection D1001(a), and D1002.

32. I am grateful to John Truscott, on behalf of the Trustees of St Nicholas' Parish Church, for letting me have a copy of the relevant 'Conveyance of the Advowson of Sevenoaks', dd 8 November 1911.

33. For example Kenneth Prior, *Christians in a Pagan Society* (London, 1975), based on a series of sermons on Acts 17 preached at Sevenoaks parish church.

34. E.L. Langston, *How God is Working to a Plan* (London, 1933). See also W.Y. Fullerton, *F.B. Meyer: A biography* (London, 1939), pp.157-9.

35. Julia Cameron, *St Nicholas Sevenoaks: the church that went under* (Carlisle, 1999).

36. See *Sevenoaks Chronicle*, 1 May 1982.

37. Church magazines, originating in the 19th century, are a splendid source for information on the wide range of church activities. Unfortunately there are few extant copies for churches in the district.

38. Brown, *Death of Christian Britain*, p.142, although his comments may be too swayed by Scottish practice.

39. Nick Spencer, *Beyond Belief* (London Institute of Contemporary Christianity, 2003).

PART TWO: CHURCHES AND CHAPELS, MISSIONS AND MEETINGS

1. ST NICHOLAS' PARISH CHURCH, SEVENOAKS, pp.69-74.

1. Alan Everitt, *Continuity and Colonization: The evolution of Kentish settlement* (Leicester, 1986), p.270.

2. John Dunlop, *The Pleasant Town of Sevenoaks: a history* (Sevenoaks, 1969), pp.82-3.

3. See John Rooker, *Notes on the Parish Church of St Nicholas, Sevenoaks* (Sevenoaks, 1910).

4. Leslie Stephen and Sidney Lee, eds., *Dictionary of National Biography*, vol.VII (London, 1921-22), pp. 1136-7.

5. Nigel Yates, 'A Kentish clerical dynasty: Curteis of Sevenoaks, Part I: 1716-1861', *Arch. Cant.*, vol.CVIII (1990); Part II: vol.CXVII (1997). In 1750 the Revd Thomas Curteis bought up the tithes of the vicar and thereafter incumbents were both rector and vicar.

6. Julia E.M. Cameron, *St Nicholas Sevenoaks: the church that went under* (Carlisle, 1999).

2. ST MARY THE VIRGIN, RIVERHEAD, pp.75-7

1. John Newman, *West Kent and the Weald* (Penguin Buildings of England series, Harmondsworth, 2nd edn, 1976), p.469.

2. See further the church guides: *Guide to the Church of St Mary the Virgin Riverhead* (1968) and *St Mary the Virgin, Riverhead 1831-1931* (1931). Also the National Association of Decorative and Fine Arts Societies, *St Mary the Virgin, Riverhead, Kent, Record of Church Furnishings* (London, 1994).

3. H.W. Standen, *Kippington in Kent: Its history and its churches* (Sevenoaks, 1958), pp.16-18.

3. ST MARY, KIPPINGTON, SEVENOAKS, pp.78-81

1. Diana and Keith Atkinson, *Guide Book to St Mary Kippington* (Sevenoaks, 1998). H.W. Standen, *Kippington in Kent: Its history and its churches* (Sevenoaks, 1958). H.P. Thompson, *Guide Book to St Mary and St Luke, Kippington* (Sevenoaks, c.1919).

4. ST JOHN THE BAPTIST, SEVENOAKS, pp.82-4

1. D. Clarke, *A Brief History and Guide to the Church of St John the Baptist* (Sevenoaks, 1970).

2. Nigel Yates, 'A clerical dynasty: Curteis of Sevenoaks. Part II: 1874-1907', *Arch. Cant.*, vol.CXVII (1997), pp.170-1.

5. ST LUKE'S, SEVENOAKS, pp.85-8

1. H.W. Standen, *Kippington in Kent: Its history and its churches* (Sevenoaks, 1958).
2. Beneath the stone is a glass bottle containing a copy of the *Daily Telegraph*, 22 July 1903, the *Kippington Parish Magazine* for July, and current coins.
3. Lee's plans provided for clerestory windows and a hammer-beam roof. A recent authoritative history is John Newman's *Saint Luke's Parish Church Sevenoaks: A centenary history* (Sevenoaks, 2003)
4. Standen, *Kippington in Kent*, p.33.
5. The oil painting by Albani (1578-1660), a gift of W. J. Thompson, originally hung above the communion table. It has been cleaned and now hangs on the north wall.
6. The Mulberry Centre houses severely handicapped people.
7. Standen, *Kippington in Kent*, p.48.
8. The hope in 1957 that St Luke's could become a separate parish from St Mary's was dashed by the Church Commissioners who argued that the church had no endowment, the building was incomplete, the boundaries presented difficulties and the population was too small; see Standen, *Kippington in Kent*, p.55.
9. This has a coloured emblem of a dove designed by Lawrence Lee of Penshurst. The window on the east wall depicting the Ascension was designed by J. Egan of Wardour Street.
10. The electoral roll was then 261; in 1979 it was 202. By 2001 it was 307.

6. VINE BAPTIST CHURCH, pp.89-92

1. British Library ADD.MS 36,709: 'A Register Booke or Record of the Congregation of Jesus Christ inhabiting in and about Speldhurst and Pembury in Kent', fol. 4r. [usually known as the Bradbourne-Sevenoaks church book], quoted in Ruth Butterfield, 'The Royal Commission of King Jesus: General Baptist expansion and growth 1640-1660', *Baptist Quarterly* XXXV, 2 (1993), p.63.
2. The history of the Baptists can be followed in B.R. White, *The English Baptists of the 17th Century* (Didcot, 1996); Raymond Brown, *The English Baptists of the 18th Century* (London, 1986); and J.H.Y. Briggs, *The English Baptists of the 19th Century* (Didcot, 1994).
3. W.R. Newton, *The Vine Baptist Church Sevenoaks 1748-1948* (Sevenoaks, 1948); L.J. Lane, *Baptists in Sevenoaks – Our Story* (Sevenoaks, 1998).

7. QUAKERS: THE SOCIETY OF FRIENDS, pp.93-5

1. Gillian Draper, 'The first hundred years of Quakerism in Kent', Part I, *Arch. Cant.*, vol.CXII (1993), and Part II, vol.CXV (1995); R. Vann, *The Social Development of English Quakerism 1655-1755* (Cambridge, MA., 1969).
2. Draper, 'The first hundred years', Part. I, p.329.
3. CKS Canterbury [East Kent] Monthly Meeting Book 1668-1777, N/FMc 1/1, 2.
4. See Library of the Society of Friends, London. Cranbrook Monthly Meeting's 'Condemnations for Misdemeanours' (1668-1712).
5. CKS, Sevenoaks. U 1000/20/P10, Z 8. Maps and papers relating to Quakers Hall.
6. CKS, Sevenoaks N/FP/6/1. Sevenoaks Preparative Meeting Minutes 1953-60.

8. METHODISM IN SEVENOAKS, pp.96-9

1. Walter D. Judd, *The Record of Wesleyan Methodism in the Sevenoaks Circuit 1746-1932* (London, 1932); William D. Horton, *The Story of Methodism in Sevenoaks from 1746*, unpub. lecture, 1979.
2. The origins and development of Methodism can best be followed in the official history edited by R. Davies, A.R. George, and G. Rupp, *History of the Methodist Church in Great Britain*, 4 volumes (London, 1965-88). For John Wesley see Henry D. Rack, *Reasonable Enthusiast: John Wesley and the rise of Methodism* (London, 3rd edn, 2002).

9. ST JOHN'S HILL, UNITED REFORMED CHURCH, pp.100-103

1. J.E. Salmon, *Sevenoaks Congregational Church: a brief history* (Sevenoaks, 1967)
2. For Morley see Edwin Hodder, *Life of Samuel Morley* (London, 1887).
3. Named after Dorcas, an early Christian disciple who 'was always doing good and helping the poor', Acts 9: 36.

11. VINE EVANGELICAL CHURCH, pp.107-109

1. For the origins and history of the Brethren see F.R. Coad, *The History of the Brethren Movement* (Exeter, 1968).

12. The Catholic Church of St Thomas of Canterbury, Sevenoaks, pp.110-15

1. A.C. Ryan, 'Some recusant and church papist families of Sevenoaks' (Kent Recusant History Society, 2002).
2. *Sevenoaks Chronicle*, 11 March 1881.

13. First Church of Christ, Scientist, Sevenoaks, pp.116-18

1. M.B. Eddy, *Retrospection and Introspection* (Boston, 1891), p. 24.
2. M.B. Eddy, *Church Manual of the First Church of Christ, Scientist in Boston, Massachusetts* (Boston, 1895), p.17.
3. Still published as a daily newspaper, *The Christian Science Monitor* was founded by Mrs Eddy in 1908.
4. Christian Science Publishing Society, *Church A Living Power* (Boston, 1980), p.31.

14. Sevenoaks Town Church, pp.119-21

1. See further Carol Gillard, *Like a Mighty Army. The story of Biggin Hill Christian Fellowship* (Biggin Hill, 1991).

16. Bessels Green Baptist Church, pp.125-7

1. W. Groser, *Memoirs of Mr John Stanger, late Pastor of a Baptist Church at Bessels Green, Kent* (London, 1824).
2. E.A. Payne, 'The venerable John Stanger of Bessels Green', *Baptist Quarterly*, vol.27, 7 (1978).

17. Bessels Green Unitarian Church, pp.128-31

1. Epitaph in Warwick Unitarian Church to the Revd William Field (1768-1854), Unitarian minister at Warwick 1789-1843.
2. Bessels Green Church Book 1697-1813. The original is in Sevenoaks Public Library Local History Section.
3. Shirley Burgoyne Black, *The Old Burying Ground at Crockenhill, Kent* (Otford, 1981).
4. Trueman Abbe, and Hubert Abbe Howson, compilers, *Robert Colgate the Immigrant: A genealogy of the New York Colgates and some associated lines* (New Haven CN., 1941).

18. Chevening, pp.132-6

1. CKS, Maidstone. XX 336.2. *Taxatio Ecclesiastica* P. Nicholai 1291 (transcribed 1802).
2. CKS, Maidstone. P88/5/1.
3. I. Watson, ed., *A History of the Parish of Chevening* (Chevening, 1999).
4. M. Roake, ed., *Religious Worship in Kent: The census of 1851* (Maidstone, 1999) p.127.
5. CKS. P/88/6/1.
6. CKS. Q/SRm/15. Quarter Session Reports. We owe this reference to Lionel Cole.
7. Roake, *Religious Worship in Kent*, p.128.

19. Halstead, pp.137-40

1. Lambeth Palace Library MS1115. Archbishop Wake's Survey of Peculiars, 1717.
2. Annotation in Streatfeild's copy of *Hasted's History of Kent*, BM ADD MS 33880.
3. *Bromley Journal*, 20 August 1885.
4. See further Geoffrey Kitchener, *Millennial Halstead. A Kentish village history* (Halstead, 2000).
5. Letter, Mrs G.C. Griffiths to G.T. Aslachsen, 11 October 1952, in author's possession.

21. Otford, pp.144-8

1. Dennis Clarke and Anthony Stoyel, *Otford in Kent: a history* (Otford, 1965), pp.163-4.

22. Seal, pp.149-52

1. S. Crookshank, *St Peter and St Paul, Seal* (Seal, 1974), p.3.
2. A.D. Stoyel, 'Norman abacus at Seal church', *Arch. Cant.* LXXXV (1970), pp.267-8.
3. Alan Everitt, *Continuity and Colonization, the evolution of Kentish Settlement* (Leicester, 1986), p.265.
4. T.S. Frampton, 'List of Incumbents at St Peter's, Seal', *Arch. Cant.* XX (1897), pp. 258-75.
5. M. Stevens, *Past Generations of Seal and Kemsing* (n.d. *c*.1970).
6. L.L Duncan, *Testamenta Cantiana: a series of extracts from sixteenth and seventeenth century wills relating to church building and topography, West Kent* (London, 1906).

7. M. Stevens, *Thomas Theobald, A Son of Seal* (n.d. *c.*1975).

8. M. Duncan Leland, 'The renunciation of Papal authority by the clergy of West Kent', *Arch. Cant.*, vol.XX (1897), p. 299.

9. Jean Fox, 'Seal, Kemsing and Ightham – 1560- 1650', *Arch. Cant.*, vol.CXII (1993), and 'Sevenoaks, Seal and Ightham, 1560-1650', *Arch. Cant.*, vol.CXVI (1997).

10. Jean Fox, 'Sevenoaks to 1650' (forthcoming).

11. Sevenoaks Local Studies Library. Gordon Ward Notebooks, Seal 3.

12. A. Whiteman, ed., *The Compton Census of 1676: a critical edition* (London, 1986), p.408.

13. Deeds etc. of sale of site to Largent Wilson (in parish church); Walter F. Judd, *The Record of Wesleyan Methodism in the Sevenoaks Circuit* (Sevenoaks, 1932).

14. Drawings signed and dated from Scott's office and preserved in the parish church.

15. M. Stevens, *Past Generations of Seal and Kemsing* (n.d. *c.*1970).

24. SHOREHAM, pp.157-9

1. The history of Shoreham is splendidly covered in Malcolm White and Joy Saynor, *Shoreham: A Village in Kent* (Shoreham, 1989). For the parish church see the various histories and guides: A. Payne, *A History of the Parish Church of St Peter and St Paul, Shoreham, Kent* (1930), G.S. Simpson, *The Parish Church of St Peter and St Paul, Shoreham, Kent* (n.d.), P. Gliddon, *St Peter and St Paul, Shoreham, Kent,* and D.E. Benbow, *Shoreham Church* (Shoreham, 1968).

27. WEALD, pp.169-72

1. Weald History Group, *Sevenoaks Weald: a brief history* (Weald, n.d. *c.*1999).

2. Edward Hasted, *The History and Topographical Survey of the County of Kent* (Canterbury, 1797; Wakefield reprint edn, 1972), vol. III, p. 60.

3. See further Pauline Strivens and Beryl Higgs, *History of St George's Church Weald* (Weald, 1989).

Select Bibliography

Aston, M., *Lollards and Reformers* (London, 1984)

Atkinson, Diana and Keith, *Guide Book to St Mary Kippington* (Sevenoaks, 1998)

Bassett, S., ed., *The Origins of the Anglo-Saxon Kingdoms* (Leicester, 1989)

Bebbington, David, *Evangelicalism in Modern Britain. A history from the 1730s to the 1980s* (London, 1989)

Beddard, Robert, 'The privileges of Christchurch, Canterbury: Archbishop Sheldon's enquiries of 1671', *Arch. Cant.*, Vol.LXXXVII (1972)

Bede, *A History of the English Church and People* (Harmondsworth, Penguin edn, 1968)

Behr, Charlotte, 'Origins of kingship in early medieval Kent', *Journal of Early Medieval Europe*, vol.9, 1 (2000)

Bell, Christopher, 'The Speech from the Throne, 1901', *English Catholic History Association Newsletter*, 2, 18 (March 2003)

Benbow, D.E., *Shoreham Church* (Shoreham, 1968)

Birch, W.G., ed., *Cartularium Saxonicum*, 3 vols (London, 1885-91)

Black, Shirley Burgoyne, *The Old Burying Ground at Crockenhill, Kent* (Otford, 1981)

Blair, J., ed., *Minister and Parish Churches. The local church transition* (Oxford, 1989)

Bliss, W.H., ed., *Calendar of Papal Registers.*, vol. II (London, 1895); Bliss and Tremlow, J.A., eds., *Calendar of Papal Registers*, vol IV and V (London, 1902 & 1904)

Bolton, J.L., *The Medieval English Economy, 1150-1500* (London, 1980)

Brandon, P. and Short, B., *The South East from A.D. 1000* (London, 1990)

Briggs, J.H.Y., *The English Baptists of the 19th Century* (Didcot, 1994)

Brown, Callum G., *The Death of Christian Britain* (London, 2001)

Brown, Raymond, *The English Baptists of the 18th Century* (London, 1986)

Buckingham, Christopher, 'Where have all the Papists gone? Or the Catholics of the Shoreham deanery in the Rochester diocese', *Kent Recusant History*, vol.3, 4 (1995)

Butterfield, Ruth, 'The Royal Commission of King Jesus: General Baptist expansion and growth 1640-1660', *Baptist Quarterly*, vol.XXXV, 2 (1993)

Cameron, Julia, *St Nicholas Sevenoaks: the church that went under* (Carlisle, 1999)

Chamberlain, Jeffrey S., 'The limits of moderation in a Latitudinarian parson: or, a High-Church zeal in a Low Churchman discover'd', in Roger D. Lund, ed., *The Margins of Orthodoxy: Heterodox writings and cultural response, 1660-1750* (Cambridge, 1995), pp. 195-215

Clark, F.L., *The Peronnets of Shoreham* (London, 1984)

Clark, Peter, *English Provincial Society from the Reformation to the Revolution: Religion, Politics and Society in Kent 1500-1640* (Hassocks, Harvester Press, 1977)

Clark, Peter, 'The Proselytising Movement in Kentish Towns during the 1570s', *Arch. Cant.*, vol. XCIII (1977)

Clarke, Dennis and Stoyel, Anthony, *Otford in Kent, a History* (Otford, 1975)

Clarke, D., *A Brief History and Guide to the Church of St John the Baptist* (Sevenoaks, 1970)

Clarke, D., *The Medieval Hospital of St John the Baptist, Sevenoaks* (Sevenoaks, 1971)

Coad, F.R., *The History of the Brethren Movement* (Exeter, 1968)

Collinson, Patrick, *The Religion of Protestants. The Church in English Society 1559-1625* (Oxford University Press, 1982)

Colley, Linda, *Britons: Forging the nation 1707-1837* (New Haven, 1992)

Cosgrave, R.A., 'English anti-clericalism: a programmatic assessment', in P. A. Dyken and H. A. Oberman, eds., *Anticlericalism in Late Medieval and Early Modern Europe* (Leiden,1993), pp.569-81

Crookshank, S., *St Peter and St Paul, Seal* (Seal, 1974)

Curteis, Thomas, *A Letter to the Right Honourable Sir Robert Peel, Bart., on the Principle and operation of the New Poor Law* (London, 1842)

Darby, H.C. and Campbell, E.M.J., *The Domesday Geography of South-East England* (Cambridge, 1962)

Davidoff, Leonore, and Hall, Catherine, *Family Fortunes: Men and women of the English middle class 1780-1850* (London, 1987)

Davie, Grace, *Religion in Britain since 1945* (Oxford, 1994)

Davies, R., George, A.R. and Rupp, G., *History of the Methodist Church in Great Britain*, 4 volumes (London, 1965-88)

Dickens, A.G., *The English Reformation* (London, Batsford, 1964)

Dobson, Mary J., 'Original Compton Census returns – the Shoreham Deanery', *Arch. Cant.*, vol. XCIV (1978)

Draper, Gillian, 'The first hundred years of Quakerism in Kent. Part I', *Arch. Cant.*, vol.CXII (1993) & Part II, *Arch. Cant.*, vol.CXV (1995)

Du Boulay, F.R.H., 'A note on the rebuilding of Knole by Archbishop Bourchier', *Arch. Cant.*, vol. LXIII (1950)

Du Boulay, F.R.H., ed., *Registrum Thome Bourchier, Cantuariensis Archiepiscopi, 1454-86* (Canterbury and York, 1957)

Du Boulay, F.R.H., 'Late continued demesne farming at Otford', *Arch. Cant.*, vol.LXXIII (1959)

Du Boulay, F.R.H., *Documents Illustrative of Medieval Kentish Society*, Kent Records XVIII (Ashford, 1964)

Du Boulay, F.R.H., 'The Pipe Roll Account of the See of Canterbury', in Du Boulay, *Documents Illustrative of Medieval Kentish Society* (Ashford, 1964), pp. 46-7

Du Boulay, F.R.H., *The Lordship of Canterbury* (London, 1966)

Du Boulay, F.R.H., 'The assembling of an estate: Knole in Sevenoaks c.1275-c.1525', *Arch. Cant.*, vol.LXXXIX (1974)

Duffy, Eamon, *The Stripping of the Altars. Traditional religion in England c.1400-c.1580* (Yale University Press, 1992)

Duncan, L.L., 'The renunciation of Papal authority by the clergy of West Kent, 1534', *Arch. Cant.*, vol.XXII (1897)

Duncan, L.L., ed., *Testamenta Cantiana: West Kent* (London, 1906)

Dunlop, John, *The Pleasant Town of Sevenoaks. A history* (Sevenoaks, 1964)

Eales, Jacqueline, *Community and Disunity. Kent and the English civil wars, 1640-1649* (Faversham, 2001)

Everitt, Alan, *The Community of Kent and the Great Rebellion 1640-60* (Leicester, 1973)

Field, Benjamin, *Sincere Devotion Exemplified in the Life of Mrs C. E. Martin of Sevenoaks* (London, 2nd edn, 1869)

Fielding, C H., *The Records of Rochester* (Dartford, 1910)

Fox, Jean, 'Sevenoaks, Seal and Ightham 1560-1650', *Arch. Cant.*, vol.CXVI (1996)

Frampton, T.S., 'List of Incumbents at St Peter's, Seal', *Arch. Cant.*, vol.XX (1897)

Fullerton, W.Y., *F. B. Meyer. A biography* (London, 19??)

Garmonsway, A.C., ed., *Anglo-Saxon Chronicle* (London, 1975)

Gibson, William, *The Church of England 1688-1832: Unity and accord* (London, 2003)

Gill, Robin, 'Religion', in Nigel Yates, ed., *Kent in the Twentieth Century* (Woodbridge, 2001), pp. 321-33

Gillard, Carol, *Like a Mighty Army. The story of Biggin Hill Christian Fellowship* (Biggin Hill, 1991)

Gliddon, P., *St Peter and St Paul, Shoreham, Kent* (n.d.)

Goring, Jeremy, *Burn Holy Fire. Religion in Lewes since the Reformation* (London, 2003)

Graham, R., ed., *Registrum Roberti Winchelsey, Cantuariensis Archipiscopi, 1294-1313*, 2 Vols (Canterbury and York, 1952-6)

Gregory, Jeremy and Chamberlain, Jeffrey S., eds., *The National Church in Local Perspective: the Church of England in the regions 1660-1800* (Woodbridge, 2003)

Groser, W., *Memoirs of Mr John Stanger, late Pastor of a Baptist Church at Bessels Green, Kent* (London, 1824)

Haigh, C., 'Anti-clericalism and the English Reformation', *History*, vol.LXVIII (1983)

Hanley, H. and Chalklin, C., 'The Kent Lay Subsidy Roll of 1334/5', in F.R.H. Du Boulay, ed., *Documents Illustrative of Medieval Kentish Society*, Kent Records XVIII (Ashford, 1964)

Hallam, H.E., ed., *The Agrarian History of England and Wales: II, 1042-1350* (Cambridge, 1988)

Haller, William, *Foxe's Book of Martyrs and the Elect Nation* (London, 1963)

Harper-Bill, C., *The Register of John Morton, Archbishop of Canterbury, 1486-1500*, 2 Vols (Canterbury and York, 1987-91)

Harper-Bill, C., *The Pre-Reformation Church in England* (London, rev. edn, 1996)

Hasted, Edward, *The History and Topographical Survey of the County of Kent*, vol.III (Canterbury, 1797; Wakefield reprint edn, 1972)

Hill, Christopher, *The World Turned Upside Down. Radical ideas during the English Revolution* (Harmondsworth, 1975)

Hilton, John, 'A Sevenoaks church rate riot', *Bygone Kent*, vol.18, 3 (1997)

Hodder, Edwin, *Life of Samuel Morley* (London, 1887)

Homan, Roger, *The Victorian Churches of Kent* (Chichester, 1984)

Horton, William D., *The Story of Methodism in Sevenoaks from 1746* (unpub. lecture, 1979)

Hudson, A., *The Premature Reformation* (Oxford, 1988)

Hussey, A.,'Chapels in Kent', *Arch. Cant.*, vol.XXIX (1911)

Hussey, A., *Kent Chantries* (Ashford, 1936)

Johns, F.D., 'The Royalist rising and Parliamentary mutinies of 1645 in West Kent', *Arch. Cant.*, vol. CX (1992)

Judd, Walter D., *The Record of Wesleyan Methodism in the Sevenoaks Circuit 1746-1932* (London, 1932)

Kenny, A., ed., *Wyclif in His Times* (Oxford, 1986)

Killingray, David, *St Nicholas Parish Church, Sevenoaks, Kent. A brief history* (Sevenoaks, 1990)

Kitchener, Geoffrey, *Millennial Halstead. A Kentish village history* (Halstead, 2000)

Knocker, H.W., 'Sevenoaks: the Manor, Church and Market', *Arch. Cant.*, vol.XXXVIII (1926)

Lane, L.J., *Baptists in Sevenoaks – Our Story* (Sevenoaks, 1998)

Langston, E.L., *How God is Working to a Plan* (London, 1933)

Lansberry, H.F.C., *Sevenoaks Wills and Inventories in the Reign of Charles II* (Maidstone, 1988)

Lambarde, William, *A Perambulation of Kent* (1570; London, 1970)

Lindley, P. and Ormrod, M., eds., *The Black Death in England* (London, 1995)

McLain, B.A., 'Factors in market establishment in medieval England: the evidence from Kent, 1086-1350', *Arch. Cant.*, vol.CXVII (1997)

Mate, M., 'The rise and fall of markets in southeast England', *Canadian Journal of History*, vol.XXXI (1996)

Meates, G.W., *The Lullingstone Roman Villa, Vol. 1: The site* (Maidstone, 1979)

Meates, G.W., 'Christianity in the Darent Valley', *Arch. Cant.*, vol.C (1984)

Morrill, John, *The Nature of the English Revolution* (London, 1993)

National Association of Decorative and Fine Arts Societies, *St Mary the Virgin, Riverhead, Kent, Record of Church Furnishings* (London, 1994)

Newman, John, *West Kent and the Weald* (Harmondsworth, Buildings of England series, 1969; 2nd edn, 1976)

Newman, John, *Saint Luke's Parish Church Sevenoaks: A centenary history* (Sevenoaks, 2003)

Newton, W.R., *The Vine Baptist Church Sevenoaks 1748-1948* (Sevenoaks, 1948)

Obelkevich, J., *Religion and Rural Society: South Lindsey 1825-1875* (Oxford, 1976)

O'Day, Rosemary and Heal, Felicity, *Continuity and Change. Personnel and administration of the Church in England 1500-1642* (Leicester, 1976)

O'Day, Rosemary and Heal, Felicity, *Church and Society in England: Henry VIII to James I* (London, 1977)

Parliamentary Papers. Minutes of Evidence Before the Select Committee on State of Children Employed in Manufactories of the United Kingdom [397] (1816), pp. 80-3

Parsons, Gerald, Moore, James R., and Wolffe, John, eds., *Religion in Victorian Britain*, 5 vols. I *Traditions* (Manchester, 1988); II *Controversies* (1988); III *Sources* (1988); IV *Interpretations* (1998); V *Culture & Empire* (1997)

Parsons, Gerald, ed., *The Growth of Religious Diversity: Britain from 1945*. Vol. 1. *Traditions* (London, 1993).

Pateman F.R.J. and others, 'St Thomas a Becket's Well, Otford', *Arch. Cant.*, vol.LXX (1956)

Payne, A., *A History of the Parish Church of St Peter and St Paul, Shoreham, Kent* (1930)

Payne, E.A., 'The venerable John Stanger of Bessels Green', *Baptist Quarterly*, vol.7, 7 (1978)

Philp, B., *Excavations in West Kent* (Kent Archaeological Rescue Unit, 1973)

Philp, B., *Excavation in the Darent Valley, Kent* (Dover, 1984)

Platt, C., *The Parish Churches of Medieval England* (London, 1995)

Pollock, Adrian, 'Social and economic characteristics of witchcraft accusations in 16th & 17th century Kent', *Arch. Cant.*, vol.XCV (1979)

Prior, Kenneth, *Christians in a Pagan Society* (London, 1975)

Rack, Henry D., *Reasonable Enthusiast: John Wesley and the rise of Methodism* (London, 3rd edn, 2002)

Rayner, Christopher, *Sevenoaks Past* (Chichester, 1997)

Raynor, Brian, *John Frith, Scholar and Martyr. A biography* (Otford, 2000)

Roake, Margaret, ed., *Religious Worship in Kent. The census of 1851* (Maidstone, 1999)

Rooker, John, *Parish Church of St Nicholas Sevenoaks* (Sevenoaks, 1910)

Rosman, Doreen, *The Evolution of the English Churches 1500-2000* (Cambridge, 2003)

Rowse, A.L., *The England of Elizabeth* (London, 1950)

Ryan, A.C., 'Some recusant and church papist families of Sevenoaks' (Kent Recusant History Society, 2002)

Sackville-West, V., *Knole* (London, 1922)

St Mary the Virgin Riverhead (1968)

St Mary the Virgin, Riverhead 1831-1931 (1931)

Saynor, J., ed., *Bexley Mosaic, Aelfric's Colloquy*, trans. A. Watkins (Bexley W.E.A., 1977)

Salmon, J.E., *Sevenoaks Congregational Church: a brief history* (Sevenoaks, 1967)

Sharpe, Kevin, *The Personal Rule of Charles I* (New Haven, 1992)

Simpson, G.S., *The Parish Church of St Peter and St Paul, Shoreham, Kent* (n.d.)

Standen, H.W., *Kippington in Kent: Its history and its churches* (Sevenoaks, 1958)

Stevens, M., *Past Generations of Seal and Kemsing*, (n.d. *c.*1970)

Stevens, M., *Thomas Theobald, A Son of Seal* (Seal, n.d., *c.*1975)

Stoyel, A., 'Norman abacus at Seal church', *Arch. Cant.*, vol.LXXXV (1970)

Strivens, Pauline and Higgs, Beryl, *History of St George's Church Weald* (Weald, 1989)

Tacitus, *Historical Works, Vol. 1, The Annals* (Dent edn, London, 1932)

Tanner, N., 'Penances imposed on Kentish Lollards by Archbishop Warham, 1511-12', in M. Aston and C. Richmond, eds., *Lollardy and the Gentry in the Later Middle Ages* (Stroud, 1997), pp.233-5

Tanner, N., ed., *Kent Heresy Proceedings, 1511-12* (Maidstone, 1997)

Thomas, Keith, *Religion and the Decline of Magic* (London, 1971)

Thorne, Susan, 'Protestant ethics and the spirit of imperialism: British Congregationalists and the London Missionary Society 1795-1925', unpub. PhD thesis (University of Michigan, 1990)

Thomson, J.A.F., *The Later Lollards, 1414-1520* (Oxford, 1965)

Thompson, H.P., *Guide Book to St Mary and St Luke, Kippington* (Sevenoaks, *c.*1919)

Tremlow, J.A., ed., *Calendar of Papal Registers*, vol. VII (London, 1906)

Trueman, Abbe and Howson, Hubert, compilers, *Robert Colgate the Immigrant: A genealogy of the New York Colgates and some associated lines* (New Haven CN., 1941)

Vann, R., *The Social Development of English Quakerism* 1655-1755 (Cambridge, MA., 1969)

Walker, John, *The Sufferings of the Clergy* (London, 1714)

Wallenberg, J.K., *The Place Names of Kent* (Uppsala, 1934)

Walsh, John, Haydon, Colin and Taylor, Stephen, eds., *The Church of England c.1689-c.1833: From toleration to Tractarianism* (Cambridge, 1993)

Walsh, R M., 'Recent investigations at the Anglo-Saxon cemetery, Darenth Park Hospital, Dartford', *Arch. Cant.*, vol.XCVI (1980)

Ward, G., 'The list of Saxon churches in the *Textus Roffensis*', *Arch. Cant.*, vol.XLV (1933)

Ward, J., *Women of the English Nobility and Gentry, 1066-1500* (Manchester, 1995)

Watson, I., ed., *A History of the Parish of Chevening* (Chevening, 1999)

Watts, Michael, *The Dissenters: From the Reformation to the French Revolution* (Oxford, 1978)

Weald History Group, *Sevenoaks Weald. A brief history* (Weald, n.d. *c.*1999)

Wesley, John, *The Journal of the Reverend John Wesley*, 4 vols (Longman edn, London, 1906)

White, B.R., *The English Baptists of the 17th Century* (Didcot, 1996)

White, M. and Saynor, J., *Shoreham, a Village in Kent* (Shoreham, 1989)

Whiteman, A., ed., *The Compton Census of 1676: a critical edition* (London, 1986)

Williams, Ann and Martin, G.H., eds, Domesday Book: a complete translation (Penguin Classics, Harmondsworth, 2003)

Witney, K.P., *The Jutish Forest: a study of the Weald of Kent from 450 to 1380 AD* (London, 1976)

Wood-Legh, K.C., ed., *Kentish Visitations of Archbishop Warham and His Deputies, 1511-12* (Ashford, 1984)

Yates, Nigel, 'A Kentish clerical dynasty: Curteis of Sevenoaks. Part I', *Arch. Cant.*, vol.CVIII (1990), and Part II, CXVII (1997)

Yates, Nigel, ed., *Kentish Sources VII. Kent and the Oxford Movement. Selected documents* (Gloucester, 1993)

Yates, Nigel, ed., *Religion and Society in Kent 1640-1914* (Woodbridge, 1994)

Zell, Michael, ed., *Early Modern Kent 1540-1640* (Woodbridge, 2000)

INDEX